D1622806

100 THINGS
ROUGHRIDERS FANS
SHOULD KNOW & DO
BEFORE THEY DIE

100 THINGS ROUGHRIDERS FANS SHOULD KNOW & DO BEFORE THEY DIE

Rob Vanstone

30 YEARS

TRIUMPH
BOOKS

No part of this publication may be reproduced, stored in a retrieval system, or transmitted in any form by any means, electronic, mechanical, photocopying, or otherwise, without the prior written permission of the publisher, Triumph Books LLC, 814 North Franklin Street, Chicago, Illinois 60610.

Library of Congress Cataloging-in-Publication Data available upon request.

This book is available in quantity at special discounts for your group or organization. For further information, contact:

Triumph Books LLC
814 North Franklin Street
Chicago, Illinois 60610
(312) 337-0747
www.triumphbooks.com

Printed in U.S.A.
ISBN: 978-1-62937-644-8
Design by Patricia Frey
Photos courtesy of the *Regina Leader-Post*

For Mom, who took me to "The Little Miracle of Taylor Field" in 1963. I was born four-and-a-half months later.

Contents

Foreword

Over my years of involvement with the Canadian Football League, a number of books have been written about its players, its teams, past championships, and the league itself. The quantity of books published since the CFL's inception in 1958 is actually quite amazing, considering the size of the league, the population base of Canada, and the fact that the CFL is uniquely Canadian in its rules and history.

If you were to compile a list of books written about the CFL, you would also find that one team seems to have had more written about its exploits than, well, all the other teams combined—and that is our very own Saskatchewan Roughriders. One of those books was even written by a Roughriders season ticketholder who lives in Minnesota! So why, exactly, are there so many books about the prairie Riders? Well, since you are already leafing through another book about Canada's Team, you likely understand that the Riders' fan base is generally a little more rabid than other teams' fans in its pursuit of anything to do with the home team.

As my career was winding down, I considered writing a book. In preparation, I purchased as many books as I could find regarding Canadian football. I then read each of them (and there were a surprising number of good ones) to determine what I should or should not include for my book to be just as entertaining as the ones I had read. From that, I determined that I wanted my book to have plenty of stories about games played throughout my years with the team and as many anecdotes as possible. It also needed to have plenty of "inside" stories about teammates—without, of course, getting any of them into trouble.

In your hands right now is another book about your team, written by a longtime friend of mine. He has written about the guys in green previously, and I am not referring to the thousands of daily and weekly columns that have appeared over the years in the *Regina Leader-Post* newspaper. I am, however, referring to his two *Before, Then & After* books—about the Grey Cup champions of 1966 (*West Riders Best*) and 1989 (*The Greatest Grey Cup Ever*). Perhaps I enjoyed them because I knew many of the personalities and players personally; however, I also enjoyed them because they were well-researched, well-written, and about my favourite football team.

When people pick up a book, they either want to learn something or to be entertained. As you read Rob's latest book, I promise you will find it both informative and enjoyable. There is little about the Roughriders organization, its players, and its history that isn't covered. And I feel comfortable saying that, to me, it is...*sort of...* the definitive "fan book" on things you absolutely need to know if you believe you are a diehard fan.

The book is loosely organized in numerical fashion, but it's not all about numbers. Chapter 23 is about Ronnie and Chapter 34 is about George, exactly as you might expect, but not every player who wore a particular number is highlighted (until Chapter 100). But the players whom fans identify with a particular jersey number are for the most part there. Harley is Chapter 81, Narco is 80, Geno is 60, and some old kicker got Chapter 36. Bill Baker gets a chapter, as does Roger Aldag, and there are other players.

But again, it isn't all about jersey numbers. There are chapters dedicated to the Grey Cup victories of 1966, 1989, 2007, and 2013, and to some of our more painful Cup losses. There are chapters about the Plaza of Honour and about Rider Pride. Labour Day Classics are chronicled, as are many other facets of the team and its history.

The chapters aren't particularly long, which means you will move along at a pretty good pace, but I promise you this—you won't get bored and you will have a tough time putting this book down once you get started.

Personally, there were several aspects of the book I very much enjoyed, like reading about the first black player who ever suited up for the Riders—Robert Ellis Jackson, way back in 1930. And I was shocked to read how the local media tried to *delicately* word (without much success) news of his arrival and play. I also loved reading that following the home-field Grey Cup win in 2013, Darian Durant went directly from Mosaic Stadium to Albert Street and took part in all the revelry.

When Glen Suitor and I went back to our hotel following our 1989 Grey Cup win in Toronto, we sat in the room talking about how wild it would be to be out celebrating with the fans on the streets in Regina and Saskatoon and Moose Jaw and all the small towns around the province that particular evening, and while we could only imagine what it was like, Darian was actually able to go out and be with the team's fans as they celebrated. I loved that story! It also made me appreciate how much he enjoyed being a part of the province.

I also enjoyed reading about Piffles Taylor. My goodness, what a great Canadian! Not only did he fight for his country during The Great War, but he was also shot down, lost an eye, spent time as a prisoner of war, and came home to eventually move on to even bigger and better things in the province he called home, including having a stadium named in his honour—a stadium in which I was lucky enough to play for 14 seasons.

There's so much more you will learn from picking up this book. I promise you will discover many things you never knew about the team you thought you knew everything about.

Enjoy.

—Dave Ridgway
Saskatchewan Roughriders, 1982–1995

Introduction

Choosing the first 99 topics for this book was, to use football parlance, a snap.

The problem: there was a 476-way tie for No. 100.

Eventually, the issue was resolved and the content was determined, as evidenced by the fact that you are holding a copy of *100 Things Every Roughriders Fan Should Know & Do Before They Die*.

On days when writer's block was seemingly lethal, I wondered whether I would complete the 100 chapters before encountering mortality. It is, after all, a daunting task to address so many topics. Early on, the "12 down, 88 to go" assessment reminded me of how much material needed to be covered. There were also days when 12 became 19, and 84 became 53, and when 100 changed by the hour. The mandate was broad, the list of possible subjects was infinite, and ideas for new chapters sprung up every time I completed an interview or revisited an aspect of the team's rich history.

Some of the chapters were automatic. How could Chapter 23, for example, not be about Ron Lancaster? Chapter 34 and George Reed were a natural tie-in. Overall, I derived fabulous fun from linking numbers to names. Oh, and there was also the unavoidable linkage of Chapter 13 to...uh...well...*ahem*...you know.

Yes, some infamous moments in Roughriders history are revisited, as is inevitable when you consider the history of a team that has weathered telethons, a one-win season, repeated Grey Cup heartbreaks, 11 consecutive non-playoff seasons, and, tragically, the deaths of four Riders players in a 1956 plane crash.

But most of the space is devoted to a celebration of great games and names. As someone who grew up in Regina during the Ronnie and George era, I had nearly 50 years of firsthand viewing experiences upon which to draw.

I also drew upon the friendship and support of loved ones.

My wife, Chryssoula Filippakopoulos, was endlessly patient as I pleaded for another "book night"—a visit to a local coffee emporium, at which she would read voraciously and I would write furiously, detached from the world due to some fine jazz (thank you, Oscar Peterson) and noise-cancelling headphones (thank you, Sony).

Thank you as well to my publisher, Triumph Books, with which I enjoyed a first-time association that was devoid of headaches (at least on my end, anyway). I am extremely grateful to them for approaching me with this opportunity.

Profuse thanks as well to everyone who consented to be interviewed, as well as to the people whom I thoughtfully conscripted as uncompensated, yet invaluable, proofreaders: Bob Calder, Dr. Mark Anderson, Jennifer Ackerman, G. Helen Vanstone-Mather—who is more commonly referred to as Mom—and, of course, Chryssoula (who was especially adept finding missing words—omission intentional, in this case).

In collaboration with Garry Andrews, Bob Calder wrote *Rider Pride*, the first history book on the Green and White. Published in 1984, *Rider Pride* remains a must-read for any fan of the club, or of football in general. So, imagine my elation when Bob consented to proofread this book. He went above and beyond to assist me, in return for a free lunch (well, breakfast consumed at lunchtime) and some Saskatoon Blades tickets.

There could not be a greater friend than Dr. Anderson, the principal at Regina's Luther College High School. I am indebted to him in more ways than the space allotted for this book would allow me to describe. (Mr. Calder also has a Ph.D. in English, so let's just say that this book has been doctored.)

Profuse thanks, as well, to Jack Morrow of Edmonton—a fountain of CFL knowledge who offered so many valuable suggestions.

Thanks to Dave Ridgway, who became a great friend in the days when I didn't even cover football for the *Leader-Post*, for consenting to write the foreword—and for The Kick, which I witnessed from a 500-level seat at Toronto's SkyDome. "Robokicker" split the uprights on a Sunday. My voice returned the following Thursday.

Thanks to *Leader-Post* editor-in-chief Heather Persson and managing editor Tim Switzer for allowing me time to work on this project.

And thanks, especially, to you for investing valuable money and time in this project. I sincerely hope that you enjoy the latest addition to the written historical record of the Roughriders—even if we may disagree on who should have been recognized in the 100th, and final, chapter. And yet, isn't that the sheer fun of it all?

But, before we start debating Chapter 100, onward to Chapter 1.

1 A Grey Cup and a Half

Darian Durant's celebratory comment was as accurate as the precise passes he threw for the Saskatchewan Roughriders during the 2013 Canadian Football League playoffs.

When asked to describe the significance of that year's home-field Grey Cup triumph, the legendary Roughriders quarterback replied, "It was the best moment in Rider history, hands down."

That is saying something, considering that the Roughriders have had an assortment of highlights—and, yes, an inordinate number of gut-wrenching lowlights—since their inception as the Regina Rugby Club in 1910.

Saskatchewan's Cup conquest in 2013 produced only the fourth championship in franchise history, one that is replete with memorable moments.

The Grey Cup titles of 1966, 1989, and 2007 are also up there, along with the careers of icons such as quarterback Ron Lancaster and fullback George Reed—both of whom are honoured with statues outside new Mosaic Stadium. The Roughriders' very survival—and their transformation from a virtual charity case into a Canadian football Goliath—is a story in itself. Also consider a fan base that is unsurpassed in terms of passion and, at times, patience.

Roughriders supporters have endured desperation telethons and, sadly, the deaths of four players in a 1956 airplane crash. Rider Priders also weathered a CFL-record 11 consecutive non-playoff seasons, along with an unmatched number of Grey Cup defeats (15). Among those losses are the heartbreakers of 1972 and 1976, championship contests that were decided in the waning seconds.

Most notably, there was the devastation of November 29, 2009, when a seeming victory suddenly evaporated as the Roughriders were called for too many men on the field after the Montreal Alouettes' first attempt at a last-second, game-winning field goal was unsuccessful. Given a second try, from 10 yards closer, Damon Duval's kick was true—leaving crestfallen Rider rooters to wonder whether what they had just witnessed was, in fact, real.

The Roughriders never trailed when there was time remaining on the clock…and still lost.

Backhandedly, though, the infamous "13th man" unravelling contributed to the unrestrained merriment of November 24, 2013, when all the accumulated baggage was jettisoned as the Roughriders routed the Hamilton Tiger-Cats 45–23. And it happened at old Taylor Field (which was re-named Mosaic Stadium in 2006), the full-time home of the Regina (later Saskatchewan) Roughriders from 1936 to 2016.

"You knew that it was going to be the last Grey Cup game in that stadium, and to come out the way they did against Hamilton, it was one of the great feelings that I had about the field," said Reed, who had a front-row seat.

Fittingly, the starting quarterback for the 2013 league final was Durant, who had entrenched himself as the No. 1 signal-caller four years earlier and was enjoying a storybook 2009 season until…well, you know.

As a counterbalance, there was Durant's performance in the 2013 Grey Cup game, after which he memorably hoisted the time-honoured championship trophy over his head as the green-and-white confetti flew.

"I was brought to tears, and I had only been [in Saskatchewan] eight years at the time," recalled Durant, who was a Roughrider from 2006 to 2016. "To see the emotions of everyone in that crowd, the people who have endured the tough times, who have

Saskatchewan Roughriders quarterback Darian Durant (No. 4) hoists the Grey Cup in victory at the end of the 101st Grey Cup game held at Mosaic Stadium in Regina, on Sunday, November 24, 2013. (Troy Fleece, *Regina Leader-Post*)

lived through [crowds of] 15,000 people, max, at the stadium, the telethon days, the heartbreaks of 2009, the plane crash, all the heartbreaking moments in Rider history…you could see everyone's emotions come out and they let it all go. I guarantee you that out of the 40,000 people in that stadium, 30,000 of them shed a tear that night."

The emotion in the stands was felt by Regina-born Lori Dattilo, now of Surrey, British Columbia, who flew back to her hometown to attend the game.

"Grey Cup 2013 was perfection," Dattilo said, recalling "the prairie sky, the sea of green fans, the crisp air, the Roughriders running out as a group during the player introductions, [Roughriders legend] Kent Austin coaching the Tiger-Cats, and vindication on the home field after what happened in 2009."

Long after the game, fans remained in the stands to savour a once-in-a-lifetime experience—a hometown Grey Cup victory on Taylor Field.

"It was like celebrating with old friends who you had been through the war with," Dattilo said. "At first, you did not believe it, because of the Calgary memories [from 2009].

"No one wanted to leave. We wanted the feeling to never end. When the win seemed certain, I thought that I was now witnessing history."

Eventually, the fans left the stadium and joined the revellers on the streets. One of them turned out to be Durant, who had just finished the 2013 postseason with eight touchdown passes in three games.

"I went home and changed clothes as fast as I could," the victorious quarterback said. "I had to be a part of the celebration. It was an historic moment. Of course, the celebration in the locker room lasts forever, with the champagne and cigars and all that stuff. Then I met with [former teammate and ex-Roughriders quarterbacks coach] Marcus Crandell and gave him a big hug. Then we went out to Albert Street and then we went to Dewdney Avenue. We walked up and down with the fans and took pictures and we were a part of the festivities."

For Durant, it wasn't a "look-at-me" moment or an attempt to revel in adulation. He simply wanted a long-awaited, firsthand look at what was occurring when Regina, and Saskatchewan, came unglued in peaceful, joyous fashion.

"I stayed low-key, for sure," he said. "I wasn't in the middle of it, but I definitely was able to get out there and experience it."

That was to the astonishment of some revellers who, in the recollection of Durant, "couldn't believe it."

"I was actually telling people, 'Yes, this is me,' because most people were drinking their butts off and they weren't in their right mind," he continued. "They were saying, 'Is this really you?' I said, 'It's me!' They're wiping their eyes like they've seen a ghost. It was crazy.

"There's no way I was going to miss being a part of that. I had to enjoy it."

As did the fans.

"It was one of the greatest days of my life," said Dylan Earis, who was born in 1993 and began following the Roughriders nine years later. "To watch that team struggle through the years and to think that a day like that would never happen, it meant the world to me when it did.

"I cried. I hugged and high-fived a lot of strangers, and I will never forget running up and down Albert Street in my wheelchair. My brother Evan said, 'We're going to the street,' and I said, 'Are you kidding?!' Some drunk guy was bouncing up and down on his truck bed. I don't think he made it out alive."

Rider Nation, by contrast, was very much alive—on a day when the accumulated misfortune was forgotten, or at least shelved, as fans rejoiced in the streets leading to the site of the landmark conquest.

"Winning it at home," Saskatoon-based Roughriders fan Don Rice reflected, "felt like a Grey Cup-and-a-half."

2 Visit Ronnie and George

One of the livelier Roughriders-related debates pertains to the team's greatest player: Ron Lancaster or George Reed?

But there was little debate when the time came to pay tribute to the icons outside new Mosaic Stadium, which officially opened in 2017.

Lancaster and Reed were both honoured with statues. After all, as former Roughriders president-CEO Jim Hopson put it, "You never say Ronnie without saying George. Ronnie and George… George and Ronnie."

Both arrived in Saskatchewan in 1963 and enjoyed illustrious playing careers well into the 1970s—with Lancaster, wearing No. 23, routinely handing off to Reed, No. 34.

It eventually reached a point where a CFL career record was established every time Lancaster threw a pass or Reed accepted a handoff.

Standards were also set away from the field as a result of myriad contributions to a city, and a province, with which they became synonymous despite being born in the United States.

The all-around excellence was such that Reed in 1976 became the first recipient of the CFL Players' Association's Tom Pate Memorial Award, presented annually to a player who demonstrates outstanding sportsmanship while making a significant contribution to his team, his community, and the union. Appropriately, Lancaster was the second recipient.

And to think that their careers in Saskatchewan, and in Canada, were nearly abbreviated.

Lancaster and Reed had clashed with Bob Shaw, who was the Roughriders' head coach in 1963 and 1964. With Shaw contractually obligated to return in 1965, Lancaster and Reed had both decided to remain in the States. However, the Toronto Argonauts ended up wooing Shaw, offering him far more money than he could have received from the penurious Roughriders, so he was released from his contract by general manager Ken Preston.

Preston proceeded to promote Eagle Keys, a former Edmonton Eskimos field boss who had been a Saskatchewan assistant under Shaw in 1964. One of Keys' first moves as the head coach was to reach out to Lancaster and Reed and express confidence in both players, enticing them to return to Saskatchewan.

The rest is history. In 1965, Reed established an enduring franchise single-season record by rushing for 1,768 yards in

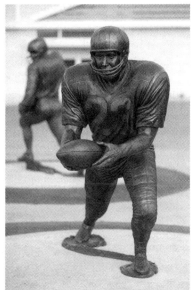

Statues of George Reed and Ron Lancaster stand by Mosaic Stadium.
(Troy Fleece, *Regina Leader-Post*)

16 games. That performance enabled him to become the first Roughrider to be named the CFL's most outstanding player. Not to be outdone, Lancaster received the league's most-coveted individual award in 1970 and 1976.

But for both players, personal accolades were not the objective. Neither was financial enrichment. Each of them could have commanded more money from another team but, as Reed put it, "I came, I played, I stayed."

Lancaster, from tiny Wittenberg College (now Wittenberg University) in Springfield, Ohio, spent his first three seasons of professional football with the Ottawa Rough Riders before being traded to Saskatchewan in 1963 for a mere $500, with the stipulation that he would not be dealt to a team in the Eastern Conference without Ottawa's approval.

Ronnie and George, NHL Version

Regina-born National Hockey League referee Brad Watson quietly, meaningfully, paid tribute to Ron Lancaster during more than 1,500 big-league games before retiring as an official in 2019.

Watson wore No. 23, which the Little General donned for the Roughriders from 1963 to 1978.

The numerical options were limited in 1996, when Watson debuted in the NHL. While looking at the possibilities, however, he was quick to make an emphatic call.

"When I was choosing a number, there was 18 left, along with 15 and 23," Watson recalled in 2014. "I said, 'I like 23,' because with Ronnie Lancaster the number was pretty well-known in Saskatchewan. I circled 23.

"Ideally, I would have taken something like Number 4, because I was a big Bobby Orr fan, but that wasn't happening. I love my number. It means a lot. I always think of Ronnie Lancaster. In the States, 23 is well-known for Michael Jordan. In Saskatchewan, 23 is Ronnie Lancaster.

"It's funny when [Saskatoon-born referee] Brad Meier and I work together, because he's [No.] 34. It's the Ronnie and George Show."

Reed was recruited by the Roughriders out of Washington State University, at which he had played fullback and linebacker. He was also recruited by the Los Angeles Rams after his senior season.

"If I'd had a feeling that I had to play in the National Football League, then I would have gone there," Reed said. "The only reason I came up here was because they offered me a little bit more money than they were going to give me in the National Football League. In those days, it was good up here because the dollar was worth more and they offered me a bigger contract."

As first-year Roughriders, Lancaster and Reed played pivotal roles in one of the CFL's most memorable comebacks. After losing 35–9 to the host Calgary Stampeders in the opener of a two-game, total-points first-round playoff series, the Roughriders won Game 2—played in Regina—by the requisite 27 points (39–12). Lancaster threw for 492 yards and five touchdowns before handing off to Reed for the winning major in what was quickly dubbed "The Little Miracle of Taylor Field."

Even though the B.C. Lions ended up representing the West in the 1963 Grey Cup, that classic comeback was a prelude to the Roughriders' first championship-game victory—a 29–14 conquest of Ottawa on November 26, 1966. Lancaster threw three touchdown passes in that game and Reed rushed for 133 yards (including a 31-yard score that effectively cemented the victory).

Reed remained a Roughrider until surprisingly retiring at age 36 as training camp loomed in 1976, despite having registered his third-best single-season rushing-yardage total (1,454) in 1975. In fact, no running back in the CFL West matched that total in any of the following eight seasons.

After Reed retired, Lancaster played for three more seasons, fittingly winning his final game thanks to a patented fourth-quarter comeback.

Lancaster spent the following two seasons as the Roughriders' head coach before becoming an outstanding analyst on CBC's CFL telecasts. He later returned to the sideline, coaching the Eskimos (1993) and Hamilton Tiger-Cats (1999) to Grey Cup victories.

A 1982 inductee into the Canadian Football Hall of Fame, Lancaster died September 18, 2008, less than a month shy of his 70th birthday.

Within months of Lancaster's passing, Reed moved back to Regina after spending 20 years in Calgary, and soon became ubiquitous in Saskatchewan once again. At one point during Reed's playing career, he was involved with 47 different charities or community groups.

"If you want to get something done, find a busy person," he said matter-of-factly.

Outside a busy Mosaic Stadium on any given day, you will find fans posing for pictures with the statues of Reed and Lancaster.

"It's a nice honour to be there with my old buddy, Ronnie, and to have him there next to me," Reed said.

It is not uncommon for fans to mingle with Reed personally, as he attends every game and is endlessly patient and accommodating with the public.

"I always looked at it from the standpoint that if someone took the time to ask me for an autograph or ask me something, then I can take the time to answer," Reed said. "Somebody else might ask me the same question tomorrow, but it's not the same person. So, you take a few minutes and you say hello to them and answer their questions and away you go.

"I had seen a few athletes who cut kids short and walked away, and I had always said that if I was ever in that position, I would take a few extra minutes."

A few minutes with the statues are certainly worth the time.

"In terms of things to do, to be able to take a handoff from Ron Lancaster [at his statue] and take a picture, or to have George Reed looking at you, because it's that famous picture of when he is so far ahead that he's looking back at where the defenders are, that's just cool," Roughriders president-CEO Craig Reynolds said. "Those are special statues and those are special memories people can make."

Reed will always cherish memories of time spent with a fellow Roughriders icon.

"I don't know if people realize how close Ronnie and I were and how close our families were," Reed said. "We did a lot of things together and I had a lot of respect for him.

"He was probably my best friend."

3 A "Wait" off the Shoulders

Roughriders fans had waited more than half a century for an elusive national championship. So, naturally, impatience took over during the obligatory latter stages of the 1966 Grey Cup game.

Only four seconds remained on the clock at Vancouver's Empire Stadium when Roughriders supporters invaded the field and rendered the remainder of the game unplayable.

Head referee Al Dryburgh wisely signalled a slightly premature end to the proceedings, calling the game. Just like that, after 56 years, the franchise had finally won a Grey Cup—courtesy of a 29–14 victory over the Ottawa Rough Riders.

"It meant a lot to the province," legendary fullback George Reed said. "I wasn't [in Regina] to see the response of the people when we won, but I saw the people who came to the Grey Cup on the train and the way they enjoyed it.

"For a small province to be able to say, 'We won the Grey Cup,' it meant a lot to the people. It meant a lot to the guys, too, but I think it meant more to the people of Saskatchewan because they were then able to stick their chests out and say, 'We're with the big boys now.'"

Ottawa, led by quarterback Russ Jackson, was favoured to win by at least a touchdown after posting an 11–3–0 regular season record and waltzing through the Eastern Conference playoffs. The Roughriders (9–6–1) had won the Western Conference, albeit not nearly as convincingly as Ottawa had dominated its division.

It appeared early in the 1966 Grey Cup that projections of doom for the Roughriders were on-target. On Ottawa's first possession, Jackson found fleet receiver Whit Tucker for a 61-yard touchdown bomb.

The eastern Riders' 6–0 lead was short-lived, however. On Ottawa's next possession, Dale West intercepted Jackson and returned the ball 41 yards to the 9-yard line. Two plays later, Ron Lancaster hit a wide-open Jim Worden for a six-yard touchdown. Jack Abendschan's convert gave Saskatchewan a 7–6 advantage only 10 minutes into the game.

The Roughriders went ahead 14–6 in the second quarter when Abendschan converted a 19-yard touchdown toss from Lancaster to Alan Ford. The pass was tipped by Ottawa defensive back Bob O'Billovich before landing in the hands of Ford as he fell to the turf in the end zone.

On the next offensive play, the Jackson–Tucker combo struck again—this time for an 85-yard score. Moe "The Toe" Racine's convert reduced Saskatchewan's lead to 14–13. Ottawa's Bill Cline subsequently completed the first-half scoring by punting for a single to create a 14–14 tie.

Thereafter, Saskatchewan took over, controlling both lines of scrimmage for the final two quarters. A robust running attack—focusing on Reed, with timely contributions from speedy halfback Ed Buchanan—allowed the Roughriders to control the football and chew up time on the clock. Moreover, the Roughriders' defence

> ### Extra Point
> 29–14 was also the score 15 days before the 1966 Grey Cup, when the Regina Rams—coached by the legendary Gordon Currie—defeated the Notre Dame de Grace Maple Leafs to win their first Canadian junior football title. The junior final, played at Gordie Howe Bowl in Saskatoon, was often referred to as the "Little Grey Cup."

was so stout that Ottawa, for all its talent, never reached midfield during the second half.

Yet, the game remained tied until the first play of the fourth quarter, when Lancaster found his favourite target—Hugh Campbell—for a five-yard major. Three defenders were in the vicinity of Gluey Hughie, but the pass was precise and his hands were typically unerring.

The Roughriders added an insurance touchdown when Reed—who in the second half amassed 102 of his 133 rushing yards—stormed 31 yards to pay dirt. Abendschan converted the Campbell and Reed majors before Ford closed out the scoring by punting for a single.

After the players were mobbed by the crowd, they returned to the dressing room and the champagne—which had figuratively been on ice since the Regina Rugby Club's inception in 1910—began to flow.

Meanwhile, television cameras had been set up near Ottawa's dressing room. As the story goes, CBC producers were so certain of an Ottawa victory that little, if any, thought had been given to situating the cameras elsewhere. The Roughriders, of course, didn't mind taking some extra steps in order to be interviewed following a ground-breaking victory.

"They've got a great defensive ball club," Reed told CBC's Ernie Afaganis, referencing the eastern Riders. "They've got a great ball club altogether, but I think we were a little irritated all week. The press kind of built them up to be superhuman and we didn't have a chance. We just wanted to prove that we had a good football team, also. I think you saw two good football teams fighting it out, and the better team of the day won."

The next day, the Roughriders returned home to an enormous welcome from 6,000-plus merrymakers at the Regina Armoury. The celebration raged throughout the winter and, in a sense, never really stopped. Consider the outpouring of affection for the players when the Roughriders, with Jim Hopson as the president-CEO, held a 40th anniversary reunion for the 1966 champions.

"They were like the touchstone," Hopson said. "They are the ones who brought us our first championship and made us believe that we could be as good as anybody."

And, on the final Saturday of November in 1966, nobody was better.

4 A Franchise Is Born

The team that eventually became the Saskatchewan Roughriders was formed without the fanfare that now accompanies virtually any noteworthy development relating to the beloved team.

On September 13, 1910, a meeting was held at city hall for the purpose of organizing the Regina Rugby Football Club. In the span of a few productive hours, a team was formed, and a practice was scheduled. (In fact, specific players were invited to the introductory practice via the newspaper. Those were the days…)

One day earlier, *The Morning Leader* had reported that "the original intention was to make it a rowing club, but so much general interest has been created that the later plan was adopted."

As efforts continued to solidify a league, the Regina team conducted regular practices.

"Regina has a husky squad of athletes from which to pick a team," *The Morning Leader* reported on September 16, "but as much as the material is green, hard and faithful practice, with generous coaching from the established players, is necessary."

The progress was such that, on September 19, it was reported that "several well-known eastern players now residing in Regina have gladdened the hearts of the officers by coming forward and signifying their intention of getting into the game again."

The only remaining question, and not an insignificant one, was: Who would they play?

A *Morning Leader* report on September 7 had noted that the local rugby side hoped to "form a league with Moose Jaw, Saskatoon, and possibly Winnipeg."

Plans for a Winnipeg team did not come to fruition. Furthermore, during a September 22 meeting in Saskatoon, a delegation from that city indicated that it was "impossible" to assemble a team for the autumn of 1910, meaning that the Saskatchewan Rugby Football Union would consist only of Regina and Moose Jaw.

An opening game was scheduled for October 1 in Moose Jaw. "The fourteen to line up in the first game will be selected from those attending practices most regularly from now out," *The Morning Leader* reported.

Interest in the first game was such that an excursion to and from Moose Jaw was organized. The cost for a round-trip ticket on the Canadian Pacific Railway was $1.25.

Some "one hundred and fifty lusty-lunged supporters," as described in a newspaper article written "BY OUR OWN REPORTER," took advantage of the offer and made their presence known at Moose Jaw's baseball grounds, where 750 spectators turned out.

Fight, Fellows, Fight...

The Regina Rugby Club's second season included some Rioter Pride.

Mayhem erupted in the second game, which Regina won 9–0 in Saskatoon. Officials called the game as a result of the tumult.

The *Leader* described the imbroglio as follows:

> In one of the most disgraceful exhibitions of lack of sportsmanship ever witnessed on a western football field, the rugby game Saturday came to an untimely close. Crowds have broken out upon the field before this the continent over, but when the crowd is led by the manager of one of the teams and a member of the police force, the thing passes the realms of the inexcusable.
>
> Except for a small portion of the crowd, that which instigated the riot, the whole affair came suddenly and unexpectedly. The first warning to most of those who witnessed it was the sight of a small figure running up the field with a mob of a hundred or more people in hot chase. In an instant the whole Regina team was surrounded by several hundred bloodthirsty hoodlums of Saskatoon, and for a time it looked warm for the visiting boys. Indeed, had it not been for the good services of the Mounted Police, the Regina boys would certainly have had some rough usage.
>
> The city police were easily the worst of the crowd. Even the chief himself was threatening right and left to arrest players who so much as commented on the methods employed by his men. Not once did any of them make any attempt to restore order, and the threats and language they were using rather excited the crowd than otherwise.

The horde of unruly spectators eventually rendered the field unplayable. After some deliberations, the victory was awarded to Regina.

The hostility did not carry over to the competing teams, which dined together that evening at Saskatoon's Flanagan Hotel.

It was not an auspicious debut for the purple-and-gold-clad Regina team, as the Moose Jaw Tigers prevailed 16–6.

The lone touchdown for Regina—managed by Allan Westman and captained by C.M. Galvin—came when Ted Porter intercepted a Moose Jaw pitchout and raced 80 yards for a score. *The Morning Leader* noted that the Regina players were "by no means disheartened" by the outcome.

"Next Saturday Moose Jaw comes to Regina," it was added, "and the local boys expect to revenge their defeat of Saturday last."

No such luck. Moose Jaw won the rematch 7–6 at Dominion Park, despite a strong effort by Regina player-coach Fred Ritter. The difference was a missed convert attempt following Regina's touchdown. The attendance was not reported.

The teams met twice more that season. On October 15, Moose Jaw won 38–0 at home to clinch the provincial title. A formality of a finale, played October 23 in Regina (which then had a population of 30,000), ended in a 13–6 Moose Jaw win.

Regina had been outscored 74–18 over four games, but a football foothold had been established.

The Regina Rugby Club opened its second season on September 23, 1911, by registering its first victory—a 15–11 conquest of Moose Jaw at Dominion Park. The 1911 edition won four of five regular season games before downing Moose Jaw 21–11 to win the provincial title.

To cap the 1912 campaign, Regina blanked the host Winnipeg Rowing Club 5–0 to win the Hugo Ross Trophy—awarded to the Western Canada Rugby Football Union champion—for the first time.

Another landmark was celebrated in 1913, when Regina won a Western Canada title at home, shutting out Winnipeg 29–0. That was the first of four consecutive Western Canada championships for the RRC, which also captured seven successive provincial crowns.

5 What's in a Nickname?

Two prominent Canadian football teams shared a nickname long before they shared a field.

The Saskatchewan Roughriders and Ottawa Rough Riders were both established franchises when they first crossed paths in a meaningful contest in 1951, in the 39th Grey Cup game.

A 21–14 loss to Ottawa at Toronto's Varsity Stadium was the first championship-game appearance for the Roughriders under the Saskatchewan label. The franchise had initially appeared in the national final as the Regina Rugby Club, which in 1923 lost 54–0 to Queen's University. The following year, the rugby club's name was changed to Regina Roughriders, who appeared in (and lost) the Grey Cups of 1928, 1929, 1930, 1931, 1932, and 1934.

From a Regina/Saskatchewan perspective, the impetus for using the Roughriders nickname has long been a matter of some speculation.

Bob Calder, the preeminent Roughriders historian, wrote that the nickname "began to appear, without any fanfare or announcement," in Regina newspaper reports in November of 1924. *The Leader*, Calder added, had also made one reference to the Roughriders back in 1915, but the name did not stick at that point (when a local lacrosse team had that label). By then, Ottawa had long been associated with the nickname, although a two-word appellation was used in the nation's capital.

Calder—in collaboration with Garry Andrews—wrote in the landmark *Rider Pride* history book that the Ottawa Rough Riders' name was derived from "lumberjacks who rode the logs down the turbulent rapids of the Ottawa River." The Rough Riders of Ottawa first competed in the Canadian Rugby Union in 1898.

Calder and Andrews went on to note that the Ottawa club in 1924 decided to refer to itself as the Senators, the same year the Regina side changed its name to the Roughriders. Ottawa reverted back to the Rough Riders tag three years later.

The context of the Regina/Saskatchewan Roughriders nickname has remained unclear for nearly a century. According to Calder, the likeliest scenario is that the team adopted its name as a reference to the "rough riders" who broke in horses in Western Canada. But it has also been speculated that the team was named after an American cavalry regiment—"Roosevelt's Rough Riders"—that fought in the 1898 Spanish-American War under the command of future United States president Teddy Roosevelt.

"It has been argued that the American ex-patriots in the Regina Rugby Club wanted to adopt the name in tribute to the ebullient Roosevelt," Calder wrote in *Saskatchewan Roughriders: The First 100 Years.*

The club's name was changed, again, in 1948 when the current title—Saskatchewan Roughriders—was adopted.

The Roughriders and Rough Riders coexisted in Canadian rugby and football circles for most of the 20th century. They met in the 1951 Grey Cup, won 21–14 by Ottawa, but did not collide in a regular season game until the Canadian Football League introduced interlocking play in 1961.

On August 28, 1961, the first non-Grey Cup game between the Roughriders and Rough Riders was played, with Ottawa winning 29–10 at Taylor Field.

From that point onward, the teams met at least once per year through 1996.

After that CFL season, the troubled Ottawa Rough Riders ceased operations. Professional football would twice return to Ottawa, first as the Renegades (2002 to 2005) and later as the Redblacks (2014 to present).

Green Is the Colour

The Roughriders were once the red-blacks, at least in terms of the colour scheme.

Although the Roughriders are popularly known as the Green and White, the team's colours were red and black from 1912 to 1947.

Actually, members of the Regina Rugby Club—forerunner to the Roughriders—wore purple and gold during the inaugural season of 1910.

A switch was made to blue and white in 1911, after which the red-black combo was adopted.

How did green and white come about? The best explanation is provided in *Rider Pride*, a team history written by Bob Calder and Garry Andrews and published in 1984.

The authors referenced an executive-committee meeting, chaired by Clair Warner, at which Jack Fyffe was an attendee.

"Fyffe moved that the red-and-black colours be retired," Calder and Andrews wrote. "No one could see any reason to do so, and his motion failed for a lack of a seconder, whereupon Fyffe pleaded that the executive would be more enthusiastic if he were allowed to state his reason for suggesting a change. The meeting agreed to hear him."

It turned out that Fyffe, who was in the implement business, routinely travelled to Chicago in the line of duty. One fine day, he passed by a store that happened to be holding a war-surplus sale.

"He wandered in and discovered that sets of nylon football sweaters were being offered at giveaway prices," Calder and Andrews recounted. "Since nylon was a magic word in the late forties, Fyffe knew a bargain when he saw it, and he bought two full sets of nylon football sweaters."

Both were green and white—with differing dominant hues.

"They were obviously superior to the red-and-black uniforms left over from the pre-war years," the *Rider Pride* authors wrote. "His motion passed unanimously, and the Saskatchewan Roughriders have worn green ever since."

Well, almost. Subsequent to the publication of *Rider Pride*, the Roughriders tinkered with two alternate looks.

Under general manager Roy Shivers, the Roughriders introduced black jerseys (with green numbers) in 2001. The team wore black and green periodically through 2006.

The black jerseys were unveiled on September 29, 2001, when the Roughriders' record fell to 3–10 as a consequence of a 39–19 loss to the Edmonton Eskimos.

"I like the uniforms," one caller to CKRM Radio's post-game open-line show observed. "The only problem was that they had the same players in them."

The black jerseys were worn for the final time on October 13, 2006, when the Roughriders edged the Montreal Alouettes 27–26 on Taylor Field.

Then, in 2010, the Roughriders decided to revert back to the red-black look. In conjunction with the team's centennial, it was announced that red and black jerseys would be worn for a July 17 home game against Edmonton. A total of 2,010 retro jerseys would be available to the public.

Wearing the new/old duds, the Roughriders won 24–20. Then the red-and-black jerseys were retired once again, presumably for good.

Saskatchewan was among the teams that granted conditional approval for the eventual Redblacks to join the CFL. One of the stipulations, however, was that "Rough Riders" not be used. Saskatchewan's management felt that 90 years of unbroken usage gave it the exclusive right to the name.

6 Visit the New Stadium

Mosaic Stadium was replaced by, well, Mosaic Stadium.

The same name aside, there are few commonalities between the Roughriders' homes, old and new.

Granted, the seating capacity—33,350—is in the same ballpark, so to speak. But in terms of amenities (cupholders!), spectator comfort (arm rests!), and virtually anything else you can name (men's washrooms devoid of troughs!), Mosaic Stadium 2.0—into which the Roughriders moved in 2017—is leagues apart from its predecessor.

"It's the best outdoor stadium in Canada," Roughriders president-CEO Craig Reynolds said. "It really is on par with anything its size in the world, I believe."

The previous facility, long known as Taylor Field, was incontestably the finest stadium in…Regina. The first incarnation of Mosaic Stadium, which received that corporate name in 2006, had served the Roughriders well since the 1920s (and continuously for 80 years, beginning in 1936), but its time had come and gone.

"It was past its prime when I played, and that was a long time ago," observed George Reed, who starred at fullback for the Green and White from 1963 to 1975.

Reed was present on July 1, 2017, when the Roughriders played their first regular season game at the $278-million pigskin palace. The home side lamented a disappointing debut, losing 43–40 in overtime to the Winnipeg Blue Bombers, but the venue-related reviews were effusive.

"It has been a great atmosphere since they opened that new place," said ex-Roughrider Weston Dressler, who caught two touchdown passes for Winnipeg to help spoil the stadium's grand opening for the host team. "To be able to go in the first game and score a couple of touchdowns was pretty cool, too."

The push for a new or dramatically upgraded stadium began as the Roughriders surged to a Grey Cup championship in 2007. Suddenly, the seats were full and the deficiencies of ol' Taylor Field—such as the need for buckets in light of the innumerable leaks—were exposed and suddenly in need of urgent attention.

"Never in the early years did I think that we would get a new stadium," recalled Jim Hopson, the Roughriders' president-CEO from 2005 to 2015. "I was optimistic that we could see a much-improved Mosaic Stadium, that we could improve the experience

Fans await the 2017 Labour Day Classic between the Saskatchewan Roughriders and Winnipeg Blue Bombers at new Mosaic Stadium.
(Troy Fleece, *Regina Leader-Post*)

for our fans. I knew the board of directors was committed and I knew that it was possible, but never did I think that it could happen. Once we started to think, 'Yes, it could,' then it changed."

By 2009, the focus had shifted to the feasibility of a domed stadium, to be constructed in downtown Regina. When sufficient funding and real estate were unavailable for such a mega-project, it was back to the drawing board. A modified blueprint called for an open-air stadium located at city-owned Evraz Place (Regina's exhibition grounds).

The deal for a new stadium was formally announced on July 14, 2012, shortly before a home game against the B.C. Lions. Early in 2017, the Roughriders began moving into their state-of-the-art lodgings.

"It really is a fantastic building," Reynolds marvelled. "I'll go on our little deck and look around and I'm just in awe of what we've built here, especially when you compare it to the old stadium.

"Everybody loves the old stadium. It has its charm. But it was just so difficult in many ways. The difference between old and new is so dramatic. It's just amazing."

7 "The Kick" Did the Trick

The Roughriders had only one point at one point. Taking note of the Hamilton Tiger-Cats' double-digit lead early in the 1989 Grey Cup game at Toronto's SkyDome, Roughriders kicker Dave Ridgway was inclined to take some mental photographs.

"We were down 13–1 and I remember at that time being fairly dejected," recalled Ridgway, who was then a 30-year-old veteran of eight CFL seasons. "It had taken me so long to get to a Grey Cup, and here we are, down 13–1. I thought, 'Uh-oh, this isn't going the way I anticipated,' and I knelt down and took the time to look around the stadium.

"It was a brand-new stadium. It was beautiful. It was packed. I tried to drink in the noises and the sights and things like that.

"And then, all of a sudden—bang!—we were on the scoreboard."

Instantly, the game turned into a classic—the catalyst being a wild second quarter in which the teams combined for five consecutive touchdown drives.

"And there were no more foreign thoughts," Ridgway continued. "It was too busy."

The excitement reached a crescendo with two seconds remaining in the fourth quarter, when Ridgway kicked a 35-yard field goal to give Saskatchewan a 43–40 victory on the 23rd anniversary of the team's first (and previously only) championship-game victory.

But the 77th Grey Cup received a kick-start, energy-wise, during that scintillating second stanza. The pace was such that the Tiger-Cats were still celebrating a 30-yard touchdown pass from Mike Kerrigan to Derrick McAdoo when Saskatchewan struck back in immediate, emphatic fashion—courtesy of a TD bomb from Kent Austin to Jeff Fairholm. (Scoring, er, drive: one play, 75 yards.)

"When Jeff got that touchdown, it was almost like, 'Game on. Here we go,'" Ridgway reflected.

Austin also threw scoring strikes to Ray Elgaard and Don Narcisse during the second quarter, but more air power was required for the Roughriders to pull out a victory.

Last-minute heroics were necessary after Hamilton's Tony Champion made a gravity-defying, nine-yard touchdown catch on a third-and-goal gamble with 44 seconds remaining. Champion, who was being tightly covered by cornerback Harry Skipper, turned 180 degrees toward the football and extended himself while falling backward.

"When I turned around, he was laid out almost horizontally catching the ball," Skipper said.

Hamilton's prolific pass-catcher then maintained control despite hitting the turf with a painful thud, especially remarkable considering that he had been injured earlier in the game but had refused to leave the contest.

"Even if it was a preseason game, you'd be like, 'Holy cow,'" Kerrigan marvelled. "And with the fact that he had cracked ribs, it just made it all the more spectacular."

After Paul Osbaldiston's convert created a 40–40 tie, the Tiger-Cats kicked off to Saskatchewan and Austin went to work from his team's 37-yard line. Following a first-down incompletion,

Elgaard Stands On Guard for Thee

The 1989 Grey Cup was a classic even before the opening kickoff.

Just ask Ray Elgaard, who was particularly moved and impressed by Liberty Silver's pregame rendition of "O Canada."

"Everyone, I guess, has their one moment from the game that signalled something meaningful to them," the Roughriders' Hall of Fame slotback recalled. "For me, it was the national anthem.

"I was always a respectful anthem guy and felt it was appropriate to take that time and think about past sacrifices that Canadians have made so that people like me could make a living playing football.

"When that particular national anthem began, it had a strange, calming effect on me, as I stood stoically on the sidelines. I remember thinking how well it was being sung and how passionate the singer was about it, and that she was another Canadian on the national stage, doing her thing.

"By the time it was over, I was geeked to get going, as the whole building had reached a crescendo of energy that seemed to explode at that moment."

The Roughriders' offence did not explode until the second quarter, in which Elgaard caught the first of Kent Austin's three touchdown passes in Saskatchewan's 43–40 victory over the Hamilton Tiger-Cats.

The Roughriders' victory triggered pandemonium and, even to this day, the thriller is celebrated as one of the greatest games in CFL history.

Although Elgaard appreciated the magnitude of the game from the outset, he was quick to put it in perspective once the national anthem had concluded and the teams prepared to play.

"I was still calm and composed as I considered that trivialness of our sacrifices that day, compared to ones made by others in more difficult times," he said.

"I always had that grounded sort of feeling that no matter how much attention we got for what we did, in the end we are really just grown men running around in tight pants and that the attention we received was quite silly.

"I felt that my contribution to the world around me was minor in the bigger scheme of things, and this was a source of personal humour for me."

Austin found Elgaard for 20 yards. Mark Guy, typically a forgotten component of the Saskatchewan offence, then made back-to-back receptions for gains of 18 and 10 to put Saskatchewan in field-goal range.

Ridgway, who was nicknamed Robokicker for a reason, took it from there. Bob Poley snapped the ball, Glen Suitor pinned it, and Ridgway was precise from 35 yards away.

"When I did see the ball in flight, I knew it was going through the posts," Ridgway said. "By then, Glen had jumped up and we were hugging each other. Polecat joined in. My eyes felt like silver dollars. They felt that huge.

"I said to Glen, 'Oh my God. We did it!'"

One play later, the Roughriders were suddenly in the unaccustomed role of champions.

"That game was just back and forth, with great play after great play after great play," Fairholm said. "Luckily, the time ran out when it did, or I would have been scared that Hamilton would have scored again. Time was on our side. It was just our time to win."

Amid the pandemonium on the field after the game, Osbaldiston—stationed in the end zone in case Ridgway's kick had been wide and it was necessary to punt the ball out in the other direction to avert a game-winning rouge—approached his opposite number and gave him the ball from "The Kick."

People also flocked toward Austin, who was named the Grey Cup's most valuable offensive player after throwing for 474 yards.

"Everybody talks about defence winning championships, but the reality is that there were 83 points scored in that 60-minute period," Ridgway noted.

Although the game was a shootout, the performance of Roughriders defensive tackle Chuck Klingbeil was worth noting. The future NFL player was named the defensive player of the game after twice sacking Kerrigan.

The next night, the Roughriders were honoured during a massive, long-awaited celebration at Taylor Field. The last players to be introduced were Poley and fellow Roughriders offensive lineman Roger Aldag, both of whom had debuted for the team in the 1970s and had therefore endured a succession of lean years.

It seems like yesterday to anyone who experienced the game, either as an employee of one of the competing teams or someone who watched the classic Cup, but 30 years have elapsed since Ridgway's climactic kick.

"I guess it has become a part of me now," he said. "To think that I got a chance to play in the game that a lot of people consider to be the greatest Grey Cup ever is a real thrill."

8 Lamb's Last Laugh

The Roughriders were widely expected to be playoff flotsam as they prepared to oppose the prohibitively favoured Edmonton Eskimos in the 1989 West Division final.

Edmonton, after all, had set an enduring CFL record for regular season victories (finishing with a 16–2 record), while Saskatchewan had placed third in the division at a mediocre 9-9.

Although the Roughriders had defeated the host Calgary Stampeders 33–26 in the West semifinal—the difference being a 50-yard touchdown run by Brian Walling late in the fourth quarter—the formidable Eskimos were lying in wait for the lucky (?) winner of that first-round contest.

"People are expecting us to blow them out of the water, but the bottom line is, I'm expecting us to blow them out of the water," Eskimos defensive tackle John Mandarich told Norm Cowley of the *Edmonton Journal* only days before the game. "It's not being arrogant and it's not being cocky, but it's being determined, because there's no reason why we shouldn't blow them out of the water."

Dave Elston, a cartoonist with the *Calgary Sun*, was of a like mindset. Leading up to the West final, Elston drew a cartoon he titled "The Sacrificial Lamb." The unfortunate lamb, a mangy-looking creature, was wearing a ba-a-a-attered Roughriders helmet.

"I thought, like everyone else, that they were going to get their butts kicked," recalled Elston, whose cartoon was also published in a sister paper, the *Edmonton Sun*.

It appeared early in the game that Mandarich, Elston, and countless others had been prophetic. The Eskimos scored a touchdown on their opening possession and fattened that lead to 10–0 midway through the first quarter at Commonwealth Stadium.

Saskatchewan's Dave Ridgway responded with a 44-yard field goal to conclude the first-quarter scoring, whereupon the Eskimos—quarterbacked by Tracy Ham, who would soon be named the league's most outstanding player for 1989—were on the march once again. They advanced 45 yards in seven plays before Eddie Lowe took over.

For starters, the veteran Roughriders linebacker sacked Ham to put the Eskimos in a second-and-15 predicament from Saskatchewan's 30-yard line. Ham then dropped back to pass, only to be greeted by a blitzing Lowe. A Lowe blow to the Edmonton quarterback dislodged the ball.

Middle linebacker Dave Albright scooped up the ball and slowly…rumbled…62…yards for a game-changing touchdown.

"Dave Albright wasn't Jeff Fairholm when it came to speed," then-Roughriders play-by-play man Geoff Currier said, referencing the speedy Saskatchewan slotback. "It was like, 'He's at the 10…the nine…the eight…'"

Ridgway provided the convert and suddenly, shockingly, the game was tied 10–10, even though the Eskimos enjoyed a 13–2 advantage in first downs at that point. Until Lowe levelled Ham, the Eskimos had dominated in net offence (169 yards to 18) and plays from scrimmage (25–9).

Contrary to popular perception, Ham and company were far from cooked after the Lowe-Albright ambush. In fact, Edmonton assumed a 20–17 third-quarter lead before Saskatchewan took control with back-to-back touchdown passes by Tom Burgess, who had replaced an injured Kent Austin in the second quarter.

The Roughriders ended up winning 32–21 to advance to the Grey Cup game (in which they defeated the Hamilton Tiger-Cats 43–40).

"In a lot of ways, I think that's when we won the Grey Cup," Fairholm said of the West final, in which he caught a touchdown pass. "The Eskimos were 16-and-2 and they were yakking, and there was all that stuff in the paper about the sacrificial lamb."

The readers took note as soon as the outcome of the West final became apparent.

"We started getting phone calls in the newsroom from people going, 'Nice cartoon!'" Elston remembered. "I'm going, 'Oh my God….' Then [sportswriter] Al Ruckaber comes in and says, 'I guess your sacrificial lamb was a wolf in sheep's clothing,' or something like that. I thought, 'There's my out right there.'"

Elston ingeniously produced a sequel to "The Sacrificial Lamb" depicting a wolf's head poking out of a sheep's costume, with a mangled Eskimos helmet sitting on the ground.

"It's funny because so many people said, 'That was really clever for you to think of that, bang-bang, with two cartoons in a row,' but it was totally a fluke," Elston said. "Valuable lesson. I never went out on a limb like that again."

Or on a lamb, for that matter.

Eskimos offensive lineman Blake Dermott wasn't inclined to immerse himself in media accounts of the game.

"I went home that night and obviously I wasn't feeling very good over what had happened," he recalled. "I decided I was going to hang low that day [after the game]. I didn't want to talk to anyone and I knew, being one of the guys that lived in Edmonton year-round, that I would have to answer a lot of questions many times over the next few weeks.

"Anyhow, my son—he was three at the time—goes out with my wife. He comes home and asks me to come with him because he wants to show me something. We walk to the corner and there is an *Edmonton Sun* newspaper stand. On the cover, there's a picture of me sitting on the bench with my head in my hands, and it looks like I'm crying. My son looks at me and says, 'That's you, Daddy! That's you!' I just said, 'Yeah, it is...'"

9 "Go Crazy, Saskatchewan!"

The 2007 season—culminating in Saskatchewan's third Grey Cup championship—sparked a transformation in Rider Nation.

In fact, the benefits are still discernible.

If not for that season, would there be a new stadium? Would the Roughriders be the financial envy of the CFL? Would there even be a cause to write this book? Or purchase it? (Thank you, by the way.)

The Green and White has always been immensely popular in Saskatchewan and far beyond, but the 2007 campaign elevated the appeal of the Roughriders to a tier that was previously unimaginable.

By mid-season, sellouts were automatic. So, it seemed, were victories—as the Roughriders won five games in a row after a 2–2 start. That fifth consecutive victory, a 31–26 conquest of the visiting Winnipeg Blue Bombers on Labour Day weekend, fuelled speculation that the Roughriders were a team of destiny.

"I think the turning point was the Labour Day game," quarterback Kerry Joseph said. "After that, we didn't expect to lose."

The classic contest was punctuated by a game-winning, 27-yard touchdown run by Joseph, who scored on a quarterback draw with six seconds remaining in the fourth quarter.

Joseph went on to be named the CFL's most outstanding player—becoming the first Roughrider other than Ron Lancaster or George Reed to receive that honour.

Kent Austin was an obvious choice for coach-of-the-year laurels after altering the team's fortunes and the fans' mindset.

The media hung on his every word, his every eloquent statement. There was an instantaneous buy-in from the players, who understood that Austin established a high standard but also appreciated the way he made lofty goals sound attainable.

Even before the Grey Cup game, in which Saskatchewan defeated Winnipeg 23–19 at Rogers Centre in Toronto, Austin was regarded as a rock star who carried a whistle—and considerable clout—instead of an instrument.

"Kent set the tone," recalled Rod Pedersen, CKRM Radio's voice of the Roughriders from 1999 to 2018. "You ask any player from the '07 team and they'll tell you about the day before training camp opened, with the meeting they always have. Every team has it. Kent Austin said, 'If your goal isn't to win the Grey Cup, there's the door. Leave.' For whatever reason, it grabbed every player by the scruff of the neck and woke them up. You would think that would be every team's goal for every coach, but something about the way Kent Austin said it got their attention.

"I've been around enough players and in enough locker rooms and travelled with enough teams to know that you need belief [in] that guy who's leading you, and that day they all followed him because they knew that he knew what it took to get there. Guess what? He did."

Austin was an unlikely catalyst for success, considering that he had left Saskatchewan under stormy circumstances after the 1993 season—his seventh as a quarterback with the club. His demand for a trade was accommodated, leading to fan antipathy and blistering media portrayals.

Undeterred, Eric Tillman—who succeeded Roy Shivers as the Riders' general manager midway through the 2006 season—felt Austin was the best choice to coach the team the following year.

That was one of many astute moves by Tillman, who helped to build a Saskatchewan team that earned a home playoff game for the first time since 1988. The Roughriders ultimately won their first title since 1989, a season that had been capped when Austin threw for 474 yards and three TDs to pilot Saskatchewan to a 43–40 victory over the Hamilton Tiger-Cats in the very same facility at which the 2007 championship was captured.

Unlike the Grey Cup of 1989, the 2007 final was hardly a classic. A sloppy affair was decided when cornerback James Johnson made his third interception of the game—with 54 seconds left in the fourth quarter—to extinguish the Blue Bombers' final drive.

The Roughriders proceeded to run out the clock, leading to Pedersen's climactic call: "Go crazy, Saskatchewan!"

The fans were pleased to oblige.

"I was at that game with most of my family, and, as we walked out of the stadium, the CN Tower was lit up in green," Roughriders historian Bob Calder recalled. "The next day, as we walked down Yonge Street, somebody high up in a hotel room balcony was blasting 'Green is the Colour' over and over again."

High times, indeed, in Riderville.

"You Go! You Go! You Go!"

The legacy of the Roughriders' 2007 championship season lives on in the form of the Chris Knox Foundation.

To this day, the foundation helps children and young adults attend sporting, fine arts, or cultural events while undergoing cancer treatment, providing patients and their families with a respite and some treasured memories.

One of those recollections dates back to the Roughriders' 2007 Labour Day Classic, in which they defeated the Winnipeg Blue Bombers in a 31–26 thriller.

One of the 28,800 attendees was the 24-year-old Knox, who had been diagnosed with terminal brain cancer in late August of 2007. His wish to attend the sold-out contest was granted by the Roughriders, who had learned of his illness. President-CEO Jim Hopson promptly made two 50-yard-line seats available to the Knox family.

Amid the post-game pandemonium, Roughriders linebacker Mike McCullough ran into the stands at Mosaic Stadium, looking for Knox.

"You're coming with me," McCullough told Knox who, along with his father, Ron, was escorted into the team's dressing room—after which head coach Kent Austin addressed the players.

"Kent just sort of said, 'Okay, guys, can I get your attention? The first thing I want to tell you is we've got a young guy in here. His name is Chris Knox. He's got a brain tumour and he's fighting for his life. I think we should all stop and pray for him right now,'" Ron Knox said.

Following the prayers, Chris Knox was hugged by everyone on the team and presented with a game ball.

"Then they made him do a dance with the football," Ron Knox said. "They're saying, 'You go! You go! You go!' He was dancing and it was pretty incredible."

Two weeks later, Chris Knox was still marvelling at what had occurred following the Roughriders' thrilling victory.

"That was one of the best days I've had in a long time," he said in mid-September of 2007. "That was probably the biggest smile on my face that I've ever had. The seats the Riders got me were amazing. I'd never sat that close in my life. Going into the locker room was amazing. I didn't know what to say to them. I was kind of speechless, just staring at them with a football in my hand. It was just overwhelming. I don't think I could have thanked them enough."

Little did Knox suspect that he would attend an even bigger game that season—the Roughriders' 23–19 Grey Cup victory over Winnipeg.

After the Roughriders won the 2007 West Division final, a fundraising campaign was launched in the hope of generating enough money to fly Knox and his loved ones to Toronto for the Grey Cup.

More than $100,000 was donated or pledged in a matter of days. As a result, there was enough money to send 10 young Saskatchewan-based cancer patients and 20 chaperones to the Grey Cup, along with Knox.

A few hours after the Roughriders' championship-game victory on November 25, McCullough and teammates Andy Fantuz, Marcus Crandell, and Corey Grant brought the Grey Cup to Knox's hotel room. He was very weak at the time, but nonetheless in great spirits as he admired the trophy.

Knox died 12 days later, when Austin paid the following tribute: "Chris was more of a blessing to us than we were to him."

The blessings have continued since then, thanks to the formation of the Chris Knox Foundation in 2008.

The Grey Cup excursion became an annual trip, with more than 175 special recipients and guests being treated to the CFL's marquee event over 10 years.

Subsequently, a total of 45 people made the journey over two trips to Vancouver Island for a visit to the *HMCS Regina*, a Canadian Forces frigate.

As well, more than 1,600 wishes were granted for people desiring to attend Roughriders games, concerts, and children's shows.

And, as Sharla Folk (Chris' mother) reflected in 2007: "It all started from asking for two tickets to a football game."

10 The Little Miracle of Taylor Field

Rare is the playoff game that is treated like a formality, a mere obligation. Rarer still is the type of comeback the Roughriders pulled off on November 11, 1963.

That Monday evening, the Roughriders played host to the Calgary Stampeders in the finale of a two-game, total-points Western Conference semifinal. The Stampeders had earlier prevailed 35–9 on home soil, meaning the Roughriders had to win Game 2 by at least 27 points to advance in the playoffs.

Undaunted, Saskatchewan triumphed by the requisite margin of 27 and engineered "The Little Miracle of Taylor Field."

Skepticism leading up to the game was so rampant that thousands of seats were still empty at kickoff. However, the stadium began to fill up as it became apparent that the Roughriders actually did have a chance at staging a monumental rally.

"When I got to the stadium, I thought, 'What the hell are we doing here?'" recalled George Reed, who was a rookie Roughrider in 1963. "There might have been 3,500 people in the stadium." Then, at halftime, people were fighting to get into the stadium as Calgary's advantage had been pared to 10 points.

"I think that was the first love that I had for the football team," Reed added. It was great to come back from 26 points down and win the game and it was good for the city. I think it really put the Riders back on the map with the people."

The Roughriders set the tone early in the game. After their first play from scrimmage, one of the team's offensive players—Ray Purdin—acted like he was leaving the field. But he stopped just short of the sideline and remained an eligible, if initially undetected, receiver on a since-outlawed sleeper play.

As the Stampeders scrambled, Ron Lancaster found Purdin for what turned out to be a 76-yard pass-and-run touchdown.

"That started an unbelievable game," Purdin said. "You could hear the crowd screaming and yelling, because they knew something magical was happening."

Lancaster, also a first-year Roughrider, worked his magic to the tune of 492 passing yards and five aerial touchdowns. He also handed off to Reed for an unconverted, 10-yard touchdown run that gave Saskatchewan a 48–47 lead in the two-game set, with two minutes remaining.

Calgary responded by marching into Saskatchewan territory. As it turned out, the game was in the hands—or on the right foot—of the Stampeders' Larry Robinson, who attempted a game-winning, 35-yard field goal on the final play.

The future Hall of Famer barely missed the kick, which was retrieved by the Roughriders' Gene Wlasiuk. Trying to prevent a series-tying single, Wlasiuk punted the ball out of the end zone. Robinson fielded the return boot on the Roughriders' 40-yard line and, while being pressured, attempted to punt the ball back into the end zone. The desperation punt sailed out of bounds at the 25-yard line, giving Saskatchewan a 39–12 victory in Game 2.

The moment the result became clear, hundreds of spectators scaled the railings and rushed on to the playing surface, mobbing the players—such as Reed, who rode off the field on fans' shoulders.

"It was quite a scene," he recalled of the commotion on the field, "because everybody thought we had done the impossible.

"Everybody was so thrilled, and they wanted to rush and they wanted to be a part of it. We wanted to get back on the bus and get back to the exhibition grounds, where we dressed, so we wouldn't get beaten to death."

The Roughriders were eventually beaten in the 1963 play-offs, losing in the maximum three games to the B.C. Lions in the Western Conference final. In the rubber match, played in

Bummer for the Bombers

Ron Lancaster engineered another classic postseason comeback in 1972, when a Roughriders rally resulted in a Grey Cup berth.

During the Western Conference final, the host Winnipeg Blue Bombers led 24–7 in the third quarter before Saskatchewan scored the final 20 points and won 27–24.

Saskatchewan got a touchdown catch by Alan Ford, a field goal by Jack Abendschan, and a touchdown run by George Reed (who amassed 109 of his 156 rushing yards in the second half) to create a 24–24 tie.

Then came one of the wildest, weirdest finishes in CFL history.

With six seconds remaining, Abendschan attempted and missed a 32-yard field goal that would have clinched the game. Mike Law fielded the ball in Winnipeg's end zone and, to prevent Saskatchewan from notching a single point that would win the game, punted the football out of trouble.

Lancaster, the holder on Roughriders field-goal attempts, caught the ball and punted it back into the end zone, and into the hands of Winnipeg's Paul Williams.

Williams' return kick was retrieved by the Roughriders' Charlie Collins, who was instantly tackled.

One problem: the Blue Bombers had not given Collins the required five-yard cushion when he picked up the punted ball and were therefore flagged for no yards.

The penalty gave Abendschan another chance at a 32-yarder, which he hit.

Reflecting on that classic finish, Abendschan—a Roughriders guard/kicker from 1965 to 1975—said "the best game we ever played was the Winnipeg game in 1972."

The Blue Bombers had finished first in the West with a 10–6 record. Saskatchewan (8–8) was third.

"They had beaten us [two out of three times] during the regular season and they were a walk to the Grey Cup," Abendschan said of the Bombers. "We came back in the second half with Ronnie and George and everyone.

"Ronnie gave us a lot of confidence. When Ronnie stepped into the huddle he was, as they said, the Little General. You just knew. As

> the third quarter went on, we knew we were going to win. We just kept coming. That's the way we played."
>
> The Roughriders' next game was also decided by a field goal on the final play. Ian Sunter, just 19, hit a tie-breaking, 34-yard field goal to give the Hamilton Tiger-Cats a 13–10 Grey Cup victory.
>
> Sunter's decisive boot provided a measure of symmetry to the season. The Roughriders and Tiger-Cats had also met in the opening week, when Sunter's 33-yarder with 32 seconds left in the fourth quarter gave Hamilton a 20–17 victory at its home field, Ivor Wynne Stadium.

Vancouver on November 23—one day after U.S. President John F. Kennedy was assassinated—the Lions won 36–1.

Nonetheless, the 1963 postseason was (and still is) something to celebrate for Roughriders fans, such as the 1,000-plus loyalists who packed the Regina airport to welcome home the team from Vancouver—at 2:00 AM. It was, you might say, another late comeback.

11 Tales of Taylor Turf

The Roughriders did not fare well during The Farewell Season of 2016.

In their final appearance at old Taylor Field—the team's home for 80 consecutive years—they lost 24-6 to the B.C. Lions and couldn't even eke out a touchdown.

Then the real show began. The elaborate closing ceremony of October 29, 2016, was the most memorable aspect of a largely forgettable season, one in which Saskatchewan won just five of 18 games.

Recollections of happier times marked a 30-minute post-game presentation that peaked when Roughriders greats George Reed, Roger Aldag, Gene Makowsky, and Darian Durant were introduced.

"Being there and knowing that it was the last game, it was kind of neat to see the stands full of people and to be one of the players representing different eras," Reed said.

The Grey Cup trophy was passed from one legend to the other, finishing with Durant (who, as it turned out, had just played his final game in green and white). He addressed the sellout crowd of 33,427, receiving a warm ovation, and everyone felt as positive as could be despite having witnessed another dreary game.

As people filed out of the stadium, "Happy Trails to You" played on the public-address system. It was a long, long road, indeed, to the final Saturday of October in 2016.

The Roughriders were founded 106 years earlier, as the Regina Rugby Club (RRC). That side's venue was Dominion Park, located near the intersection of Broad Street and 7th Avenue.

Dominion Park remained the RRC's home facility, despite $18,000 in damage sustained in a 1912 tornado, through 1916, after which play was suspended due to the First World War.

When competition resumed in 1919, the RRC was based at Regina's exhibition grounds.

Two years later, the club moved to Park Hughes, part of the eventual Taylor Field site (located on a tract of land bordered by Cameron and Retallack streets and 9th and 10th avenues).

While at Park Hughes, the team in 1924 played its first game as the Regina Roughriders. Park Hughes was the team's primary home until 1928. That year, a new gridiron was installed on what became the Taylor Field complex, which by then incorporated Park Hughes and the adjacent Park de Young.

The latter name applied to the Roughriders' venue in 1928 but would not be associated with the team for the seven seasons that followed. The Roughriders played at the exhibition grounds from 1929 to 1935.

In 1936, at long last, there was stability. The Roughriders moved back to Park de Young, which had been upgraded. More improvements were made leading up to the 1947 season, before which another major change occurred.

In the spring of that year, former Roughriders player, coach, and executive Neil Joseph "Piffles" Taylor died suddenly at age 52. The decision to rename the stadium in his honour followed soon after.

Taylor Field remained the official name until 2006, when a corporate deal was struck with The Mosaic Company. Just like that, Mosaic Stadium was born. The playing surface, however, was still known as Taylor Field, with the Mosaic Stadium label applying to the structure as a whole.

In 2017, the Roughriders moved into new Mosaic Stadium, and demolition of the old yard began. By 2018, there wasn't any sign of the stadium on a vast, unoccupied stretch of land, but Taylor Field was still near and dear to the hearts of so many people.

That was evident on May 11, 2018, when Durant—who had quarterbacked the Roughriders to three Grey Cup appearances, including a home-field championship-game victory in 2013—announced his retirement from football.

"I named my daughter Amayah Taylor after Taylor Field," Durant wrote on his website. "It meant so much to me to be able to play in the last game at 'old' Mosaic Stadium. It's also very fitting to me that I played the last game of my career in Regina last fall [with Montreal], and was able to see and hear the fans one last time from the playing field.

"I look forward to one day showing my family around Regina, and showing my daughter where her father won a championship in front of Rider Nation on 'Taylor' Field."

The Tale of Taylor

The loss of an eye would not prevent Neil Joseph "Piffles" Taylor from playing the game he loved for a team with which he became synonymous.

The gentleman after whom Taylor Field—the Roughriders' longtime home—was eventually named served his club and his country with distinction.

In 1917, while a fighter pilot with the Royal Flying Corps in the First World War, Taylor's airplane was shot down in a dogfight with the Germans' Deutsche Luftstreitkrafte. He lost his right eye in the confrontation.

Despite having blood in his eyes, Taylor succeeded in nosing his Bristol fighter plane into a French field.

He spent 13 months as a prisoner of war before the armistice was signed in 1918. Many of his fellow Canadian pilots had been killed, including his older brother (Samuel) and several close friends.

Samuel Taylor was involved in the air battle that brought down the Red Baron—Manfred von Richthofen—in 1918, but was killed in the final weeks of the war.

"Piff was very fortunate, indeed, to survive," said Judith Milliken, Piffles Taylor's granddaughter.

"Prairie people had lost so much as a result of World War I—whether it be husbands, brothers, fathers, or sons. The community had suffered great loss. Those like Piff, who made it home, were highly valued."

Taylor was born in Collingwood, Ontario, but moved to the small community of Yellow Grass, Saskatchewan, with his family when he was eight. The Taylors later moved to Regina, where "Piff" completed high school at Central Collegiate before enrolling in the University of Toronto.

He had played for the Regina Rugby Club in 1915 (appearing in one game) and 1916 (two games) before again heading eastward and beginning his military service.

"Piffles Taylor, the busy little soldier quarterback, will call the signals and the way he can fool the fellows [is] laughable," the *Leader* reported leading up to one RRC game. "He's always rarin' to go and the speed with which he gets plays away is marvelous and he has yet to be found guilty of not knowing the other fellow's weak spots and taking advantage of them."

After the war, Taylor rejoined the Regina Rugby Club and, in 1919, played in one particularly memorable game when the team was in Calgary.

"[Taylor] suddenly halted the game and ordered everyone to stay back," the *Leader-Post*'s Dave Dryburgh reported. "He went to his knees, searched the ground, and came up with what he sought.

"It was his glass eye…which had been jarred loose by a terrific tackle. He put it back where it belonged, called time in, and started barking signals and trading tackles with fellows twice his size again."

Taylor was also a lawyer and businessman in Regina. He managed the Drake Hotel and, in that capacity, was known to provide lodgings for players in need.

In terms of the gridiron, he coached with the Roughriders and eventually became the president of not only the team, but also of the Western Interprovincial Football Union and the Canadian Rugby Union. He was also a supporter of the Roughriders being labelled a provincial team.

Even with all the demands on his time, he served on Regina city council for five years.

On May 24, 1947, Taylor died suddenly in his sleep at age 52 in a suite he shared with his wife, Mabel, at the Drake Hotel. Park de Young was formally renamed Taylor Field, in honour of Piffles, on September 6, 1947. What was the origin of the moniker?

"It's an expletive he used," grandson Sam Taylor explained. "In those days, when you thought someone was full of it, you'd say, 'Ahhh, piffles!'

"It's dated. It's from that period. I was told that he started using that when he was studying at the University of Toronto around 1914 or 1915, and it just stuck.

"Piffles became a name that he was known by by his friends and eventually by all his family. To us, we would always refer to him as Grandpa Piff."

Actually, he was called "Piff" more often than "Piffles," but the latter nickname predominates in historical accounts of Taylor and his contributions.

Taylor was posthumously inducted into the Canadian Football Hall of Fame (1963), the Saskatchewan Sports Hall of Fame (1987), and the Roughriders' Plaza of Honour (1993).

"What has become apparent to me over the years, in discussing Piff with those who knew him, was that he was very much a people person—a thoughtful, generous, and humorous man," Milliken said. "For those reasons, Piff was very well beloved."

12 Dobberville

Some football executives would give an arm and a leg to have a player like Glenn Dobbs—who used an arm and a leg to great effect with the 1951 Roughriders.

In addition to throwing 28 touchdown passes in 14 regular season games—in an era when the aerial game was seldom emphasized to the extent that it is today—Dobbs averaged 44.2 yards per punt. Twenty of his 90 punts produced a single point during one of the most memorable years in franchise history.

The charismatic Dobbs ensured that the memories began well before the season. Shortly after signing with Saskatchewan, he was introduced to the people of Regina at a Quarterback Club gathering. February 25, 1951, was an especially frigid winter day, but undeterred Roughriders fans filled the Grand Theatre and lined up outside, thrilled as they were to welcome the team's new quarterback.

"I remember thinking, 'That'll be nice. There won't be too many people,'" Dobbs recalled in 1998, four years before his death at age 82. "Wouldn't you know it? The darned place was packed and the lineup outside was a block long."

Talk about a starting lineup! And talk about a personality! Even though the temperature was minus-30 and a patented Prairie blizzard was howling, Dobbs unhesitatingly left the comfort of the great indoors and met the shivering supporters. He was comparably cordial the following spring, when he helped fans paint the Taylor Field fence.

"My second time up there, everyone got a paintbrush," Dobbs remembered from his home in Tulsa, Oklahoma. "The whole team

Glenn Dobbs joined the Roughriders in 1951 and proceeded to lead them to the Grey Cup, earning MVP honours in the west. (Courtesy of *Regina Leader-Post*; origin unknown)

showed up. I've never seen so many people. We painted the whole stadium in one day. We didn't do a bad job, either.

"Before, I had played in Brooklyn and Los Angeles. You'd see people at the games, especially in California. There would be 50 or 100 kids lining up for autographs. You'd see them, but you'd never see them again. In Regina, you knew those people. You knew everybody. You'd call everybody by their first name.

"It was wonderful. It was a blessing. It was the greatest part of my career."

A Heisman Trophy candidate and an All-American at the University of Tulsa, Dobbs was a first-round draft choice (No. 3 overall) of the NFL's Chicago Cardinals in 1943. However, he enlisted in the air force and played military football, after which he spent his first four professional seasons in the old All-America Football Conference, earning league MVP honours with the 1946 Brooklyn Dodgers.

Dobbs was 31 by the time he flew north to join the Roughriders, after declining an offer from the NFL's Chicago Bears and their legendary leader, George Halas.

"I was going to sign with the Riders or the Bears," Dobbs said. "I asked Mr. Halas if he could match the offer. He didn't come up to my expectations, so I told him, 'I'm signing with Saskatchewan.' He wished me good luck. I turned around and shook hands with the guys on the Roughriders' board and that was it. I enjoyed it. It worked out beautifully."

Did it ever. Dobbs helped the Green and White post an 8–6 record in 1951 and, for the first time, earn top spot in the Western Interprovincial Football Union.

He was so phenomenally popular, so quickly, that Regina was dubbed "Dobberville." Letters simply addressed to "Dobberville, Saskatchewan" found their target, much like Dobbs when he was throwing the football like nobody in Saskatchewan had seen to that point.

"Those were great times," Dobbs reflected. "We used to go to church with the people and visit their homes and their schools. Little kids would come to the door, wanting autographs. We'd say, 'Sure, come on in!' We were the hard-workingest bunch of guys you ever saw."

With Dobbs leading the way, the Roughriders advanced to the 1951 Grey Cup—their first championship-game appearance since 1934—before losing 21–14 to the Ottawa Rough Riders at Varsity Stadium in Toronto.

Dobbs was among several prominent Roughriders players who battled injuries leading up to and during the 1951 final. As he put it during a 1960 sports dinner in Regina, the Roughriders went to the Grey Cup "on a diet of novocaine to deaden the hurts that came with winning the Western title."

He spent two more seasons in Saskatchewan, performing double duty as a player-coach in 1952, but—due in large part to a knee injury—he never reprised the staggering success he enjoyed in Year 1. Even so, his phenomenal popularity was unaffected.

"I was here only three years," Dobbs told the dinner crowd in 1960, "but this province will always be my home."

The Unluckiest 13

The Roughriders have celebrated one more Grey Cup championship than they have won.

For a few fleeting seconds, there was jubilation on the sideline as several Roughriders players thought they had defeated the Montreal Alouettes in the 2009 Grey Cup game. Then everyone stopped, suddenly, as they saw flags on the field at Calgary's McMahon Stadium.

The Alouettes' Damon Duval had just missed a 43-yard attempt at a game-winning field goal. Time had expired. But the Roughriders, as it turned out, had too many men on the field—a very unlucky 13—and were penalized as a catastrophic consequence.

Given one more chance, from 10 yards closer, Duval made the kick and the Alouettes won 28–27. The Roughriders' emotions, meanwhile, ranged from devastation to disbelief.

"That loss in the Grey Cup is really a heavy burden for me, even to this day," lamented Ken Miller, the Roughriders' head coach from 2008 to 2011. "I think about that situation and that game often, and sometimes I can't bear to watch football on TV when the game is close. I just cringe, still feeling the emotion of that game."

The situation is rife with irony, considering that a Roughriders marketing campaign, celebrating the franchise's fervent fans, declared that "the 13th man makes all the difference."

The victorious quarterback on November 29, 2009 —Anthony Calvillo—happened to wear No. 13. He rallied the Alouettes from a 27–11 fourth-quarter deficit and put his team in position for Duval to attempt, and eventually deliver, the game-winning field goal.

Oddly enough, the Roughriders never trailed when time remained on the clock, but they still suffered a gut-wrenching defeat.

"We had it won," said Darian Durant, who in 2009 was in his first full season as Saskatchewan's starting quarterback. "It was just a terrible, terrible error. It will probably go down as one of the worst moments in championship-game history, in any league. It was devastating."

The Roughriders' dressing room was like a morgue, although the silence was interrupted on occasion—once by offensive lineman Gene Makowsky.

"Geno has always been the quietest guy in the room," Durant observed. "He never said a word. He came to work every day. He was the ultimate professional. He never complained. The thing I'll remember is him just yelling and screaming, and the pain he felt. He understood how hard it was, first of all, to just reach that game, but winning it once you get there.

"Just seeing his pain, I had to leave the locker room. I went back in the training room, myself and Andy Fantuz. We were just talking to each other about it, and we just couldn't believe it, but the thing I'll always remember is Geno's reaction. Even on the field, the most he would give you was a fist-pump. He wouldn't show much enthusiasm at all. To see him going through that, that really hurt me. I just couldn't watch it anymore. I had to leave."

Meanwhile, throughout Rider Nation, the fans were dealing with despair.

"Leaving the stadium was surreal," Roughriders historian Bob Calder said. "It was deadly quiet, as if everyone was leaving a funeral. Forty-three thousand of the 45,000 fans were Roughrider supporters and they just trudged out, heads down, barely comprehending what they had just seen. Usually there is cheering after a game because at least one side has won, but there were so few Alouette fans there that there was simply silence."

Back in Regina, though, the anguished reaction of Roughriders fan Dylan Earis was audible.

"I remember crying about it," said Earis, who was 16 at the time. "I didn't realize the flag was on the field, so I thought we had won the Cup. My brother got up and punched the wall and left the house. I cried for five more minutes the next morning before I went to school. My English teacher, who knew I was a big Rider fan, asked if I was okay. My friends were checking on my well-being."

That same Monday, the Roughriders returned to Regina and were welcomed home by thousands of fans at Mosaic Stadium. In other centres, a team that lost so ignominiously might be vilified, booed, or simply shunned, but the show of support provided as much solace as could be derived at the time.

Also worth noting were the 2009 Roughriders' accomplishments leading up to the Grey Cup.

They finished first in the West Division, snapping a 33-year pennant drought, and secured a championship-game berth by defeating the visiting Calgary Stampeders 27–17. Then the Roughriders, who posted a 10–7–1 regular season record, came as close as possible to upsetting the 15–3–0 Alouettes.

"If we would have been blown out in that game, everyone probably would have said, 'It was a hell of a year,'" receiver Rob Bagg noted. "But because we were so close and because of the manner in which it ended, it seems like we lost more than we gained that season. In retrospect, it certainly wasn't the case."

That game, that season, became building blocks and rallying points—as did the "13th man" slogan. The Roughriders returned to the Grey Cup the following year, losing 21–18 to Montreal.

"We almost overcame [the spectre of the 13th man] the very next year and then, in 2013, we got rid of that," said Jim Hopson, the Roughriders' president-CEO from 2005 to 2015. "At the time, it was devastation, but in retrospect winning in 2013 helped to make up for that loss in many, many ways."

Yet, some of the pain endures.

"I was recording the 2009 Grey Cup on a VHS tape," Earis said. "After the game, I threw the tape under the bed.

"I still haven't watched it."

14 "Doubles" Dealing

It was the ultimate two-for-one deal—one in which the Roughriders obtained a pair of eventual Grey Cup-winning quarterbacks in one game-changing transaction.

On April 12, 2006, Roughriders general manager Roy Shivers consummated a blockbuster trade with the Hamilton Tiger-Cats, obtaining the first overall pick in a dispersal draft involving players from the defunct Ottawa Renegades in return for tailback/returner Corey Holmes, safety Scott Gordon, and a first-round pick in the 2007 CFL draft (who turned out to be defensive lineman J.P. Bekasiak, selected No. 4 overall).

With considerably less fanfare, the teams also exchanged negotiation-list quarterbacks, with Darian Durant's rights going to Saskatchewan in return for those of Reggie Ball.

Shivers proceeded to select Kerry Joseph to open the dispersal draft. Joseph went on to have a solid season with the Roughriders of 2006—a campaign in which Shivers was fired—before quarterbacking Saskatchewan to a championship the following year.

The celebration was short-lived in one sense. Joseph was dealt to the Toronto Argonauts in March of 2008, a move that eventually opened the door for Durant to become the Roughriders' No. 1 quarterback—a capacity in which he led Saskatchewan to three league finals and one title.

Durant's CFL rights initially belonged to the Renegades. Their general manager, Eric Tillman, added Durant to the negotiation list when he was the University of North Carolina Tar Heels' starting quarterback. Once the Renegades folded after the 2005 season, the CFL held a negotiation-list dispersal draft and Hamilton claimed Durant.

As a first-year Roughrider in 2006, Doubles (as he was eventually nicknamed due to his initials of DD) was used sparingly. He completed his only pass, for 14 yards, and added a 20-yard run for a Danny Barrett–coached Saskatchewan team that also employed Joseph, Marcus Crandell, and Rocky Butler at quarterback.

"Danny Barrett was very supportive of me," Durant said. "Kerry and Marcus were great. I have to give a lot of credit to [offensive co-ordinator] Tommy Condell as well. He was one of my best coaches ever. Between Kerry and Tommy, they taught me so much about the X's and O's of the game, how to use your abilities, how to use your eyes to move defenders. I always felt like I was a pretty cerebral quarterback, so I picked up things quickly.

LegenDarian

Darian Durant carried a team on his shoulders and, a fortnight later, hoisted the Grey Cup even higher.

The 2013 season culminated when the Roughriders, quarterbacked by Durant, defeated the Hamilton Tiger-Cats 45–23 to win the CFL championship on Taylor Field. But, if not for a signature performance by Durant in the West Division semifinal, the Green and White would have been ingloriously one-and-done in the playoffs.

Entering the fourth quarter, the host Roughriders trailed B.C. 25–16. The Lions had contained Saskatchewan's formidable running back, Kory Sheets, and the fans were understandably restless.

Star receiver Weston Dressler took note of the surroundings and approached Durant—a.k.a. Doubles—with a succinct message: "Dubs, we've got to make a play."

Durant proceeded to make a succession of big plays and take over the game, to the extent that one individual can influence the proceedings in a team sport, and helped the Roughriders score all 13 fourth-quarter points to win 29–25.

"It really was something, because you could just see it and you could feel it," former Roughriders president-CEO Jim Hopson said. "He was not going to be beaten. He basically put the team on his back. Whether he was running the ball or throwing the ball, he was going to win the game."

On the final play of the third quarter, Durant ran for 15 yards to extend a drive. Two plays later, in another second-and-10 situation, he took off on a 35-yard run to set up a 10-yard touchdown pass to Dressler.

The Roughriders' next possession—an eight-play, 49-yard march—ended with a 45-yard Chris Milo field goal that put the home side ahead 26–25.

Durant used his legs yet again late in the fourth quarter, running for gains of 28 (once more on second-and-10) and 13 (on second-and-7) to put Saskatchewan in position for a 28-yard field goal by Milo, who concluded the scoring with 51 seconds remaining.

Not long afterward, one fan went on Twitter and aptly called the quarterback's performance "LegenDarian."

"It was a pretty special performance," Dressler said.

Durant completed 19-of-23 passes for 270 yards and two touchdowns (both to Dressler) and rushed six times for a game-high 97 yards (91 of which were amassed on those four second-down runs).

"[The Lions] were fired up up front, taking away Sheets," recalled Durant, who worked closely with offensive co-ordinator George Cortez. "They had great coverage on our receivers downfield. I told Coach Cortez, 'Anytime it's second down, let's call the quarterback draw. If I see man coverage, I'm just going to take my drop and set up and take off and run and find a lane.'

"It definitely was a conscious decision, and I give Coach Cortez a lot of credit for just calling my number and believing in me, because I hadn't run a lot that year. Of course, having that game at home and knowing that the Grey Cup was at home, there was no way I was going to let us go down—not after everything I had been through over the years before that.

"There was no way I was going to let us lose that game."

"With their help, I was able to have some success. I made the practice squad. Marcus got hurt late in the season. I was able to come in. I completed my first pass.

"It was just a great experience being with a guy like Kerry, because a lot of quarterbacks are selfish and they don't want to teach the young guys the ropes and how to get it done in the league. I have to give Kerry a lot of credit. He didn't have to do what he did. I'll always love him for that."

Durant was the Roughriders' third-string quarterback, behind Joseph and Crandell, in 2007 and did not play a down despite dressing for every game of that championship season. Butler was traded to Hamilton in January of 2007.

To begin the 2008 campaign, Durant was again No. 3— behind Crandell and Steven Jyles—but everything changed July 4 when Crandell was injured early in a road game against the B.C. Lions. Jyles was next in line but was ineffective. At halftime, head coach Ken Miller decided to switch to Durant, who cautiously but unerringly operated the offence as the Roughriders won 26–16.

Eight days later, Durant made his first start and piloted Saskatchewan to a 33–28, come-from-behind victory in Hamilton.

"It was a great example of where preparation meets opportunity," Miller said, remembering a game in which Durant completed 23-of-32 passes for 339 yards and two touchdowns, one of which was the first scoring reception by emerging Roughriders star Weston Dressler.

One week later, Durant threw for 349 yards and three majors in a 41–33 victory over the visiting Montreal Alouettes. He was again the starting pivot in the Roughriders' next game—a 28–22 home-field victory over Toronto—but missed most of that contest due to a rib injury that forced him to sit out several weeks and essentially derailed a promising season.

By the fall of 2008, the Roughriders' quarterbacking situation had become a mess—on a good day. Michael Bishop, a mid-season acquisition from Toronto, had joined an equation that also included Jyles and Durant, Crandell having been released. It was almost a pick-a-quarterback-out-of-a-hat scenario. What could possibly go wrong?

After an ugly home playoff loss to B.C., Bishop was summarily released. The Roughriders made plans to proceed with younger quarterbacks, most notably Durant. He was named the starter for the 2009 training camp and never relinquished the reins, guiding Saskatchewan to first place in the West Division—a feat that had not been accomplished since 1976—and a Grey Cup berth.

"Even when you look at going to the Grey Cup in '09 and '10 and back in '13, it really was an amazing run he had as the leader of our team and the organization, and he was the face of the organization for so, so long," Roughriders president-CEO Craig Reynolds said. "As time goes on, his legacy will grow."

15 Flight 810

For the longest time, the Roughriders had retired only four player numbers—40 (belonging to Mel Becket), 55 (Mario DeMarco), 56 (Ray Syrnyk), and 73 (Gord Sturtridge).

They were killed on December 9, 1956, in what was then the worst aviation disaster in Canadian history.

Becket, DeMarco, Syrnyk, and Sturtridge were among nine people affiliated with the Roughriders who had travelled to Vancouver for the East-West Shrine All-Star Game.

Sturtridge (a defensive end) and Becket (centre) were in the lineup at Empire Stadium and helped the Western All-Stars blank the East 35–0. Syrnyk (defensive tackle) and DeMarco (guard) were among the spectators, having travelled to Vancouver to watch the game.

The next day, Becket, DeMarco, Sturtridge, and Syrnyk boarded Trans-Canada Air Lines Flight 810, which was to make stops in Calgary, Regina, Winnipeg, and Toronto.

The plane, a Canadair North Star, encountered a problem with one of its four engines over the Rocky Mountains and crashed into 8,200-foot Mount Slesse (near Chilliwack, B.C.). Icing of the wings and fuselage were cited as contributors to the crash.

All 62 people aboard—59 passengers and three crew members—were killed, including Sturtridge's wife (Mildred), Roughriders director Harold McElroy, and Winnipeg Blue Bombers player Calvin Jones.

The crash was huge news across Canada, especially in Saskatchewan.

"The whole city [of Regina] was in shock," longtime Roughriders fan John Lynch recalled more than 60 years later. "Nobody talked.

It was almost creepy how quiet it was on the streets. Everyone was walking with their heads down."

As news circulated about the plane's disappearance, there was also a semblance of hope.

"For a day or two, you thought, 'Well, they've crashed on a mountain. They'll find it. Maybe there's a lot of people alive,'" Sandy Archer, the Roughriders' trainer from 1951 to 1980, said in a 2006 interview.

A lengthy, extensive search for the missing aircraft was futile at first. Eventually, however, mountaineers happened to find the wreckage on May 12, 1957.

The determination was that the plane had crashed directly into the mountain, with the impact and explosion instantly killing everyone. Flight 810 missed clearing Mount Slesse by no more than 100 feet, and perhaps as few as 50.

In 1995, the debris field was declared an official heritage site by B.C.'s provincial government. Some of the debris remains visible after the snow melts.

There were visible and frequent reminders for Reg Whitehouse—a Roughrider from 1952 to 1966—who ended up settling in Chilliwack.

"I can see Mount Slesse from where I'm sitting," he said in a 2006 interview.

Whitehouse, who died in 2008, played in the 1956 All-Star game—in which he kicked five converts—but took a different flight home, as did several other participants in the East-West contest.

Whitehouse was part of a Roughriders team that posted a 10–6 record in 1956, only to miss the playoffs four times in a five-season span that followed the air disaster.

The Slesse Memorial Trail now includes a plaque that honours the victims of the crash.

16 Labour of Love

The Labour Day Classic isn't actually played on Labour Day, nor is it an automatic classic.

It doesn't matter, really. In good years and bad, and regardless of how the annual long-weekend showdown between the Roughriders and Winnipeg Blue Bombers unfolds, it invariably feels like playoff football in September.

"Besides the Grey Cup, that's the best game-day environment, hands down," former Roughriders quarterback Darian Durant said. "Winnipeg fans find tickets and they're able to get in. Even though they have small spaces in the stadium, you can hear them cheering when things go well for their team. The atmosphere on Labour Day is just so electric."

Since 1982, the Roughriders and Blue Bombers have annually collided in Regina on the Sunday of Labour Day weekend. But the Classic, in a sense, dates back considerably further.

In 1951, for example, a Taylor Field record crowd of 12,028 watched Jack Jacobs come off the bench and throw three fourth-quarter touchdown passes to give Winnipeg a 24–22 victory over Glenn Dobbs and the Roughriders.

The 1983 game was another gem—one in which Saskatchewan's Ken Clark, whose forte was punting, was pressed into duty as a placekicker due to an injury and ended up kicking a 41-yard, game-winning field goal, shortly after returning from the bedside of his dying mother.

In 1986, Ray Elgaard caught a 56-yard touchdown pass from Joe Paopao in the final minute to give the Roughriders a 34–30 comeback victory over Winnipeg, which had defeated Saskatchewan 56–0 nearly two months earlier.

Kicker Labels Banjo Pickers

The string of games bearing the Banjo Bowl label began in 2004, the impetus being comments by Winnipeg Blue Bombers placekicker Troy Westwood.

Leading up to a 2003 playoff matchup between the Roughriders and Blue Bombers, Westwood jokingly referred to Saskatchewan fans as "banjo-picking inbreds." In fact, Westwood even doubled down two days before the West Division semifinal.

"I had referred to the people of Saskatchewan as a bunch of banjo-picking inbreds," he said after summoning a group of newspaper reporters, revelling in the moment. "I was wrong to make such a statement and I'd like to apologize. The vast majority of the people in Saskatchewan have no idea how to play the banjo."

Saskatchewan did play football very well on the subsequent Sunday, defeating Winnipeg 37–21. During the game, the Roughriders' Bobby Perry had a tussle with Westwood, who was repeatedly trash-talked by another Saskatchewan linebacker, Terrence Melton. However, Roughriders defensive tackle Nate Davis was indifferent toward Westwood.

"He's a kicker, so I don't listen to him," Davis said after the game, during which he celebrated at one point by kneeling on the turf and lifting a leg, as would a dog at a fire hydrant.

"I've always done that," Davis noted. "I'm marking my territory."

Despite the outcome, the Bombers decided to mark the tradition by labelling the Roughriders' annual visit as the Banjo Bowl—to the extent that a trophy was even presented. The Green and White has typically downplayed the event, wishing the game's nickname would simply go away.

"I hate that name: Banjo Bowl," former Roughriders president-CEO Jim Hopson wrote in his book, *Running the Riders*, adding, "I'm all for great sports rivalries, but true rivalries don't need garbage marketing to sell themselves."

Maybe so, but the Banjo Bowl tag is still applied—not always in the intended manner, mind you.

In 2012, Blue Bombers fans' discontent with general manager Joe Mack prompted one wag to suggest that the Saskatchewan-Winnipeg game should be known as the "Ban Joe Bowl."

The next year, Brad Wall—a fervent football fan who was the premier of Saskatchewan from 2007 to 2018—fuelled the fire leading up to the 10th annual Banjo Bowl. He appeared on a YouTube video, one that quickly went viral, and made a statement while strumming a banjo. "Oh, hi," Wall told the viewers. "I was just playing the banjo. You know, it's funny. I practise a lot. It turns out that I'm just not very good at it. Kind of like the Bombers...at football."

The plucky Bombers proceeded to win 25–13, thereby improving their record to 2–8.

Another compelling chapter was added to the storybook in 2002, when Rocky Butler—who had been Saskatchewan's fourth-string quarterback at one point in the season—made his CFL debut and ran for three touchdowns to help the Riders win 33–19.

Many fans cite the 2007 Classic, in which Kerry Joseph scored on a game-winning, 27-yard quarterback draw with six seconds remaining, as the best of them all.

But there are times when the game almost seems secondary to the spectacle. In many years, the Roughriders usually sold out only one game per season—the Classic, which traditionally signals the unofficial end of summer and, for many fans, the start of the real football season.

Each year, Regina is invaded in late August or early September by Winnipeg fans who, despite their allegiance, are warmly received (albeit with some good-natured ribbing). Roughriders and Blue Bombers supporters typically socialize and schmooze long before and after their teams clash.

"The whole weekend, that's the granddaddy of all regular season games, for sure," said Roughriders offensive lineman Brendon LaBatte, a former Bomber. "There's passion on both sides. For the most part it's a competitive, friendly rivalry, but it goes past that in some instances, too. For the whole weekend, it always builds an atmosphere that I don't think can be beaten."

17 The Superstar Next Door

When the Roughriders were knocking on the door, they often looked to Joey Walters in the end zone.

When the team's fans were knocking on the door, Walters—one of the most spectacular receivers in franchise history—would cheerfully oblige.

It wasn't unusual for young Roughriders supporters to visit Walters' home and ask for autographs. When time permitted, he would even join in for some pickup games of touch football.

It isn't surprising, then, that people who were youngsters in the late 1970s and early 1980s have fond memories of the Roughriders' No. 17.

"How do we explain what Joey Walters was, how he played, to anyone under 50 years old?" wondered longtime fan Ron Podbielski, who was born in 1964. "You can't look up Joey Walters on YouTube. You can't see the breathtaking, thrill-racing, spectacular way he could play the game and manipulate defences into complete frustration. You have to take our word for it."

You can see the numbers, which are some of the most impressive in Saskatchewan football history. For example, the former University of Clemson Tigers receiver caught 91 passes for 1,715 yards (still a team single-season record) and 14 touchdowns during a 1981 campaign in which he had 100-plus yards in 11 of the Roughriders' 16 games.

The following year, Walters caught 102 passes (then a CFL record) for 1,692 yards in his sixth and final season with Saskatchewan. Also in 1982, he made one of the most dazzling catches anyone can remember—a diving, one-handed touchdown grab of a John Hufnagel aerial in Taylor Field's south end zone.

Roughriders receiver Joey Walters against Hamilton in 1977. (Roy Antal, *Regina Leader-Post*)

Another noteworthy grab was on October 29, 1978—Walters' 24th birthday—when he caught Ron Lancaster's 333rd and final touchdown pass as the iconic quarterback fittingly completed his career by guiding Saskatchewan to a 36–26 comeback victory over the Eskimos in Edmonton.

Walters did not limit his brilliance to the CFL. In 1983, he signed with the Washington Federals of the United States Football League and instantly became a star in that short-lived circuit. The 1984 season, in which he caught 98 passes for 1,410 yards and 13 touchdowns, was reminiscent of his CFL production. After two years in Washington, he spent the 1985 campaign with the Orlando Renegades, finishing his three-year USFL career with 219 catches for 3,153 yards and 24 touchdowns.

Jeff Pearlman, whose *Football for a Buck* (about the USFL) is one of the finest sports books ever written, ranked Walters 14th among all players who suited up in that league. Podbielski feels that Walters, who was among the San Francisco 49ers' final cuts in 1980 and was a replacement player with the Houston Oilers during the 1987 NFL strike, had the ability to shine at an even higher tier.

"It's just my opinion, but he could have played anywhere and at any level and been a star," Podbielski said. "Had he been in the NFL, he would have been a superstar, not just a star. We were blessed to grow up with him and watch him."

In those days, too, there wasn't much else to watch. The Roughriders missed the playoffs for a CFL-record 11 consecutive seasons, beginning in Walters' rookie year of 1977. On many a day, an amazing play or three by Walters was a silver lining for fans who had endured yet another Roughriders loss. And anyone who met this spectacular human being off the field was a fan for life.

"I'm so thankful for the people of Regina and Saskatchewan, especially going through the two-win seasons," Walters said. "They stuck with us and continued to cheer us on and encourage us. That was unbelievable in itself. Then for them to take a liking to me, that was really special to me. I tried to show them that by being a friend and signing autographs and going to schools and doing things out in the community to let them know that they meant something to me as well."

18 Fast Feet Fuelled Fairholm's Fantastic Football Feats

Catching up with Jeff Fairholm these days is much easier for an author than it was for a defensive back during the game-breaking receiver's playing career.

The ever-obliging Fairholm was known for his blazing speed during six seasons—1988 to 1993—with the Roughriders.

Nobody who watched the team during that span has any recollection of Fairholm being caught from behind. If he had even half a step, he would emulate the Road Runner and unfailingly leave everyone in the dust en route to the end zone. *Beep beep!*

"I always said that once I got the ball and I was running, I was able to kick it into some other gear," Fairholm recalled. "I don't think I was ever caught from behind, other than in college. I remember one in college but, in pro, I don't think I ever was.

"When I go to golf tournaments, some people will come up to me and say, 'You were never caught from behind.' The one guy who says it to me every year is [Hall of Fame quarterback] Damon Allen. It makes me feel good. That's kind of what I did. I don't know how I did it, or why. Certainly, I wasn't the fastest guy in the league, but for some reason I was able to kick it into another gear when I caught the ball in the open."

The Roughriders were hoping for such a player when Fairholm was selected second overall in the 1988 CFL draft, out of the

University of Arizona. However, his statistics as a senior did not foreshadow the superlative pro career that followed.

Over his first two NCAA seasons, he had 46 catches for 722 yards and three touchdowns. But in his graduating season, the son of former Montreal Alouettes defensive back Larry Fairholm had just six catches for 112 yards—totals the Roughriders' No. 18 often exceeded during a CFL game. (He was even capable of doubling those numbers, registering single-game highs of 13 catches and 240 yards with Saskatchewan.)

In fact, Arizona star defensive back Chuck Cecil—a future NFL player—had more interceptions (nine) than Fairholm had receptions (six) in 1987, as the team switched to a run-oriented attack.

Fairholm could still run, anyway, finishing the 40-yard dash in a brisk 4.43 seconds leading up to the 1988 CFL draft. The Roughriders took notice and quickly reaped the rewards from making Fairholm a high draft pick as he was named the West Division's rookie of the year.

The following season, Fairholm had 11 touchdown catches and was named the West's most outstanding Canadian. Most notably, he scored on a 75-yard touchdown bomb from Kent Austin—despite being interfered with on the play—to help Saskatchewan defeat the Hamilton Tiger-Cats 43–40 in a classic Grey Cup.

Austin and Fairholm combined for another long-distance major the next season—a 107-yarder during a 55–11 victory over the Winnipeg Blue Bombers on September 2, 1990. That remains, as of this writing, the longest offensive play in Roughriders history.

Despite Fairholm's prowess over the first three seasons, his best numbers were to come. From 1991 to 1993, he averaged 72 receptions for 1,325 yards per season, while scoring 28 touchdowns over those three years. And those touchdowns were something to behold.

Jeff Fairholm in 1988. (Don Healy, *Regina Leader-Post*)

"You don't feel the rush until you're sitting on the bench, or until you've crossed the goal line," Fairholm reflected. "It's nice to be able to watch it on film and know that you've contributed to your team. It's a great rush to score a touchdown and help your team. That's where I come from."

19 "Fake 34, Tight End Flag"

There is not a nicer person in the history of Canadian professional football than Tony Gabriel. Even so, the mere mention of his good name can induce despair, anger, or any number of emotions in Roughriders fans.

That is because Gabriel figured prominently in two of the team's most heartbreaking losses—the Grey Cup defeats of 1972 and 1976.

In 1972, the future Hall of Fame tight end made three key receptions, totalling 54 yards, on a fourth-quarter drive that culminated in a game-winning field goal. Ian Sunter split the uprights from 34 yards away as time expired to give the Hamilton Tiger-Cats a 13–10 victory over Saskatchewan at Hamilton's Ivor Wynne Stadium.

Four years later, Gabriel caught a 24-yard touchdown pass from Tom Clements—on a route called "Fake 34, Tight End Flag"—with 20 seconds remaining in the game to give the Ottawa Rough Riders a 23–20 victory over Saskatchewan in Toronto.

"Everybody in the world knew they'd be going to Gabriel," Saskatchewan quarterback Ron Lancaster lamented after the game. "They've run the play 64 times, and then they make it work."

The closest defender on the play, safety Ted Provost, summed it up succinctly after the game: "One damn play and it ruins the whole season."

Although Provost was devastated by the loss, Lancaster reflected several years later that there were numerous contributing factors to the defeat.

"Poor Ted Provost still takes a heck of a riding or is still being blamed for something that wasn't his fault," the Little General said. "We had so many chances to win that football game."

In the second quarter, for example, Saskatchewan was stopped on a third-and-1 gamble deep in Ottawa territory.

It also did not help that tailback Molly McGee suffered a rib injury in the first half and was consequently shelved, a situation that left the Western Conference champions without a multipurpose weapon.

Marking the Occasion

On the evening of November 24, 2013, the Roughriders were finally on even footing with Mark Kosmos.

By winning the fourth Grey Cup in franchise history, the Roughriders were, at long last, part of as many championships as Kosmos' footwear.

Respected as a linebacker and a leader, Kosmos donned the same pair of cleats in four CFL finals, winning each time. He was victorious with the Montreal Alouettes (1970), Hamilton Tiger-Cats (1972), and Ottawa Rough Riders (1973, 1976). Saskatchewan was the losing team in 1972 and 1976.

Following the 1976 game, Kosmos—the Ottawa captain—was the first to receive the Grey Cup trophy.

"I remember standing on the rails and giving the old Richard Nixon victory sign," said Kosmos, rewinding to November 28, 1976, at Toronto's Exhibition Stadium. "There were thousands of people still in the stands. They just cheered and I thought, 'My god, I'll never have this experience again.' It was as if I was leading an orchestra."

Saskatchewan's offence completely evaporated after a 51-yard Bob Macoritti field goal had increased the lead to 20–10.

Nonetheless, the Roughriders' defence—the CFL's finest during the 1976 regular season—held a potent Ottawa offence in check until late in the game.

Ottawa's penultimate possession stalled on the 1-yard line, when Clements was stuffed on third-and-1. Desperately needing a first down on the ensuing possession, the Roughriders could not move the chains and had to punt. Ottawa ended up scrimmaging the ball on Saskatchewan's 35-yard line, setting the stage for Gabriel's grab.

For Roughriders fans, it was a shocking conclusion to a season that seemed destined to culminate with a championship—which would have been only the second in franchise history.

Saskatchewan had cleared an important hurdle in the 1976 Western final, defeating the visiting Edmonton Eskimos 23–13. Edmonton had downed Saskatchewan in the previous three conference finals, played in the Alberta capital, before the Roughriders exacted revenge against the Eskimos on home turf.

"We beat them and, in a way, it felt like the Grey Cup because we had lost to them in the previous years," recalled Rhett Dawson, Saskatchewan's star receiver at the time. "We got to go to the Grey Cup and fought our asses off and we got beat by a good team. It's just the way it happens sometimes."

Ottawa—which had lost 29–16 to the visiting Roughriders in regular season play—wasn't expected to be as difficult an opponent as was Edmonton. For much of the 1976 league final, the Roughriders were indeed the superior team. But when it really counted, there was Gabriel—again—and the losing side was left to digest a devastating loss, the effects of which are still being felt.

In fact, it was the most excruciating loss in Roughriders history until November 29, 2009, when the 13th-man meltdown occurred (see Chapter 13). Gabriel, as it turned out, was in the stands at Calgary's McMahon Stadium for that game.

As Roughriders fans disconsolately shuffled out of the stadium, Gabriel and his friend Frank Brodeur hoped to board a rapid-transit train. There was a lengthy lineup, so Gabriel and Brodeur went in search of a restaurant.

"Finally, about a 20-minute walk away, we get into this restaurant that looks fairly decent, and it has one table available," Gabriel said. "We're standing in line and these two ladies say, 'Why don't you join us?' We sat down and one of the ladies said, 'Oh, no! You're Tony Gabriel from 1976!' Then some other Roughriders fans came in and started the cheers. All of a sudden, the whole restaurant breaks out with chants of 'Next year!' and cheers for the Roughriders.

"It was incredible. They were depressed, but all of a sudden they're cheering for their team. And one of them said, 'Now that this one has been stolen from us, we can forget about Tony Gabriel.'"

20 The Green Army

The dedication of Rider Nation is something to behold.

In good times and bad, Roughriders fans have stood by their team—revelling in its greatest moments, weathering the adversity, and embracing its heroes.

"Rider fans are awesome," Saskatchewan quarterbacking legend Darian Durant said. "They come from everywhere. They support their team, no matter what.

"I remember that, during our tough times, there were a couple of boos here and there, but we'd still have 28,000 fans at the stadium. I'm not sure what happened before I got there with the telethon days and all that stuff, but from my experience they're super-loyal.

"I've been through bad seasons, losing seasons, and the fans have been there every step of the way. They're the best in the world."

Durant alluded to the telethons, such as ticket blitzes in 1987 and 1997 that sustained the community-owned franchise through some of its darkest hours.

Resilient Rider rooters have also endured devastating Grey Cup losses—heartbreakers in 1972, 1976, 2009, and 2010—and droughts such as 11 consecutive non-playoff seasons and 19 years without a postseason home game.

One fine day—October 28, 1979—an overflow crowd of 28,012 congested Taylor Field for the Roughriders' home finale and watched the B.C. Lions fall 26–12. The woeful team's second and final victory of the season offered a rare respite from the misery of the season during the landmark "Rider Pride Day"—an occasion marked by a then-record crowd.

A year later, Saskatchewan posted a second successive 2–14 record but attendance increased, and a rare profit was realized. Also consider the 1981 and 1982 seasons, during which the Roughriders played to more than 100 per cent capacity without even making the playoffs.

"You can't say enough about our fans," president-CEO Craig Reynolds said. "It's just amazing, the passion they have for this team. There's the support that they've given to this team through thick and thin. They've always been there.

"They're so passionate, and that goes every which way. They're passionate when you win, and they're so excited and so happy, and then they're very passionate when you lose and they wear their hearts on their sleeves."

Jim Hopson, Reynolds' predecessor as president-CEO, can attest to that.

"I love the fans," Hopson said. "They are passionate. That's the word I always think of—passionate. I'd remind myself of that when I'd be with some less-than-happy fans.

"The passion made them cheer and paint their faces and sit in terrible weather and follow the team through thick and thin and all the good stuff. But also, when things went bad, they felt they had the right to express their unhappiness.

"You're dealing with a million owners. That's what you've got. You've got people who have ownership of the team. That's tremendous. It's the buy-in. They're not just fans. They're owners. It's part of their DNA, so to speak."

The Regina-born Hopson, a Roughriders player from 1973 to 1976, has seen countless examples of fandom that extend far beyond the norm.

"There are a number of stories of people asking to be buried in their Riders jerseys or being buried in the casket with the Rider flag on it," he noted. "I remember visiting people at the end of their lives and them telling me what the Riders have meant to them and their family.

"The Riders are sort of woven into the fabric of people's lives. It's part of who they are, and they pass it on. We're now talking third and fourth and fifth generations of Rider fans who continue to be the best out there, I think. I had the good fortune to travel across Canada so much, and the Rider fans in Ottawa are just as passionate as the Rider fans in Lucky Lake. They care."

They care to an extent that their emotional temperature is affected by the team's performance.

"It has a huge impact on how people are doing," Weyburn-born Roughriders guard Brendon LaBatte said. "Moods change

Making Noise About Noise

It has long been considered acceptable for a loud home crowd to make life difficult for the visiting quarterback and his offensive cohorts.

Messages on video boards at sporting venues routinely exhort the fans to Make Some Noise! (Translation: on the count of three, be spontaneous!)

But there was a time when some members of the football fraternity felt it was poor form for noise from the gallery to affect the proceedings.

Such was the sentiment among members of the Ottawa Rough Riders' coaching staff on September 10, 1967, following a 32–23 loss to Saskatchewan before a sellout crowd of 21,696 at Taylor Field.

For starters, Rough Riders assistant coach Al Bruno blasted the officiating.

"Awww, never mind the officiating," Rough Riders assistant coach Kelley Mote told Laurie Artiss of the *Leader-Post*. "I'm not complaining about that. It's the fans! You call these fans here great? Why, they're from Hicksville!

"That hollering when we were trying to call plays is ridiculous, and the poorest sportsmanship I've ever seen. We prepared well for this game...we knew what their defence was going to do and we had check-offs to everything. Not only couldn't we use audibles, but our guys couldn't even hear the signals!"

Mote, by contrast, was easily heard.

"It was a disgrace!" he snorted. "If they can beat us fair and square, then fine, but this wasn't either. They should be ashamed of themselves. Maybe they'd smarten up if other cities did the same to their team, and I hope it's us, because the next time we face 'em, we're going to whip 'em good."

Ottawa head coach Frank Clair was also whipped up after the game—and "The Professor" was not known for emotional outbursts.

"The sorriest thing is that Canadian football has no rule to prevent that," Clair said. "Sure, you can call a time-out once, and the clock stops. But the second time you must put the ball into play and you know the screaming would have been louder if we tried that."

The din made it virtually impossible for Ottawa quarterback Russ Jackson to call audibles at the line of scrimmage.

"Sure, it hurt that we couldn't check off," Clair said. "But I might have been happy if our players could have heard just the original signals. Look how many times we were called for offensive offside, simply because our linemen couldn't hear the numbers. And we had backs running into each other because they were missing their count.

"Everybody says we need more scoring in our game and they even suggest four downs. Here we were giving them a great scoring game and the crowd just killed it. I'm not saying we would have won, because Regina played a fine game, but I think we, or any visiting club, deserve an equal chance."

when the Riders are doing good or bad. That's the importance of this team to the province."

The province's importance to the team is also worth acknowledging, considering that playing in Regina, in front of rabid Roughriders fans, can present a daunting challenge for members of the visiting side.

"From the moment they get off the plane, it's palpable," said Rod Pedersen, the play-by-play voice of the Roughriders for 20 seasons. "Why do the people take it so seriously? People can say it's all we have. They're probably right, and who cares? We don't have to apologize for that. It puts us on the national stage. It unites everybody. We all have that one common thing. What I laugh about is when guys like [former Roughriders general manager] Eric Tillman say we've got a million assistant GMs. Actually, it's millions. It's not just the people who live in the 306. It's all around the world."

21 "The Crisis Is Real"

Rider Pride nearly died.

It seems unfathomable now, considering the Roughriders' vast financial resources, but the CFL team was on death's door as recently as 1997.

On March 15 of that year, a province-wide, buy-or-die telethon was held with the objective of selling the equivalent of 200,000 tickets. The ticket blitz became a last-ditch initiative after a 1996 season in which $1.7 million in losses put the community-owned franchise $2.6 million in debt.

"Our debt exceeds our line of credit," Roughriders president Fred Wagman said during a sombre media conference on December 11, 1996. "The crisis is real. I'm convinced that if we don't meet these two components, we'll be shutting down."

The words were jarring, although not entirely surprising. After the Roughriders' regular season home finale in 1996, there was some speculation as to whether the last CFL game on Taylor Field had just been played. After all, the Green and White was in dire straits and the league was on life support.

The week of the 1996 Grey Cup game, played in Hamilton, felt like a wake. It was impossible for even the most optimistic observer to ignore the grim financial realities that were facing the league—issues that were mirrored in Saskatchewan.

It was a tense winter as the Roughriders gradually approached their goal. Then, on the morning of the telethon, team treasurer Tom Shepherd announced that an anonymous benefactor, labelled "a consortium of private companies," had donated $500,000—an amount that translated into 29,412 single-game tickets.

That contribution, as it turned out, put the Roughriders over the top. To conclude the five-and-a-half-hour telethon, it was announced that 215,222 tickets had been sold.

The financier, it turned out, was the NFL. It had reached a working agreement with the CFL that included a U.S. $3 million loan, the Roughriders' share working out to $500,000 in Canadian currency.

The Roughriders, throughout their history, have faced and overcome financial challenges. After the First World War, for example, the Regina Rugby Club had 30 cents in its bank account. A fundraising campaign soon boosted that amount to $2,265, according to the 1984 team history *Rider Pride* by Bob Calder and Garry Andrews.

In 1937, a *Leader-Post* headline screamed, THE 'RIDERS NEED HELP!

"Start the money rolling in," read part of a Depression-era advertisement. "If it is not available, the present tough times on these Saskatchewan plains may drive Regina out of the big Western football picture—for the first time in a quarter century."

Once again, the day was saved, although the team's existence was not an easy one for the longest time.

Consider the events of 1961, when back-to-back dreadful seasons—over which the Roughriders won only three games—had created a financial crisis.

The team was $78,000 in debt, a monstrous total in those days, when Bob Kramer—the Roughriders' president from 1951 to 1953—returned for a term that would last from 1961 to 1965. Kramer, who was eventually inducted into the Roughriders' Plaza of Honour and the Canadian Football Hall of Fame, spearheaded a successful ticket campaign.

The debt load became suffocating once again by the mid-1980s. The Roughriders' rainy-day fund had been exhausted after they lost

$723,000 on their 1986 operations. They were $600,000 in debt when the management committee met to plot out the future.

One key move was the appointment of former Roughriders defensive lineman Bill Baker, then a member of the club's executive, as general manager. Shortly after assuming the GM's post, he began restructuring the organization, with an emphasis on cost cutting.

Late in April 1987, Baker met the media and declared that the franchise's future was tenuous, to the extent that it could be broke by late August or early September if there weren't improvements on the field and at the gate.

"Nobody quite believes it," Baker told reporters, "but I tell you, it can really happen."

At that point, the Roughriders had 11,500 season-ticket holders. They needed an average attendance of twice as many customers to make ends meet.

While encouraging fans to purchase tickets, the Roughriders endeavoured to slash expenses by $1 million. An individual salary ceiling of $70,000 was imposed, meaning that star players such as future Hall of Famers Ray Elgaard and Roger Aldag accepted pay cuts to help the team.

Baker issued an update in May 1987, when slightly fewer than 13,000 season tickets had been purchased. He warned that one of the necessary lifesavers would be the sale of another 100,000 game tickets.

"I don't think people realize how fragile it is," said Baker, echoing his refrain of the previous month. "I don't think people really believe it will happen—that the club might not be here."

As a means of selling those tickets, a telethon—a 16-hour event that aired June 13 and 14—was scheduled. The team ended up selling 77,138 ducats, which left them shy of the 100,000 objective, but the infusion of ticket revenue along with some concessions from city hall greatly improved the Roughriders' chances of survival.

Dan Rambo, the team's director of player personnel at the time, credits Baker for his stewardship during a perilous period.

"He is probably considered by many to be the architect, along with the board of the day, of the modern-day revival of the Saskatchewan Roughriders," Rambo said.

Even so, there was not an immediate improvement on the field in 1987. The Roughriders posted a 5–12–1 record, compared to 6–11–1 the year before.

Nonetheless, a foundation for future prosperity was established under first-year head coach John Gregory with the arrivals in 1987 of quarterbacks Kent Austin and Tom Burgess, and receiver Don Narcisse. Plus, placekicker Dave Ridgway rejoined the Roughriders (who had traded him away earlier in the year) via a dispersal draft when the Montreal Alouettes folded, and second-year rush end Bobby Jurasin blossomed into a star (registering a franchise-record 22 sacks). Two years later, the Roughriders won the Grey Cup.

In 1997, a year that began with apprehension about the team's future culminated in an unexpected berth in the Grey Cup game. Saskatchewan had an 8–10 regular season slate before upsetting the Calgary Stampeders and Edmonton Eskimos in the West Division playoffs, with quarterback Reggie Slack emerging as an unlikely hero. The storybook was slammed shut in the Grey Cup, though, when Doug Flutie and the Toronto Argonauts easily won 47–23.

Despite the disappointment, considerable solace could be derived from the stirring postseason run, and from the sheer financial survival of the Roughriders and the CFL.

22 See the Riders on the Road

Even far away from Mosaic Stadium, Roughriders fans tend to make themselves at home.

That is especially true at Calgary's McMahon Stadium, where a green invasion occurs every time the Roughriders visit. Based upon crowd noise, it is often difficult to discern whether Saskatchewan or the host Calgary side has made a big play.

"I wouldn't say it's neutral, but it's very close," said Roughriders receiving great Jeff Fairholm, who resides in Calgary. "There's a lot of Saskatchewan-born people in Calgary, and their Rider Pride lasts. It seems like half the stadium is in green and white. Edmonton's the same way. It's the same everywhere you go. It's crazy."

Although some of the host teams would no doubt prefer to see more of the seats occupied by their own fans, revenue generated as a result of visits by the Roughriders is happily accepted across the league.

"There are few more gratifying pure 'Canadian' experiences than attending a Roughrider game in an opposing stadium anywhere in Canada," Roughriders fan Ron Podbielski said. "To some, this may be a stretch, but if you want one way of understanding why this is such a wonderful, tolerant, and beautiful country to live in, you can do few better things than don a Roughrider jersey and see a game in Vancouver, Edmonton, Toronto, or Calgary.

"Sure, you hear the stories of Rider fans being abused on the road—having beer spilled on them, their children insulted, their game experience a misery—and I don't doubt that this stuff happens. The back-and-forth catcalls I have heard between Rider and Bomber fans simply walking to Mosaic on Labour Day Sunday...what starts out as a polite interaction can become beer- and frustration-fuelled and evolve into something else. But my experiences have been so much more uplifting."

In the summer of 2013, for example, Podbielski watched the Roughriders—who concluded that season with a home-field Grey Cup triumph—defeat the Eskimos, whereupon he returned to his hotel via Edmonton's Light Rail Transit.

"A lovely couple wearing Eskimos jerseys sat down beside me and my family on the way home from Commonwealth Stadium," he recalled. "It had been a back-and-forth encounter culminated by a Rider victory in one of [running back] Kory Sheets' memorable performances that year. It was a devastating loss for the Eskimos' fans, suffering through a tough 4–14 year.

"As we talked about the game, the couple asked me about my family, engaged with my kids, thanked me for visiting Edmonton, and then wished my team well. Where else does this happen?"

Podbielski also remembers taking the subway to a game in Toronto. He was seated near a father-son duo, resplendent in Argonauts jerseys. "Hey, Rider fan…the best fans in the world," the dad said to Podbielski. "Glad to see you come here to our stadium."

Such was the ignition of an extended conversation about everything they shared as Canadian football fans.

"I thought to myself, 'In this cosmopolitan city, considered snobby and too big for the CFL, this man and his 20-something son are still into talking about what binds us together—Canadian football,'" Podbielski marvelled. "The Argo fans are few in number, but mighty in spirit."

A comparable experience was savoured in Vancouver in 2010. Podbielski travelled to the stadium via a jam-packed bus on which, according to his estimate, Roughriders fans outnumbered B.C. Lions supporters by a 60-to-40 ratio.

"We all started singing 'Green is the Colour,'" Podbielski said of the Roughriders' fight song. "The Lions' fans, smaller in number but louder in an attempt to compensate, started singing the terrible B.C. fight song. But instead of catcalls, what erupts afterward is a chorus of laughter and high-fives between the Lions fans and the Rider fans. Where else but Canada could this ever happen?

"If you want to understand how sport can transcend itself and mean something more than just wins or losses, go to a Rider road game and take public transit. Your faith in what Canadian football means to this great country—hell, why we have a great country—will be completely restored."

23 "We Want Ronnie!"

The 1978 Roughriders finished last in the West with a 4–11–1 record but, nonetheless, the ending was absolutely perfect.

Ron Lancaster's final CFL game as a quarterback was the definition of poetic justice, considering the nature of his playing career and the way his farewell appearance at Taylor Field had unfolded.

Improbably, and still unfathomably, the Little General was booed by some of the home "fans" one week before he received multiple standing ovations on the road—to the extent that Edmonton Eskimos supporters were actually cheering against their own team, which had secured first place in the West before it played host to Saskatchewan on the penultimate week of the regular season. (The Roughriders had a bye in the final week.)

A Commonwealth Stadium crowd of 42,673 wanted to see the legendary No. 23 one more time, and Roughriders head coach Walt Posadowski eventually obliged.

Rookie pivot Larry Dick, Lancaster's heir apparent, had started the game and played reasonably well—throwing two touchdown passes—but the only story on October 29, 1978, was the final appearance of a 40-year-old CFL icon.

With less than 11 minutes remaining in the fourth quarter, Lancaster removed his warmup jacket and entered the game with his team trailing 26–20. As he walked on to the field, Lancaster received a handshake from Edmonton cornerback Larry Highbaugh and a standing ovation from the Eskimos' fans.

Lancaster would soon engineer a trademark fourth-quarter comeback—one of 50 in his 16 seasons with Saskatchewan—as the Roughriders won 36–26.

For starters, Lancaster threw a game-tying touchdown pass to Joey Walters, with Bob Macoritti's convert putting the visitors ahead to stay.

Lancaster added an insurance major when, shortly after completing his final pass (to Brian O'Hara), No. 23 scored on a one-yard quarterback sneak in a third-and-goal situation.

"I figured when you get close, you should give it to your best back," Lancaster, always quick with a quip, told a swarm of reporters.

The postgame picture had been dramatically different one week earlier, when the Winnipeg Blue Bombers won 13–7 at Taylor Field. On that occasion as well, Posadowski had replaced Dick with Lancaster in the fourth quarter, but he threw two interceptions and some fans' displeasure went overboard.

"If you can believe it or not, here at Taylor Field, they're booing Ron Lancaster," analyst Mike Wadsworth said, incredulously, during CTV's telecast of the game.

Columnist Bob Hughes was suitably appalled and made his feelings known in the October 23, 1978, edition of the *Leader-Post*.

"This is a guy who has given almost half his life to the Saskatchewan Roughriders," Hughes wrote. "This is a guy who came in here when they were nothing, when they were down, when they seemed to run out of life, and he made them into a dynasty

The Little General Stands Tall

The odds were never too long for a quarterback who was thought to be too short.

Ron Lancaster, at 5-foot–9¾, became a giant figure in the CFL despite his modest dimensions, and in spite of some skeptical coaches who felt that he wasn't tall enough.

Bob Shaw, the Roughriders' head coach in 1963 and 1964, was among the doubters—at least at the outset of Lancaster's 16-season tenure behind centre for the Green and White.

In 1963, the Roughriders auditioned a number of other quarterbacks—Bob Ptacek (who was also an excellent linebacker and defensive back), Lee Grosscup, M.C. Reynolds, and a warmed-over Frank Tripucka—in addition to Lancaster before finally settling on the latter.

Ptacek was the opening-day starting quarterback before Shaw turned to the newly acquired Lancaster, who was at the controls for six consecutive games. Lancaster was then left off the travelling roster as the Roughriders went to Calgary and started Grosscup—a first-round draft pick of the New York Giants in 1959—against the Stampeders. When Grosscup struggled, Shaw turned to Ptacek once again, with little change in the results (or lack thereof).

The situation became even more confused leading up to a September 21 home game against the Edmonton Eskimos. Tripucka, approaching 36, was brought back for a third stint in Saskatchewan. At his peak, he was one of the premier passers in franchise history, and his success carried over into the fledgling American Football League as an original member of the Denver Broncos.

By 1963, however, Tripucka was all but done. He was quoted as saying, "I've only got 10 good throws left in me. Do you want me to use them all up in one quarter?"

Upon arriving in Regina, only 30 hours before the Edmonton game, Tripucka told the *Leader-Post*, "I just hope they're not expecting miracles."

Lancaster was reinstated as the starter against Edmonton, but when the offence continued to falter, Tripucka soon entered the game. At that point, as the *Leader-Post's* John Robertson observed, "More than a few fans were wondering not only whether Lancaster was through for the evening, but if he had just about run out the string as a Rider."

It was Tripucka, though, who was playing out the string. He was lifted after throwing his third interception and in came Lancaster, again, to begin the fourth quarter. The offence languished as Edmonton increased its lead to 7–1. Worse yet, the Roughriders were backed up to their one-yard line, needing a touchdown and a convert to win.

"With the wind against them, all seemed lost for the Roughriders," Robertson wrote of a team that was staring at the likelihood of a third consecutive game without a touchdown.

Sixteen plays and 109 yards later, the Roughriders had that touchdown—an eight-yard pass from Lancaster to Dale West on second-and-goal.

"I could see West in the end zone but guys kept grabbing me," Lancaster told the *Leader-Post.* "I could hear Coach Shaw yelling from the bench to throw the darn thing, but every time I raised my arm someone bumped into me. When I finally got it away, I was sure it was going to hit the goal post, but it missed by about a foot."

Reg Whitehouse's convert, with 1:35 left, provided what turned out to be the winning point. West, a star on both sides of the ball that day, sealed the victory with an interception—one of his CFL-best 10 picks that season.

Even after the 109-yard drive, Shaw was not sold on Lancaster, who handled most of the quarterbacking for the next three games.

Tripucka's final start was on October 12, 1963, when the Roughriders lost 26–6 to the B.C. Lions. Only then did Shaw turn to Lancaster again—and for good.

The rest was history, as was the Roughriders' chaotic quarterback carousel of 1963.

feared throughout the Canadian Football League. This is a guy who has turned down chances to go play elsewhere, where the money would have been bigger, turned it all down so he could stay here because it was a good place to raise a family, and he did believe in Roughrider tradition. Hell, he was Roughrider tradition.

"And yesterday, they booed him. It was sad, and it was unfair, and people around Western Canada, who watched it and heard it on television, could not believe it."

The subsequent events in Edmonton were also difficult to believe. How often, after all, is a rival player the object of so much adoration?

A banner—"Thank you, Ron, for all the good years"—was conspicuous at the Eskimos' home park throughout the afternoon. Edmonton fans burst into a "We Want Ronnie!" chant during the fourth quarter. When he put the Roughriders ahead, he received another standing ovation, as WOW! flashed on the scoreboard.

The love-in for Lancaster was such that a Commonwealth Stadium firetruck, which usually did a celebratory lap when the Eskimos scored a touchdown, saluted the Roughriders' quarterback as sirens blared. A sign reading HOO-RAY RONNIE was displayed on the side of the vehicle during the salute.

"If Ronnie had written the script himself, he couldn't have written it any better," Walters recalled. "That last game was kind of a storybook, wasn't it?"

It was the antithesis of the horror story against Winnipeg, a sad situation that Lancaster was always reluctant to discuss. But, thankfully, there was one more week, one more game, and one more riveting rally by Ronnie.

"When the game ended, no one was really happy with the season," Lancaster said 30 years later when asked about his fitting farewell to the football field. "You tried to forget it. It was tough.

"But, yeah, that was a good day."

24 Attend the Plaza of Honour Inductions

The Roughriders' Plaza of Honour is a shrine of a slightly different shine.

Although the Plaza recognizes familiar figures such as Ron Lancaster and George Reed, there is also ample room to acknowledge people of long and distinguished service who may not be regarded as icons.

"It's the Plaza of Honour—not a hall of fame," selection-committee chairman John Lipp noted. "It was purposely named Plaza of Honour because there's more to it than pure athletic excellence. That is factored into our selections, honestly, but it is broader than that."

That is part of the charm. While paying homage to legends, the Plaza also enables players, coaches, administrators, and volunteers of longstanding service and devotion to receive due commendation for their oftentimes quiet contributions to the community-owned team.

"It gives us a chance to recognize some people who played 10 or 12 years—maybe someone who wasn't a big star, but who faithfully played roles on the team," Lipp said. "It gives us a chance to acknowledge someone who might have been overlooked at times, but who was nonetheless important to the success of the team."

Consider the inductees for 2019—Kerry Joseph and Neal Hughes.

Joseph played a marquee position, quarterback, and in so doing guided Saskatchewan to the 2007 Grey Cup title. Along the way, he was named the league's most outstanding player.

Hughes, by contrast, was seldom in the spotlight during his 10 years with the Roughriders. He wasn't even drafted, but

Ken Reed (left), Gary Lewis (centre), and Rhett Dawson in front of the Saskatchewan Roughriders Plaza of Honour in 2006. (Roy Antal / *Regina Leader-Post*)

nonetheless helped the team—one he had watched as a young season-ticket holder—win two Grey Cups. As one who excelled in high school football (with the Thom Trojans), and with the junior and university Regina Rams, he is a home-grown success story, and eminently Plaza-worthy as a result.

Initially, the big, big names were accentuated. The Plaza was introduced in 1987—77 years after the franchise's inception—so there was plenty of catching up to do. But the shrine has evolved quite nicely into a mechanism for appreciating people who, as Lipp put it, "have done yeoman work in the community, in the city, and in the province."

The induction ceremony, like the shrine, is not elitist. The average fan can mingle with Roughriders stars, past and present, and with other people whose bond is a passion for their green team.

25 "Huddle Up" and the Cup

One momentous Grey Cup prompted talk of another.

After the Roughriders defeated the Hamilton Tiger-Cats 43–40 in the 1989 championship game, Phil Kershaw took over as president of the Green and White and immediately began to think big.

"As we held our annual meeting in early December, right after the big win, I was thinking of a bold stroke—something to capitalize on the euphoria that enveloped the province at the time," Kershaw recalled. "I thought, 'Why can't we host the Grey Cup?'

"Remember, we had neither hosted nor even applied to host it at the time, for the simple reason that Regina and the area didn't have the requisite accommodations to put on a major event.

"Frankly, some of my colleagues probably wondered if I should be impeached for forwarding such a loony concept, but I felt it was time for the Riders to step up and be bold."

Kershaw initially proposed that Regina play host to the 1993 Grey Cup, an idea that was greeted with skepticism.

"Everybody thought it was unrealistic," said John Lipp, the Roughriders' president from 1993 to 1995, who did not fall into the category of "everybody."

Lipp had attended the 1988 Grey Cup, played in Ottawa, and took note of how the capacity of Lansdowne Park was increased by temporary seating.

Emulating Ottawa, he figured, could allow the Roughriders to meet the minimum seating requirement of 44,000. (Taylor Field had 27,637 permanent seats at the time.)

Prairie weather in November was also viewed as a potential negative but, again, Lipp took note of precedent. If a Grey Cup could be held in Winnipeg, as was the case in 1992, why not Regina?

Lipp raised the issue with CFL commissioner Larry Smith during 1993 Grey Cup week in another prairie city, Calgary.

"I told him, 'Larry, we're going to try to bid for a Grey Cup,' and that we had been able to overcome the stadium thing," Lipp recalled. "He said, 'Sure! Why don't you? Give it a shot.' He was very encouraging."

It was more than Lipp service. The Roughriders president proceeded to meet with the team's board of directors and discussions intensified about a possible bid, which soon became reality.

Presentations were made to the CFL's board of governors on March 3, 1994, in Sacramento, California. Saskatchewan and Winnipeg were the aspiring hosts, with the winner requiring two-thirds approval from the 10 governors.

Saskatchewan was ahead on the first ballot, but only by 6–4. At that point, Calgary Stampeders owner Larry Ryckman recommended a half-hour break, during which the candidates could possibly tweak their proposals. Lipp used the respite to chat with Saskatchewan premier Roy Romanow, who was part of the delegation, and said, "We need to sweeten our offer just a bit," and a little extra was added—in the form of additional dollars that increased Saskatchewan's guarantee to the CFL to $3.2 million.

"We went back in, took another vote, and got the required seven votes," Lipp said.

There was still the matter of limited hotel space in Regina but, again, ingenuity won out. "Huddle Up In Saskatchewan" was warmly received by Reginans who responded to the plea to open up their homes to out-of-town Grey Cup attendees.

With slightly more than a year and a half before the big game, the organizing committee—chaired by Bob Ellard—immersed

The City of Taylor Field

Records are supposedly meant to be broken, but one Roughriders standard is certain to last.

On October 14, 1995, an unprecedented, unmatchable crowd of 55,438 watched Saskatchewan defeat the Calgary Stampeders 25–20 at Taylor Field.

For three hours on a Saturday afternoon, Taylor Field was the third-largest city in Saskatchewan, behind Saskatoon and Regina.

"That was a great day—a highlight of my career," recalled Dan Farthing, who caught a touchdown pass in that game to help Saskatchewan improve its record to 6–10.

"We let the crowd get to us," Stampeders offensive lineman Bobby Pandelidis told Murray Rauw of the *Calgary Herald* after the game.

For part of the 1995 season, the seating capacity of Taylor Field was doubled by temporary bleachers that were erected for the first Regina-based Grey Cup game.

Calgary also played in that year's championship game, losing 37–20 to the Baltimore Stallions on November 19, 1995, before 52,064 onlookers—more than 3,000 fewer than had watched the October 14 spectacle, when five per cent of the people who were in Saskatchewan that day were at the stadium.

"I was on the field before the kickoff," said John Lipp, who was the Roughriders' president at the time. "I looked up in the stands, saw that many people, and got choked up. It was overwhelming."

It is impossible to imagine the Roughriders again playing before such a gathering, or anything close, at home. The new Mosaic Stadium, which opened in 2017, has 33,350 permanent seats and can be expanded to 40,000 for special events, such as a Grey Cup. Although the surroundings are state of the art, the sea of humanity of October 14, 1995, will never be rivalled.

itself in the preparations and ultimately staged a spectacularly successful event.

Regina was alive during the week leading up to the game, as fans flocked to various venues that included a tent that was erected downtown. The streets were jammed for the Grey Cup parade. And the game was played before 52,064 spectators at Taylor Field, where the Baltimore Stallions defeated Calgary 37–20.

The major hurdle, as it turned out, involved actually starting the game. There was talk of postponement due to howling winds that, had they persisted, could have posed a hazard to fans sitting in the towering temporary seats.

"When we arrived about an hour and a half before the game, we weren't let into the stadium," Roughriders fan Ron Podbielski recalled. "The ticket-taker told me, 'The wind is so high, there is fear the temporary seating might collapse. In all likelihood, the game is going to be cancelled until tomorrow, but hang around as we don't know for sure.'

"I thought, '*WHAT?*', thinking about our city's biggest nightmare. Here we had done a fabulous job hosting our first-ever Grey Cup week, and 'Huddle Up In Saskatchewan' was going to morph into a Monday Grey Cup hangover, with a small viewing audience and the big-city doubters snickering at Regina."

The go-ahead was eventually given and the gates were opened. The game was uneventful, save for the fact that Baltimore became the first (and only) U.S.-based Grey Cup champion. The CFL's three-year American experiment was ashcanned after the 1995 season.

Expansion to the United States provided much-needed money, in the form of franchise fees, at a time when the league was desperately clinging to life.

The Roughriders, who were also in dire financial straits, realized a $1.1-million profit from the 1995 Grey Cup. On top of that, a point was proven. Regina could, in fact, play host to a Grey Cup festival—and a wildly successful one at that.

Subsequently, the question changed from *if* Regina could stage a Grey Cup to *when* the next one would be. Sure enough, the championship game returned to Regina in 2003, and again a decade later.

In 2013, the Roughriders registered their ultimate home-field victory, defeating the Hamilton Tiger-Cats 45-23 in the 101st Grey Cup game—another happening that, once upon a time, was thought to be impossible.

The Grey Cup game is to return to Regina on November 22, 2020, when new Mosaic Stadium will play host to a CFL championship game for the first time. The 2020 Grey Cup was awarded to Saskatchewan on February 21, 2019. The event will be held in conjunction with the Roughriders' 110th anniversary season.

26 Cold Discomfort

The painful memory is frozen in time for anyone who was at Taylor Field on November 22, 1970.

Improbably, Larry Robinson kicked a 32-yard field goal—directly into a forbidding, chilling wind that was gusting up to 60 kilometres per hour—on the final play to give the Calgary Stampeders a 15–14 victory over Saskatchewan in the third and deciding game of the Western Conference final.

"I didn't think there was a chance," Robinson reflected. "I tried kicking into the wind from there before the game and never even got one to the goal line. When I did kick it, I thought it was going to make the goal line but go wide. Then a gust hit it and, whew, it went through."

And the Roughriders' finest season *was* through.

Saskatchewan had dominated the CFL in 1970, registering a 14–2 record, and appeared poised to continue on its roll during the playoffs.

Then everything that could go wrong, did. Although Saskatchewan won 11-3 in Calgary to force a third game, Ron Lancaster—who was named the CFL's most outstanding player in 1970—suffered cracked ribs and a bruised muscle in his back and was therefore sidelined for most of the rubber match.

Another factor was the weather, which was somehow braved by 18,385 onlookers, including Lorne Kazmir.

"At halftime, the guy behind me offered $10—and then $20— for the palm-sized, chrome hand-warmer that I had," recounted Kazmir, a longtime fan. "Keep in mind that $20 could be more than a day's wages back then. I thought about it briefly, but then decided that I couldn't spend $20 if I froze to death."

Kazmir also remembered another icicle of a fan saying, "If I die here today, do you think they will find my body before spring training?"

Mind you, many fans were heated up by controversial officiating decisions.

Shortly after an interception by Bob Kosid late in the third quarter, Gary Lane—starting at quarterback in place of Lancaster— rolled out to the left and ran toward the end zone from Calgary's 12-yard line. Lane, whose helmet was torn off during the play, thought he had scored but was ruled out of bounds at the 1-yard line.

The bad news continued from there. Lane fumbled on first-and-goal from the 1-yard line, the result being a half-yard loss.

On second down, Lane planned to hand off to George Reed, but the star fullback slipped on the icy turf. Lane then took off

Earning the Stripes

Ironically, Gary Lane's abbreviated tenure with the Roughriders is notable for some controversial decisions by the officials—calls that Lane himself questioned at the time.

Lane later became an accomplished NFL official, working in that capacity from 1982 to 1999 and being on the field in two Super Bowls (1989 and 1999) along the way.

His career as a player included a stint with the 1970 Roughriders, for whom he was the starting quarterback in Game 3 of the Western Conference final due to an injury to Ron Lancaster.

Lane thought he had scored not once, but twice, against the Calgary Stampeders late in the third quarter of that game, which the Roughriders ultimately lost 15–14. Afterward, he pointed the finger at (guess who?) the officials.

"They took it away from us twice," he told the *Leader-Post*. "I stepped into the end zone inside the flag on that run...I know I did."

He was referring to a run from the 12-yard line, on which he thought he had scored, and felt the same way about a subsequent lunge toward the goal line from one-and-a-half yards out.

"I made it," he insisted. "I was lying across the goal line when the whistle stopped play. They ruled me out again."

Lane starred for the University of Missouri Tigers before spending three seasons in the NFL—two with the Cleveland Browns and one with the New York Giants.

He retired as an NFL official leading up to the 2000 season after failing his physical, the result of a heart problem. Sadly, he died of a heart attack in 2003 at age 60.

Lane is one of two former Roughriders quarterbacks who went on to enjoy a long and successful career in officiating.

Montreal-born Jim McKean, a member of the Green and White for part of the 1966 season, later changed his focus to umpiring and ended up working American League games from 1973 to 1999. He also umpired in three World Series (1979, 1985, 1995) and three Major League Baseball all-star games (1980, 1982, 1993).

himself and lunged toward the end zone. As was the case on his 11-yard run, it was very close, but a touchdown did not result.

"We didn't get the call when we needed the call," lamented Reed, who felt Lane was in the end zone both times.

Lane fumbled on third-and-goal from the 1-yard line, and a golden opportunity was squandered.

Even so, Saskatchewan was ahead 14–12 after the third quarter. That lead held up until Robinson's climactic kick.

"The best team we ever had was in 1970," Hall of Fame centre Ted Urness said in 2006. "[Calgary] never should have won it."

Eagle Keys, the Roughriders' head coach from 1965 to 1970, still marvelled at Robinson's kick more than three decades later.

"We didn't think he had a chance in the world to make the thing," Keys said. "It was like somebody took the ball and dropped it over the goal posts. We felt like we should have won that one and gone to the Grey Cup again."

Instead, Calgary advanced to the national final against the Montreal Alouettes, who won 23–10—with future Roughriders great Jeff Fairholm in the stands, watching his father (Larry) play defensive back for the winning side.

It was hardly the championship matchup anyone expected. Saskatchewan, after all, was the only CFL team to reach double digits in victories during the 1970 regular season. Calgary and the Edmonton Eskimos each had 9–7 slates, and Montreal—which was barely over .500 (7–6–1) and third in the Eastern Conference— ended up winning it all.

27 Safety First

Roughriders safety Glen Suitor was vilified and vindicated during the championship season of 1989.

In cases where there wasn't any time remaining on the clock, he experienced, within two months, the lowest and highest moments of his professional football career.

Suitor reached a nadir September 30, when he was flagged for pass interference on a Hail Mary pass attempt by the B.C. Lions. His rare mistake put the Lions in position to win 32–30 at Taylor Field.

Once the playoffs arrived, Suitor was able to savour sweet redemption and, ultimately, the taste of champagne.

In order to do so, he had to get past a nightmarish Saturday night in September.

It appeared that a Saskatchewan victory was a mortal lock. The Lions had the ball on the Roughriders' 53-yard line with just five seconds remaining in the fourth quarter. The only option for the visiting side was a desperation pass.

As the final few seconds ticked away, Matt Dunigan threw a bomb in the direction of three receivers, each of whom was far away from the end zone. Even if the ball was caught, all the Roughriders had to do was make the tackle and win the game. It was as simple as that.

There was only one problem: Suitor crashed into B.C.'s David Williams well before the ball arrived. It was a no-brainer of a pass-interference call.

Because a game cannot end on a penalty, the Lions were given one more play, from the Roughriders' 18-yard line. Dunigan again looked to Williams, who was interfered with in the end zone—this time by Albert Brown.

More flags. More life for the Lions. More slapping of foreheads on the part of Roughriders loyalists.

As a result of the second successive pass-interference call, the Lions were given the ball on the one-yard line. Dunigan proceeded to score on a 1-yard run—only after fumbling the snap, recovering the ball, and frantically reaching the end zone—and the Roughriders were left to bemoan an indigestible defeat.

"That's the toughest loss ever, no question," head coach John Gregory told reporters after the Roughriders' record fell to 6–7. "I don't know what else can happen to this football team, but I don't think one play by one person determines a football game. The easiest thing to do is to point fingers after a loss and to start shuffling players."

The Roughriders didn't point fingers, but the same could not be said of the fans. Suitor was excoriated on open-line phone-in shows for what he acknowledged was a "terrible decision."

The backlash was such that, for about a day, Suitor (who was then 26) debated whether to retire from football. That notion was abandoned when he met with and received an endorsement from Gregory.

"He said, 'Pretty much everybody in this province wants me to cut you, or at least make sure I bench you for the rest of the way,'" Suitor recalled. "I said, 'Coach, you might have to do that, and I deserve it. I understand.' He said, 'There's no way I'm going to do that. You made a mistake. Other guys made mistakes in the game, too.'"

Suitor was unerring, however, in how he handled the aftermath of the game. He faced reporters in the dressing room, despite being near tears, and even guested on CKRM Radio's call-in show two nights after the game.

Saskatchewan Roughriders safety Glen Suitor on September 30, 1984.
(Bryan Schlosser, *Regina Leader-Post*)

"Glen sat there for about the first 40 minutes of the show like a piñata," said Geoff Currier, who was then the radio voice of the Roughriders. "We all know how tough Saskatchewan fans can be. He had this colossal blunder, so they just whacked him. It was just brutal, and you're cringing for the poor guy.

"But as the show went on, the calls started to turn around. People started to call in and stick up for him. By the end of the show, people were kind of back on board. As tough as Saskatchewan fans are, they also have a sense of fairness about them, and compassion."

There was also an element of fairness to the culmination of the 1989 season.

Suitor starred in the West Division final in Edmonton, registering five defensive tackles, an interception, and a quarterback sack to help the Roughriders (9–9) upset the 16–2 Eskimos 32–21. He was routinely deployed on blitzes, a strategy the Roughriders had installed especially for that game, and the Eskimos could not find a way to cope.

"I was still in the mode, all the way through to and including the Grey Cup, of, I've got to make amends for that mistake [against B.C.]. Every single time, every single play, I have to give everything I have. I may still miss a tackle, but I have to go 100 per cent every play because I've got to make amends for that mistake," Suitor said.

Make amends he did, several times over, while helping the Roughriders advance to and win the Grey Cup game, defeating the Hamilton Tiger-Cats 43–40. Suitor added another interception, pinned the ball for the game-winning field goal—a 35-yarder by Dave Ridgway with two seconds remaining—and, fittingly, was the last player to touch the football during that classic contest.

Following Ridgway's field goal, the Roughriders kicked off. The Tiger-Cats' Steve Jackson fielded the kickoff at his 28-yard line and quickly punted the football back into Saskatchewan territory. Suitor retrieved the ball on the 40-yard line, near the sideline.

He scurried out of bounds while raising his hands in the air as Saskatchewan celebrated the second championship in its history.

It was the only title for Suitor, who in 1989 was named a West Division All-Star for the first of five times. A three-time league All-Star, he retired after the 1994 season—as the Roughriders' all-time leading interceptor (51)—to become an analyst on TSN's CFL telecasts, a capacity in which he excels to this day.

28 Riders' Tie to a Spy

Nearly a half-century before the term "Spygate" was coined, a future Roughriders head coach was involved in a different form of espionage.

Bob Shaw, the Roughriders' field boss in 1963 and 1964, was an assistant coach and advance scout with the Baltimore Colts when they prepared for the NFL's 1958 championship game against the New York Giants.

At the insistence of Colts owner Carroll Rosenbloom, Shaw watched the Giants' practices from atop an apartment building that overlooked Yankee Stadium.

"He asked me to go up, and I went up for the week before the game and observed them," Shaw recalled in 2008, three years before his death. "I remember getting caught by the building manager, and I told him I was a reporter and I was writing a story that I spied on the club."

Shaw acknowledged that he "certainly had a concern" about spying on an opponent's practice, to the extent that he was worried about a possible detrimental effect on his future coaching career if he was caught.

Realizing that, Rosenbloom assured Shaw that he had a job for life if, somehow, the trickery was exposed. Suitably reassured, Shaw travelled to New York and found a spot on a rooftop, where he would be undetected by the Giants.

The Colts ended up winning 23–17 in overtime, in what has often been referred to as the "Greatest Game Ever Played." Did the pregame, er, scouting prove to be beneficial?

"It helped in this regard: they didn't do anything different, and that's a good thing to know when you're playing a team," Shaw said. "It just reconfirmed that they were doing what they were doing all year long."

"Spygate," as it existed decades ago, eventually came to light. In fact, it was mentioned by Giants great Frank Gifford in *The Glory Game*, a book about the 1958 classic.

"Apparently, Rosenbloom wanted to win the game that badly—for a lot of reasons," Gifford wrote. "Supposedly Shaw reported that we didn't appear to be working on anything new. But it didn't take a rocket scientist to figure that out. We hardly ever did anything different on offence, and never on defence. In fact, we hadn't changed anything since the regular season game in November when we'd beaten them. They didn't need Shaw. They just needed some film from our first game."

The issue of spying came to the fore when New England Patriots head coach Bill Belichick was fined $500,000 by the NFL after one of his team's video assistants was caught taping the New York Jets' defensive signals during a game in 2007. The incident quickly became known as "Spygate."

"Well, he did it a little bit differently, didn't he?" Shaw said, chuckling, in reference to Belichick. "I did it firsthand. He did it with cameras and stuff."

The 1958 game represented a breakthrough for the NFL. The telecast was watched by a once-unimaginable audience of 45 million.

Even with the benefit of spying, the Colts were trailing 17–14 late in the game, at which point quarterback Johnny Unitas guided Baltimore on a long drive. That possession was punctuated by Steve Myhra's 19-yard field goal with seven seconds remaining in the fourth quarter.

The kick by Myhra—who played for the Roughriders in 1961 and 1962—forced overtime, which concluded 8:15 into sudden-death play when Alan Ameche scored on a one-yard plunge.

"It was a fantastic game," Shaw said. "I think that set the tone for the NFL."

Shaw was a part of another classic—the "Little Miracle of Taylor Field," covered in Chapter 10—in his first year with the Roughriders.

"That Calgary playoff game at Regina was a hell of a game—coming back from 26 points," Shaw reflected. "The world's championship game was a great one, too."

29 It's All Relative

Duron Carter's hands are quite the hand-me-down.

His father, you see, is legendary NFL receiver Cris Carter.

With heredity in mind, the younger Carter—who made a series of spectacular catches during one-and-a-half seasons with the Roughriders—was asked if his surehandedness was a gift from Dad.

"I pretty much think I was born with hands," Duron Carter said in 2018. "I always had an uncanny ability to catch the ball, but I think it was something that was passed down to me from him."

Cris Carter, a 2013 inductee into the Pro Football Hall of Fame, caught 1,101 passes for 13,899 yards and 130 touchdowns over 16 NFL seasons, spent with the Philadelphia Eagles, Minnesota Vikings, and Miami Dolphins.

In 2017, Duron Carter had his second 1,000-yard receiving season as a CFL player en route to being named the Roughriders' most outstanding player. Always a charismatic and controversial presence, he was released by Saskatchewan near the midpoint of the 2018 season.

He soon resurfaced with the Toronto Argonauts and was employed in the same city where his uncle, Butch Carter, once coached the NBA's Raptors. Duron now plays for the B.C. Lions.

Duron Carter is among several former Roughriders who has had notable family ties extending beyond the CFL. For example:

- George Reed is from a football family. Two of his brothers, Wayne (a halfback) and Frank (cornerback), played for the New York Giants and Atlanta Falcons, respectively. Reed's brother-in-law, Jerry LeVias, was a receiver with the San Diego Chargers and Houston Oilers. Reed's cousin, Mel Farr, was a prominent running back with the Detroit Lions. Another cousin, Miller Farr, was a defensive back with the Chargers, Oilers, Lions, Denver Broncos, and St. Louis Cardinals. And there's more. Reed's daughter, Georgette, competed for Canada in the shot put in the 1992 Summer Olympic Games in Barcelona. (Got all that? Good.)
- John Chaput, in a superlative book titled *Saskatchewan Tough*, uncovered the nugget that Steve Belichick was a guest coach at the Roughriders' training camp in 1958. You might be familiar with his son—New England Patriots head coach Bill Belichick.
- Chris Getzlaf was a Roughriders receiver from 2007 to 2015, and again in 2017. His younger brother, Ryan, is a longtime NHL star with the Anaheim Ducks.
- Rich Preston—an assistant coach with Anaheim—was a waterboy with the Roughriders in the 1960s before becoming

a successful professional hockey player and coach. His father, Ken Preston, was the Roughriders' highly successful general manager from 1958 to 1977.

- Randy Mattingly was the Roughriders' backup quarterback in 1974 and 1975. His brother, Don Mattingly, was a beloved slugger with the New York Yankees before becoming a successful major-league manager.

- Darian Durant, a Roughriders quarterback from 2006 to 2016, closely followed his younger brother's NFL career. Justin Durant was a linebacker for five teams over 11 seasons.

- Bart Hull, a running back with the 1994 Roughriders, has impressive hockey connections to his father (Bobby), brother (Brett), and uncle (Dennis), each of whom starred in the NHL.

- Linebacking was in the genes for the Lowe brothers. Eddie Lowe played for the Roughriders from 1983 to 1991. Woodrow Lowe was with San Diego from 1976 to 1986.

- Jimmy Kemp was a Roughriders quarterback in 1996, and a CFLer from 1994 to 2002. His father, Jack Kemp, quarterbacked the Buffalo Bills before embarking on a career in politics. He was the running mate for Republican presidential candidate Bob Dole in 1996. Also worth noting: Jeff Kemp, Jimmy's brother, was an NFL signal-caller from 1981 to 1991.

- Fred McNair was a backup quarterback with Saskatchewan in 1992. His brother, Steve McNair, quarterbacked the Tennessee Titans in the 2000 Super Bowl. In 2003, he was named the NFL's co-MVP (along with the Indianapolis Colts' Peyton Manning).

- Frank Tripucka, who had three stints at quarterback with the Roughriders, was an especially prolific passer during the mid-1950s. His son, Kelly Tripucka, was an NBA star from 1981 to 1991 after excelling at his father's alma mater, the University of Notre Dame.

- Carl Crennel completed his 11-year career as a CFL linebacker when he joined the Roughriders in 1981. He is a younger brother of longtime NFL coach Romeo Crennel.
- Kenton Keith, a game-breaking tailback with the Roughriders from 2003 to 2006, is a cousin of former NFL star running back Roger Craig.
- Clyde Brock was an elite offensive tackle with the Green and White from 1964 to 1975, earning CFL All-Star honours four times during that span. His son, Matt Brock, was a defensive lineman with the Green Bay Packers (1989 to 1994) and New York Jets (1995 and 1996). Talk about a chip off the old Brock!

30 Visit the Saskatchewan Sports Hall of Fame

Any Roughriders fan is certain to take a shine to a shrine.

The Saskatchewan Sports Hall of Fame, based in Regina, has a diverse and fascinating Roughriders collection that dates back to the team's formative years.

Consider the game-worn leather helmet, donned by Eddie "Dynamite" James as a member of the 1931 Regina Roughriders.

Or Gordon Barber's red and black Roughriders sweater, with a crest from 1928.

Or, rewinding even farther, a jacket bearing the insignia of the Regina Rugby Club, which became the Roughriders in 1924.

Or any number of items honouring Ron Lancaster and George Reed.

"Ronnie and George…it really doesn't get much better than that," said Sheila Kelly, the Hall's executive director.

Lancaster and Reed were among the principal figures in the Roughriders' first Grey Cup victory in 1966. Although there have been subsequent championships, memorabilia pertaining to the 1966 title is a constant even though the Hall's exhibits and displays are routinely rotated.

"There will always be something from 1966, because that was such a landmark event for the team," Kelly said. "It was the first Grey Cup team and, of course, there's that connection with Ronnie and George."

Ronnie and George also had a connection with Alan Ford, who caught a touchdown pass for Saskatchewan in the 1966 Grey Cup game. Later, as the Roughriders' general manager, Ford played a valuable role in the CFL team's alliance with the Hall.

"That was Al Ford's vision," Kelly said. "He came to realize that with every staff turnover, the Loraas Disposal bin would be pushed up against the building and everything would get thrown out. He realized there had to be a better way, so he contacted the Hall and said, 'Would you take that?' We had a good amount of Rider memorabilia before that, but that really solidified the arrangement."

In a perfect world, the Hall could display all its memorabilia, connected to a seemingly infinite number of sports and athletes, but space constraints render that impossible. The shrine is based at 2205 Victoria Avenue, in the old Land Titles Building—an edifice that has a long history but a shortage of space. Hence the rotating exhibits.

There are, however, two constants. There will always be an interesting selection of Roughriders-related items, and a hockey icon will be recognized in some way.

"Gordie Howe and the Roughriders…that's what people want to see when they come in here," Kelly said, "and then they're thrilled with everything else they see."

Kelly is thrilled that "hundreds" of Roughriders-related items are in the possession of the Hall, including some gems from the team's historic stadium.

"We have lots from old Taylor Field," she said, smiling. "We have benches, seats, lockers, and some of the turf."

Artificial turf or natural?

"We don't have the grass," Kelly replied. "If we did, then we'd need goats, and it could get messy."

31 "I Only Have Eyes for Hugh"

Hugh Campbell was dubbed Gluey Hughie—and the nickname stuck.

Campbell's remarkable hands and telepathic on-field rapport with quarterback Ron Lancaster, produced a succession of big plays for the Roughriders during the 1960s.

Opponents knew Lancaster would look for Campbell, especially near the end zone, but attempts at covering him were often futile—as evidenced by his 60 touchdown receptions over six seasons with Saskatchewan.

Teammates often extracted humour from the Lancaster-Campbell connection. Wisecracking tight end Jim Worden once told Lancaster that his favourite song was, "I Only Have Eyes for Hugh."

During one game in 1965, eight of Lancaster's 11 completions were to Campbell, who amassed 206 receiving yards in a 25–6 victory over the Winnipeg Blue Bombers. Saskatchewan's other receivers combined for three catches and 38 yards.

"I'd go to him a lot because it was easy to do," Lancaster said. "He delivered. If somebody's going to deliver, you're going to go to him more. Working together as much as we did, we knew what each other was going to do. I could throw the ball and he would go get it. You'd always take a chance with him because he would go and knock the ball down if it wasn't well-thrown. Either he got it, or nobody got it. He was reliable, dependable, durable, and he just got the job done. We had a good thing going so we weren't going to mess it up."

Campbell joined the Roughriders during the 1963 season, after being released by the NFL's San Francisco 49ers. He did not anticipate a lengthy stay in Saskatchewan.

"Bob Shaw did come out to the airport to meet the plane," Campbell said of the former Roughriders head coach. "He was nice and drove us to the hotel."

The checkout, Campbell figured, would not be far off.

"I told my wife, 'Don't unpack too much,'" Campbell continued. "We came to Regina with a suitcase each. We each had a plate, a fork, a knife, and a spoon, besides a few clothes and a cup or something. We thought, 'We're only going to be there five weeks. We'll take some stuff we can live on for five weeks.'"

How about five more seasons?

In 1964, Campbell registered his first of three consecutive 1,000-yard seasons. In 1965, he posted career single-season highs in receptions (73) and yards (1,329, then a Western Conference record) and set a league standard for touchdown receptions (17) the following year. He added another touchdown grab—the game-winner—as Saskatchewan defeated the Ottawa Rough Riders 29–14 in the 1966 Grey Cup game.

Campbell wasn't the fastest, smoothest receiver, but good luck to anyone who tried to defend him.

"I'm telling you, he'd come down on me and I had him covered, but when he broke, he'd separate," said Ken Ploen, a former Winnipeg defensive back and quarterback. "You couldn't anticipate his break, so he'd break and I'd break with him and there was the ball. Ronnie had anticipated where he was going, and he threw the ball. I didn't even know it. What can you do? Nothing. You're going to tackle the guy after he catches it—or hope you're going to tackle him.

"You were never overly concerned that Campbell's speed was going to burn you. It was the moves he put on you or lulling you to sleep. He was a very sly, intelligent football player and a great receiver. He had super hands and, running patterns and things, he was probably as good as anybody."

The same could be said of Campbell off the field. He was the Edmonton Eskimos' head coach when they won an unprecedented five consecutive Grey Cups (1978 to 1982). Tack on four more titles as an executive (1987, 1993, 2003, and 2005) and he ended up with 10 championships in the CFL. (Interestingly, Lancaster was the Eskimos' head coach when they won the 1993 Grey Cup.)

A year after the 10th title, Campbell stepped down. The Eskimos made the announcement at their annual dinner, which included one very special guest: Ron Lancaster.

The Quiet Legend

A rotation customarily ended a negotiation when Ken Preston was the Roughriders' general manager.

Contract talks were known to conclude without a word. Preston would simply make a 180-degree turn in his swivel chair and silently peer out the window of his office.

Done deal. And have a nice day.

Preston was as frugal as the circumstances dictated, considering the financial challenges the Roughriders encountered during his 20-year tenure in the GM's well-oiled chair. The team operated on a shoestring budget, but nonetheless was able to enjoy a prolonged period of prosperity during his regime.

Beginning in 1962, the Roughriders did not have a losing record while also making the CFL playoffs for 15 consecutive seasons—a span in which Saskatchewan captured its first Grey Cup title (in 1966).

All of that happened with the GM playing an integral, but often unheralded, role.

"He was really interesting—so different than any football guy I can think of today," said former Roughriders president-CEO Jim Hopson, who was an offensive lineman with the Roughriders from 1973 to 1976.

"He was quiet. He was unassuming. He was almost invisible. You seldom saw Ken at practice. You didn't see him in the locker room a lot.

"If you were going to see him, he'd call you up to his office on the second floor of the Hill Avenue Shopping Centre. He was a nice, very polite, quiet man. Yeah, he was tough to deal with. It was well-known how tight-fisted he was when it came to money, but he treated me well."

For example, Hopson began the 1974 season as a starter while perennial All-Star guard Jack Abendschan was recovering from knee surgery. Hopson had not signed for a starter's wage, but Preston took note of the situation and requested a meeting with the then-sophomore lineman.

"He called me in about halfway through the year and said, 'Jim, you're having a tremendous year and we're really happy with you. You don't have any starting bonuses in your contract. I understand that you're wanting to buy a house, so I'm going to give you the amount that we would normally give somebody for being a full-time starter,'" Hopson recalled. "It was about $3,000. That was a lot of money in 1974.

"While he had this reputation [for being penurious], he also was a decent man. The guys didn't stay here for their entire careers just because they loved the Riders and the fans. Ken took care of them. There was Tim Roth and Jack Abendschan and Ralph Galloway and Clyde Brock and Ed McQuarters, and you go through the list. It wasn't just the salaries. Guys got good jobs. Jack Abendschan was working at [Kalium] Potash and Ed McQuarters at SaskPower, and Ken was a driving force behind that."

Preston, from Portland, Ontario, was first affiliated with the Roughriders when he joined the team as a player in 1940. He returned to the Regina squad in 1943, and again for a three-year stay that began in 1946. He also coached the team in 1946 and for part of the 1947 season.

After his playing career, he purchased a paper-box manufacturing company and was successful in that venture. He remained involved in football by coaching the Regina Junior Bombers, becoming a Western Interprovincial Football Union official, and by serving as a part-time manager of the Roughriders.

Dean Griffing stepped aside as the manager—the term "general manager" was not yet in vogue—in 1958, prompting team president Sam Taylor to encourage Preston to apply for the job.

"When Sam Taylor asked me in 1958 to take over as general manager, I said I thought I could do all that was required in half a day," Preston said in a 1985 *Leader-Post* interview. "So that's what I did, and I spent the other half-day over at my paper-box plant. Of course, I was paid for half a day, too!"

Preston eventually became a full-time football executive and divested himself of the paper-box company. The stage was set for a long and successful tenure that was recognized in 1990, when he was inducted into the Canadian Football Hall of Fame. He died the following year, at age 73, and the tributes poured in.

Phil Kershaw, the Roughriders' president of the day, put it aptly in August of 1991: "Ken Preston epitomizes everything that's good about the Saskatchewan Roughriders."

33 Keys to the Victory

Eagle Keys' arrival in Saskatchewan was much like the man himself—low-key.

Little was made of his appointment as a Roughriders assistant coach in 1964, but history was soon made after he assumed the head-coaching reins.

Keys was the victorious field boss on November 26, 1966, when Saskatchewan captured its first Grey Cup title—56 years after the franchise's inception as the Regina Rugby Club. The landmark conquest came in his second year as the head coach.

"He really put it all together," said Larry Dumelie, a Roughriders defensive back from 1960 to 1967.

Saskatchewan posted a 2–12–2 record in Dumelie's first year with the team, under head coach Ken Carpenter. The Roughriders then took strides under head coaches Steve Owen (who had seasons of 5–10–1 and 8–7–1) and Bob Shaw (9–7–0, 7–7–2), all the while building the nucleus of a consistent winner.

When Shaw left for Toronto to become the Argonauts' head coach, Keys was promoted from an assistant's role and was wise enough to recognize the manner in which the team was evolving.

One of his first key moves was to express confidence in quarterback Ron Lancaster and fullback George Reed, both of whom disliked playing for Shaw. In fact, Lancaster and Reed both said they did not intend to return to Saskatchewan in 1965 if Shaw was still the coach.

Moreover, Keys had a belief in every player on the team, instilling reciprocal loyalty.

"Coach Keys' philosophy was that if you made the roster at the beginning of the year, you weren't looking over your shoulder during the season unless you really flopped," former Roughriders defensive lineman Don Bahnuik said. "You were given a vote of confidence and, all things being equal, you were going to stay a part of the team.

"That was a big confidence-builder. If you were a rookie and you made a mistake, you had the peace of mind that you weren't going to get yanked or cut because of that. That built superior loyalty to the team. The loyalty we had to Eagle was incredible. He was special to all of us."

That includes receiver Hugh Campbell.

"When Eagle came [to Saskatchewan], he was more of a players' coach,'" Gluey Hughie said. "We hit it right getting Eagle at that time, but he hit it right getting all of us at that time, because by then Ronnie had gained the confidence and could do a lot of the running of the offence. Eagle did a great job with Ronnie in the office and then, when we'd get to practice, he'd already told Ronnie what to do."

Under Keys, Reed rushed for a Roughriders-record 1,768 yards in 1965, becoming the first member of the team to win CFL most-outstanding-player honours. One year later, Lancaster fired a career-best 28 touchdown passes and was named the Western Conference's top player, before finishing that season with a championship.

The 1966 Roughriders placed first in the West at 9–6–1 before upsetting the 11–3–0 Ottawa Rough Riders in the Grey Cup.

Under Keys, Saskatchewan posted superior records in each of the next four seasons—going 12–4–0, 12–3–1, 13–3–0, and

14–2–0—and made two more Grey Cup appearances (in 1967 and 1969). However, the Roughriders were unable to repeat the feat of 1966.

Shortly after the 1970 campaign, Keys left Saskatchewan to coach the B.C. Lions.

"We'd improved every year since I got there, from 1965 until 1970," he remembered in 2006. "I just felt that there's always a time to leave. It was nothing personal or anything. You get to a point where you have a chance to do something else and you do it."

Keys' excellence as a coach was recognized in 1990, when he—along with former Roughriders GM Ken Preston—was inducted into the Canadian Football Hall of Fame.

Keys died in 2012 at age 89.

34 By George, They Did It

One Sunday in 1965 was especially memorable for the Roughriders—on the ground and through the air.

After George Reed rushed for a franchise-record 268 yards to help Saskatchewan defeat the B.C. Lions 30–14 on October 24, 1965, the Roughriders flew back to Regina and were greeted by an overflow crowd at the airport.

A throng estimated at 2,500 celebrated the fact that Saskatchewan had clinched the third and final playoff spot in the Western Conference.

Yes, even a third-place showing prompted a stampede toward the tiny terminal. Such is the longstanding enthusiasm of Rider Priders.

Naturally, the fans gravitated toward Reed, who had set the conference record for rushing yards in a game. The previous standard of 238 had been established by the Calgary Stampeders' Lovell Coleman in 1964.

Reed also threatened the CFL's single-game record of 287 yards, set by the Ottawa Rough Riders' Ron Stewart in 1960. As

George Reed with the Saskatchewan Roughriders in the 1970s. (Don Healy, *Regina Leader-Post*)

of this writing, Stewart and Reed are still first and second, respectively, on the all-time list.

"We went into the game knowing we had to win to have a shot at making the playoffs," Reed recalled. "That was a very critical game for us. The guys blocked well and I seemed to be able to run the football and do things that we needed to do.

"I always played pretty well in B.C., too. I always had that little edge because B.C. used to have my rights. I knew a lot about B.C. I didn't know a lot about Regina when they traded my rights to Regina. I'm glad it worked out the way it did. It gave me a little extra incentive against them.

"More of my family from Seattle was able to come up and see me play. They would all pile into a couple of cars and they would drive up and spend the evening with me. After the game, I was able to spend a couple of hours with them before they headed back. It was always nice that way. We tried to give them a good show."

The Lions had originally owned Reed's rights while he played fullback and linebacker at Washington State University. However, the Lions' lineup included a determined runner named Nub Beamer when Reed graduated from college.

"They thought that he was going to be their fullback for several more years, so they traded my rights to Saskatchewan," Reed said. "I don't know for what—maybe a dollar."

Reed finished the 1965 regular season with 1,768 rushing yards, still a franchise record, in 16 games. He was only 26 yards shy of the then-league standard of 1,794, set in 1964 by Calgary's Earl Lunsford.

After posting an 8–7–1 record in 1965, the Roughriders travelled to Winnipeg and lost 15–9 to the Blue Bombers in the Western semifinal. Reed, however, had one road trip remaining—to Toronto, where he was named the CFL's most outstanding player.

"To be the first Rider that did it, it's a great memory," he said.

October 34

George Reed was 36 years old with 16,116 career rushing yards and a trail of would-be tacklers behind him.

Considering that 30 is a precarious age for a ball-carrier, it shouldn't have been surprising on that basis that he announced the end of an illustrious playing career on May 31, 1976.

Nonetheless, the news shocked Rider Nation and everyone across the CFL. After all, he had signed a two-year contract extension in January 1976, not long after rushing for 1,454 yards (the third-highest single-season total of his career) and 11 touchdowns.

"The time has come, I guess," Reed told reporters. "My mental preparation for the season hasn't been right. It hasn't been what it should be by this time in the year. When that happens, you know it's time to step down."

Looking back, Reed cited the extra responsibility of serving as president of the CFL Players' Association as a factor behind his sudden retirement.

"I had signed the biggest contract that I was going to have, but it finally caught up with me," he said in 2019. "That's when I walked away. I knew that I could do one [job], but I couldn't handle both of them. If I was going to play, I was going to have all my attention on the field, as I always did.

"That probably was the turning point for me—the fight that I was trying to lead the players through with the Players' Association."

Reed's stunning announcement came only one week after he had become the first recipient of the CFL's Tom Pate Memorial Award, which recognizes outstanding sportsmanship and community involvement. (Ron Lancaster won the award the following year.)

Reed was formally honoured by the Roughriders at halftime of a home game against the Winnipeg Blue Bombers on October 24, 1976—although the date was designated October 34 in recognition of the legendary fullback and his uniform number.

He received a number of gifts, including a grandfather clock that "still ticks away" near the front door of George and Angie Reed's Regina residence.

The days leading up to the tribute were part of George Reed Week, a period that included a sold-out testimonial dinner.

One of the speakers was former Roughriders head coach Eagle Keys, who said, "Only God knows if He'll plant another seed to produce a football player as good as George Reed."

Since the most outstanding player award was first presented in 1953, a Roughrider has been called to the podium on only four occasions, beginning with Reed in 1965. Ron Lancaster received the award in 1970 and 1976. Kerry Joseph was next in line, in 2007.

35 Tale of the Tape

The Roughriders' top two all-time rushers have something in common other than excellence on the ground.

George Reed and Wes Cates also demonstrated an ability to make big gains despite the pain, especially in games of magnitude.

Consider the third and deciding game of the 1967 Western Conference final, between the Roughriders and Calgary Stampeders. Reed carried the ball 37 times for 204 yards to help Saskatchewan win 17–13, prompting veteran head coach Eagle Keys to observe, "George has never, ever run any better."

He did so despite being a walking bruise, the result of leg, shoulder, and rib injuries.

"I looked like a mummy," Reed recalled. "If you had walked into the dressing room, you would have seen both shoulders taped and my ribs taped. From my knees all the way down to my ankles, I was completely taped.

"After we won the game, it probably took me almost an hour to get all the tape off of me in the locker room there in Calgary. Then I got up and had my shower.

"But we won the game, so that was the big thing. We had everything on the line. There wasn't a tomorrow, so you go out there and play."

Reed consistently absorbed and dished out punishment while rushing for 16,116 yards in 13 seasons as a Roughrider, beginning in 1963.

"George Reed got injuries all the time and you consider that he only missed five games in 13 years," former Roughriders trainer Sandy Archer said. "That is very unusual, because he got hit a lot. He had shoulder injuries and elbows and knees. You name it, he had it, and he played. He wasn't going to quit."

That attitude prevailed even when Archer needed to administer a painkilling shot that, in and of itself, was excruciating.

"George dislocated a toe one time and, for the next six or seven games, he had to have it frozen twice a game," Archer said, flashing back to 1968. "After the game, his toe looked like a big, fat sausage. He couldn't do anything until the next Friday."

That wasn't enough to keep No. 34 out of the lineup. Sitting out was never a consideration.

"The dislocated toe might have been one of the most painful things I had," Reed said. "For the first two or three times I took shots in it, I couldn't stand the needle. I said, 'If I can't play without the needle, I won't play.' I think I played several more games on it. [The mindset] was, 'We'll just tape it up and away we go.'

"That's the way it was. I just felt that when it was time to play, it was time to play, and whether I could practise or not was not important. It was important to be ready to go on to the battlefield with the guys. That's how much I thought about the guys. I thought that if I didn't play, I would let down the other 31 guys on the football team."

Reed was forced to miss four games in 1970 with a fractured left tibia—an injury that actually bothered him for half the season. Nonetheless, he was still able to rush for 821 yards in 12 games.

In 2007, Cates also had to sit out four games—the final three regular season contests, plus the playoff opener—due to a hairline fracture in his left foot.

The injury was initially thought to be a season-ender, but Cates had other ideas. With the injured foot numbed by painkillers, he returned to the roster for the West Division final and also played in the Grey Cup, helping the Roughriders win a championship in his first of five seasons in Saskatchewan.

"There was a point where I really didn't think that I could play and I wasn't going to have an opportunity to help out my team," said Cates, whose 4,761 rushing yards place him second only to Reed on the Roughriders' career list. "To find out that I did have that opportunity, even though it was going to come with some consequences, those consequences were well worth it.

"It's something I can always look back on and say I took that extra step. I kind of put my body at risk, but it paid off."

36 The Reluctant Robokicker

Dave Ridgway is always delighted to sign autographs, but it is best not to ask him to add his nickname—"Robokicker"—to the inscription.

"When I'm asked to sign anything, I never sign Robokicker," the legendary Roughriders placement specialist said. "I may have done it once in all of the things that I have ever been asked to sign."

His signature play—a Grey Cup–winning field goal in 1989—contributed to a reputation that made the moniker applicable, if not especially palatable to its reluctant owner.

"It put a lot of pressure on me," Ridgway said, "because there was the implication that you can do a job like that with robotic accuracy."

Ridgway *was* virtually automatic by the late 1980s. So, when he was asked to snap a tie from 35 yards away in the waning seconds of the 1989 league final, there was little doubt that he would deliver.

Sure enough, Ridgway connected on "The Kick" and gave Saskatchewan a 43–40 victory over the Hamilton Tiger-Cats, only the second title in team history.

"The one thing that stands out more than anything is how enduring people's memories of that game are," Ridgway said.

Memories of Ridgway as a Roughrider date back to 1982, when he was an unheralded training-camp attendee. The door was opened when Paul Watson, who had been Saskatchewan's strong-legged but erratic kicker in 1981, tore an Achilles tendon while playing volleyball during the off-season. That left it up to Ridgway and 1982 Roughriders draftee Kevin Rydeard to compete for the kicking job.

Ridgway got the nod and proceeded to enjoy a stellar campaign, hitting 38 of 51 field-goal attempts en route to earning his first of six berths on the CFL All-Star team. He spent four more seasons with Saskatchewan before surprisingly being traded to the Edmonton Eskimos in a deal that was announced in January of 1987.

During the 1986 season, Saskatchewan had quietly dealt a first-round draft choice to the Eskimos for offensive lineman Bryan Illerbrun. Edmonton was also given the choice of claiming Ridgway or a future third-round pick, with the option to be exercised after the 1986 season. Edmonton took Ridgway, only to deal him to the Montreal Alouettes.

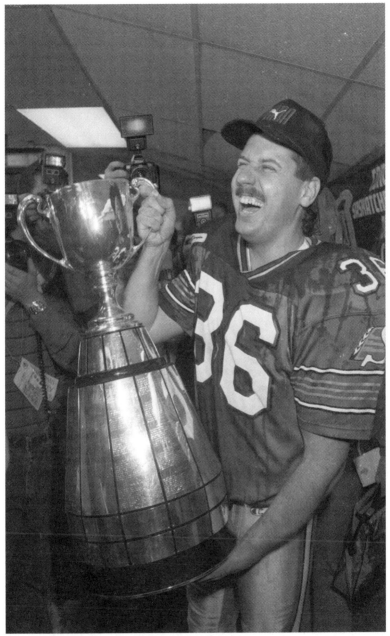

Dave Ridgway celebrates the Roughriders' 1989 Grey Cup victory.
(Bryan Schlosser, *Regina Leader-Post*)

Suddenly, the Roughriders were without a proven place-kicker. Bill Baker, who took over as the Roughriders' general manager in December of 1986, labelled the Ridgway trade (which was negotiated before the team's housecleaning) as "one of the dumbest deals I've ever heard of."

Dumb luck eventually worked in Saskatchewan's favour. The Alouettes folded as the 1987 regular season loomed, necessitating a dispersal draft—in which Baker chose Ridgway.

Upon returning to Saskatchewan, Ridgway elevated his play. Before the deal, he had connected on 68.5 per cent of his field-goal attempts. During his second stint in Saskatchewan, lasting from 1987 to 1995, he made 81.9 per cent of his kicks while acquiring—if not necessarily embracing—the aforementioned nickname.

"I matured into the position where I had very high expectations of what my performance should be, and I don't think that anybody had ever been harder on my performance than I was," Ridgway recalled. "I was self-motivated. But the kids out there today, they're kicking beyond what I did. Doing it over 14 or 15 years is different than having one or two good years."

The great years in Saskatchewan were recognized in 2003 when Ridgway was inducted into the Canadian Football Hall of Fame. As part of his acceptance speech at the ceremony, and countless times thereafter, he has made a point of thanking Roughriders supporters who allowed him to enjoy a 14-year CFL career.

"I was always treated very well by the fans," Ridgway reflected from his home in Indiana. "That was part of the motivation for me. I always wanted to perform well for the fans. If you look back, there's no doubt that other than having children and grand-children, the time that I spent in Saskatchewan was some of the most wonderful years in my life."

"It's not all sunshine and roses. There are clouds and storms, and this and that happens, but that's life. I matured to a point where you understood that you had to take the good with the bad. I was fortunate to have way more good than bad in my 20-plus years living in the province.

"Saskatchewan was very, very good to me."

37 Sad Day...Happy Ending

The lowest moment of Paul McCallum's professional football career kickstarted his transformation into the most accurate placement specialist in CFL history.

Such an evolution did not seem to be a strong possibility on November 14, 2004, when the Roughriders kicker missed an 18-yard field-goal attempt in overtime of the West Division final against B.C. The host Lions quickly countered with a 40-yard Duncan O'Mahony field goal that gave them a 27–25 victory and a trip to the Grey Cup.

"It's a living nightmare," McCallum told reporters in the trainer's room after the game. "I let everyone in the locker room down today and I have no excuse. I didn't do my job. It's kind of hard to face the guys right now. This one hurts."

The pain was also palpable in Regina, where the reaction went far over the top in some cases. Residents threw eggs at McCallum's house, dumped on a neighbour's driveway, and even uttered a threat toward the kicker's wife. The couple's two young daughters were also at home at the time.

"This is a sad day for the Rider Nation," then-Roughriders chairman Garry Huntington told the media.

McCallum ultimately turned the "sad day" into a happy ending. Thirty-four at the time of the incident, he played his final game at age 46. He retired with a field-goal percentage of 80.4, the best of any CFL kicker with at least 400 attempts.

"That miss, yeah, it was bad, but I turned around and made a positive out of it," McCallum said.

"I decided that I wasn't going to let that kick define me. Unfortunately, it had to take something like that to open my eyes to appreciate even more what I was doing for a living and to work hard at it."

After the memorable miss and its fallout, McCallum spent one more season with Saskatchewan before signing with B.C. as a free agent. It was in his home province where he became uncannily accurate.

"There's a lot of things that I did from a mental aspect—mental focus and mental training—after [2004] to make sure that it never happened again, and it worked," McCallum said. "It showed in my statistics after I left Saskatchewan."

Through the 2005 season, McCallum had made 75.1 per cent of his field-goal attempts (356 of 474). Thereafter, he was 11 percentage points higher (86.3), going 366-for-424.

Moreover, he was a two-time CFL All-Star (in 2010 and 2011), the winner of the Grey Cup's most valuable Canadian award (2006), and the CFL's most outstanding special-teams player (2011).

McCallum is second all-time in field goals made (722) and attempted (898), trailing only ageless Lions legend Lui Passaglia (who was 875-for-1,203).

Perhaps most impressively, McCallum became a virtual sure thing in the games of greatest importance.

Overcoming the devastation of 2004, McCallum never again missed a field-goal attempt in a divisional playoff game. In the postseason as a whole, he was a staggering 46-for-47 (.979) post-2004,

Paul McCallum at Roughriders training camp in 2005. (Joshua Sawka, *Regina Leader-Post*)

McCallum 12, Edmonton 3

In addition to scoring every Roughriders point in a 12–3 victory over the Edmonton Eskimos on October 27, 2001, Paul McCallum kicked the longest field goal in CFL history—a 62-yarder—in the waning seconds of the first half.

And he did so with the previous record-holder, Dave Ridgway, in attendance at Taylor Field. Ridgway had kicked a 60-yarder for Saskatchewan on September 6, 1987, in a 29–25 loss to the visiting Winnipeg Blue Bombers.

Former Roughriders offensive lineman Bob Poley—Ridgway's erstwhile long-snapper—was working as a sideline commentator for Regina radio station CKRM when McCallum made his long-distance boot (one of his four field goals on the day). Poley requested the football from a minor official and then gave the pigskin to Ridgway, who in turn presented it to McCallum.

On the 62-yarder, Jeremy O'Day snapped the ball to Dylan Ching, who pinned the ball for McCallum, who proceeded to make history.

"It all comes down to the game situation," McCallum said after the game. "We had tried some from 67 yards earlier in the week in practice, and I've hit from 65 during pregame warmups in Calgary. These chances don't come up all the time. I don't even know how much I made it by. The wind helped me a little bit, but when it's really windy, sometimes that knocks it down."

McCallum, the Roughriders' all-purpose kicker, was actually surprised to be called upon to attempt the 62-yarder, noting that head coach Danny Barrett had not voiced his intention to go for three points.

"I remember running out on to the field to punt the ball and Dylan Ching [holder] says, 'No, no! We're going to kick a field goal. Grab your tee!'" McCallum recalled. "Dylan's looking at me and going, 'Can you make this?' I'm like, 'What?' I probably ran a good four or five yards on to the field thinking I was going to punt, so I ran back and grabbed my tee. Then I hit it."

As of this writing, the four longest field goals in CFL history have been kicked at Taylor Field.

First, Edmonton's Dave Cutler set a distance mark of 59 yards on October 28, 1970. The Roughriders' Paul Watson matched that feat on July 12, 1981. Watson's share of the record stood for six-plus years until his successor, Ridgway, connected on the 60-yarder. And then McCallum, who had replaced Ridgway late in the 1995 season, stretched the standard to 62.

with the only miss—a 48-yarder that hit an upright—coming in the 2011 Grey Cup. Nonetheless, after the game, McCallum celebrated a championship for the second time in his career.

38 "Dress" for Success

The smallest player made the biggest impression at the Roughriders' camp in 2008.

From the moment 5-foot-7 Weston Dressler stepped on to the field, heads turned and tongues wagged as he sped all over the place, leaving would-be defenders in the dust.

"Even though a person or two in the organization said, 'He can't stay. He's too small,' I said, 'He looks like he's over six feet to me,' because he was really a producer and got the job done," said Ken Miller, the Roughriders' head coach from 2008 to 2011.

After starring at the University of North Dakota, Dressler arrived in Saskatchewan with little or no fanfare. He signed with the team in the spring, not long before rookie camp, and was soon introduced to the nuances of professional three-down football.

"I remember coming in," he recalled. "I was young and naïve. I didn't fully understand how the training-camp process and making the team worked. I just thought I was coming up to play some football. It was probably better that I didn't know as much or really understand what I was going to have to do in order to make the team. I was just running around, having fun playing football, and was not worried about that stuff."

Dressler eventually had great fun collaborating with quarterback Darian Durant, who also made his first start in green and white in 2008. At first glance, Durant was skeptical, but his appraisal of Dressler did a quick 180 once workouts began.

"Just seeing him, I'm thinking, 'He's just another guy,'" Durant remembered. "Of course, he's very small in stature, but once we got on that field and I saw him run right by the DB, I said, 'Wow!' Then he did it again and again and again. It was like, 'This guy is special.'"

Dressler became a Roughrider, at least from the perspective of his CFL rights being owned, when he was placed on the team's negotiation list by general manager Eric Tillman.

The move looked especially ingenious after Dressler was named the league's rookie of the year. He accepted the trophy after catching 56 passes for 1,128 yards—an average of 20.1 yards per reception—and six touchdowns.

A Roughrider through 2015, Dressler would enjoy four more 1,000-yard seasons in Saskatchewan (and a Grey Cup championship in 2013) before reaching that statistical milestone again with Winnipeg. He joined the Blue Bombers in January of 2016, shortly after being released by the Roughriders for financial reasons.

Even then, the enormously popular Dressler continued to spend his off-seasons in Regina, having settled in the community and being embraced in turn.

"There will always be that connection with the Roughriders," he said. "That's the first professional team I ever had a chance to play for. They gave me an opportunity that no one else was willing to, so for that, I'll always be grateful. I played with them for eight years. That's longer than any other team I played on throughout my entire life in any sport, any league, any age group, whatever.

"There will definitely always be a piece of the Roughriders with me, for sure."

Kory Runs to Glory

Stats sheets reflect Kory Sheets' dominance.

In both of his seasons as a Roughrider, he exceeded 1,200 rushing yards—peaking at 1,598 en route to celebrating a Grey Cup title in 2013.

Also worth noting is that the latter total was achieved in barely 14 games. While recovering from a knee injury, he sat out nearly three games and did not play in the meaningless regular season finale because the Roughriders' starters were being rested for the playoffs.

Extrapolate Sheets' totals over a full 18-game regular season and he would have approached 2,000 yards and eclipsed George Reed's franchise single-season record of 1,768, set in 1965.

Not bad for someone who, despite impressive college credentials and an NFL pedigree, was not highly touted as the Roughriders' training camp approached.

Sheets' big break occurred in Saskatchewan's 2012 preseason finale. Head coach Corey Chamblin had an intolerance of fumbles, to the extent that anyone whose ball security was questionable was liable to be benched or released outright.

Such was the fate of Brandon West, who was first on the depth chart when Saskatchewan opened camp in 2012.

Early in an exhibition date with the Calgary Stampeders, West caught a short pass from Darian Durant, fumbled, and watched Malik Jackson return the ball to Saskatchewan's 16-yard line.

That was it for West as a Roughrider, as it turned out.

Sheets entered the game, rushed six times for 81 yards (including a 34-yarder) and one touchdown, and won the job.

Simon Says...Farewell

Geroy Simon saved a first for his last game.

The Hall of Fame receiver caught his first Grey Cup touchdown pass—and then his second—on November 24, 2013, to help the Roughriders defeat the Hamilton Tiger-Cats 45–23 on Taylor Field.

"We had talked earlier in the week," recalled Darian Durant, the victorious quarterback. "I didn't believe it when he told me, but he said, 'Dubs, I've never caught a touchdown pass in a Grey Cup.' I'm like, 'What? Are you kidding me? You're the greatest receiver of all time and you've never had a touchdown reception in a Grey Cup?'"

Durant had a feeling that would change. Offensive co-ordinator George Cortez had drawn up some plays for the 38-year-old Simon, who had starred for the B.C. Lions before being traded to Saskatchewan in 2013.

Sure enough, Simon caught a 15-yard touchdown pass from Durant to give Saskatchewan its first points of the 2013 Grey Cup game. That duo later collaborated on a 42-yard major to help Saskatchewan assume a 31–6 halftime lead.

During the celebration after the game, Durant said to Simon, "I told you! I told you I was going to get you your first touchdown pass in a Grey Cup!"

Simon retired as the CFL's all-time leader in catches (1,029) and receiving yards (16,352)—totals that made him a lock for enshrinement in the Canadian Football Hall of Fame in his first year of eligibility (2017).

On induction day, much of the footage showed Simon during his 12 seasons with B.C., including 2006—a year which he was named the league's most outstanding player. But there were also images from that fantastic finish, a performance that helped Saskatchewan post its first home-field Grey Cup victory.

"It was probably the most important day in the history of this franchise, and possibly the province, knowing the amount of fans that are here in the province and how much they love the Riders and this organization," Simon said. "It was a special day, and it will never be forgotten."

He proceeded to rush for 1,277 yards and 11 touchdowns as a first-year CFLer, before following up with a banner year in which he scored 12 majors. To reward his offensive linemen, he bought them hamburgers after every game in which he rushed for 100 yards or more.

"He was a very entertaining guy with a big personality," former Roughriders president-CEO Jim Hopson said. "He wanted to be a great player and he was."

Sheets' greatness peaked in the 2013 Grey Cup game. He rushed for 197 yards en route to being named the game's most valuable player.

The Hamilton Tiger-Cats had closed the gap to 31–16 in the fourth quarter before Sheets made three pivotal plays—the first of which was a 21-yard run on second-and-19. The Riders won 45–23.

"When he made that run, I knew we were going to win," Hopson said. "Karma was with us. We could do no wrong."

Sheets followed up with a 16-yard run—on which he broke the Grey Cup game rushing record of 169 yards, previously set by the Edmonton Eskimos' Johnny Bright in 1956—and eventually scored from four yards away with 5:23 left.

The Oakland Raiders took notice, signing Sheets to an NFL contract. The former University of Purdue Boilermakers star appeared to have a roster spot locked up, only to suffer a torn left Achilles' tendon during an exhibition game on August 22, 2014.

The scenario was painfully familiar for Sheets, who had suffered a torn right Achilles' tendon at the Miami Dolphins' training camp in 2010. He was waived by the Dolphins in 2011 before spending part of that season on the Carolina Panthers' practice squad.

Then it was off to Saskatchewan, where in two years he created memories that will last a lifetime.

"I loved Regina and Saskatchewan," reflected Sheets, who never played again after suffering the injury in 2014. "I wish I would have gone left instead of right [and stayed in the CFL]. Those were the best two years of my life, whether I knew it or not. Back then, it was all about moving forward and getting to somewhere bigger or better or whatever you want to call it—just getting to another place where you thought you wanted to be."

40 The Fun Run of '81

The 1981 Roughriders were the best team that never made the playoffs.

After enduring back-to-back 2–14 seasons, long-suffering Saskatchewan fans fell in love with the '81 edition, which went 9–7 and created all sorts of excitement on and off the field.

The regular season ended in depressing fashion—with a defeat that dashed the Roughriders' playoff hopes—but the events of that year were nonetheless a tonic for everyone with allegiances to the Green and White.

Sellouts, once a rarity at an expanded Taylor Field, became automatic as the 1981 Roughriders captivated the province. The team routinely played to above-capacity crowds, with fans spilling on to "Hemorrhoid Hill"—the grassy knoll in Taylor Field's south end zone used for overflow seating with terrible sightlines.

The team was also reintroduced to the end zone after two seasons (1979 and 1980) in which the offence was a liability. Under first-year head coach Joe Faragalli, who had choreographed high-octane offences with the powerful Edmonton Eskimos, the Roughriders accentuated the pass. Fans fell in love with the air show, and with the many charismatic players on that team.

The most popular player, beyond question, was Joey Walters. The spectacular slotback amassed 1,715 receiving yards—still a franchise single-season record—in 16 games, while scoring 14 touchdowns. He was complemented by Chris DeFrance, who caught 64 passes for 1,195 yards and five TDs, including a 100-yarder.

The offensive line, which had been rebuilt over two seasons under head coach Ron Lancaster, blossomed into the CFL's finest and typically provided airtight protection for quarterbacks John Hufnagel and Joe Barnes.

Somehow, the 1981 Roughriders managed to alternate two signal-callers without having to deal with the slightest murmur of a quarterback controversy. Hufnagel and Barnes were memorably dubbed "J.J. Barnagel" by the *Leader-Post*'s John Chaput, and the label fit as well as the two quarterbacks melded into the team structure.

In 1981, Barnes and Hufnagel collaborated for 4,873 aerial yards and 33 touchdown passes—or nine more aerial touchdowns than Saskatchewan had compiled over the previous two seasons combined.

"They had a healthy relationship and very complementary styles," said Greg Fieger, who played for Saskatchewan from 1980 to 1984. "It did create a lot of stress on the opposing defence. It was a great tool we could use. I learned a lot from both of them. They parked their egos at the door. They took a role that was being asked of them and committed to it.

"These were two guys—very successful in their careers—coming into the locker room and leading in different ways. They had an ability to communicate with everyone and relate with everyone.

"It wasn't a 'Joe room' or a 'John room.' That can sometimes happen when you have two quarterbacks running the ship, but that was never an issue in that room. I think it spoke a lot for the character being built in the room at the time."

The cast of characters also included All-Star defensive end Lyall Woznesensky, whose sack dance was known as the "Woztusi."

Rival quarterbacks were pressured as well by Vince Goldsmith, who registered 17 sacks en route to becoming the CFL's rookie of the year.

As it turned out, though, Goldsmith's presence for the CFL awards presentations during Grey Cup week was the only time that a Roughrider was conspicuous in the 1981 playoffs.

Needing to defeat the B.C. Lions to earn a playoff berth for the first time since 1976, the Roughriders lost 13–5 in a torrential rainstorm at Vancouver's Empire Stadium.

"If Mother Nature is on our side that night, we would have made the playoffs," Barnes said. "I replayed that game over and over for quite a while."

The loss was especially excruciating because of the inequities of the CFL's playoff format, as it was structured at the time. The top three teams in the East and West Divisions made the playoffs, without any allowance for a crossover—such as the current provision, which grants the fourth-place team in one division admission into the playoffs if its record is superior to that of the third-place finisher in the other loop.

At 9–7, Saskatchewan had a much better record than three teams in the East—the Ottawa Rough Riders (5–11), Montreal Alouettes (3–13), and Toronto Argonauts (2–14). Even so, the Roughriders did not advance to the playoffs, which included an East semifinal between teams (Ottawa and Montreal) that combined for one fewer regular season victory than Saskatchewan had registered that year.

"To think Ottawa made the playoffs and hosted a playoff game with five wins and we were out of the playoffs after winning nine games was terrible," Woznesensky lamented. "We were mad. We had had such a great season and to see teams going into the playoffs that didn't deserve to be there while we sat out again was painful."

But that season, as a whole, was fabulous fun.

41 A Victory for Veronica

Roughriders fans have witnessed countless exciting endings, but never a finish quite like that of September 4, 1983.

The man of the moment was Roughriders punter Ken Clark who, with a game on the line against the Winnipeg Blue Bombers, was suddenly cast in the role of emergency placekicker. He had just returned to Regina from the bedside of his dying mother, Veronica.

Adding to the degree of difficulty, the field-goal attempt—Clark's first since 1976, when he was 9-for-22 on three pointers attempts as a member of the Hamilton Tiger-Cats—was from 41 yards away...and into the wind.

So, of course, he calmly split the uprights, giving Saskatchewan a 32–30 lead that held up for the remaining 43 seconds.

"I knew that kick was going through," Clark told the *Leader-Post.* "I didn't have any doubt. During the game, I felt that my mother was there for that amount of time—and gone as soon as the ball went through the uprights."

Clark was pressed into field-goal duty after Dave Ridgway was injured while making a tackle on a third-quarter kickoff return. Ridgway was taken to nearby Pasqua Hospital and diagnosed with a concussion.

At the hospital, Ridgway could hear the cheers from the stadium as his teammates mounted a late-game rally. Winnipeg led 30–29 when Saskatchewan assumed possession on its 37-yard line with 1:31 remaining. The Roughriders soon moved into field-goal range, the key play being a 37-yard pass from John Hufnagel to Chris DeFrance. Clark took it from there.

"I had to come back and play," said Clark, who had flown back to Regina from Toronto. "My mom, she was such a good fan. She wouldn't have had it any other way. This was a special day. I had dedicated it to her."

Fittingly, Clark also launched a 101-yard punt during that game. That stood as the longest punt in Roughriders history until Chris Milo unleashed a 108-yarder in 2011. Milo's boot tied a league record that Zenon Andrusyshyn had set with the Toronto Argonauts in 1977.

Clark's clutch field goal and long-distance punt were rare highlights during a season in which the Roughriders registered a 5–11 record. They entered the aforementioned Winnipeg game at 1–6.

Late in the season, general manager John Herrera traded Clark to the Ottawa Rough Riders for fullback John Park and future considerations (receiver Carl Powell). Neither Park nor Powell enjoyed a lengthy tenure in Saskatchewan, whereas Clark's finest moment as a Roughrider is fondly remembered to this day.

42 Gopher Tales

There was a time, long ago, when the Roughriders had a live mascot—a white goat named "Roughie," who was introduced in 1949.

When the team finally had a cuddly costumed character to patrol the Taylor Field sideline, he/she/it was actually a loaner.

For the 1976 Western Conference final, the Roughriders borrowed the Calgary Stampeders' mascot—Ralph the Dog. (Appropriately, the Stampeders' roster at the time included a centre named Basil Bark. But we dog-ress…er, digress.)

Ralph was on hand for the Roughriders' 23–13 victory over the arch-rival Edmonton Eskimos, a long-awaited breakthrough that propelled the Green and White into the 1976 Grey Cup game.

"A small group of members of management, including myself and a few ardent fans, were so impressed with Ralph during the Western final that we invited him to accompany the team to Toronto for the Grey Cup," former Roughriders president and management-committee member Gordon Staseson recalled. "The group paid Ralph's expenses, because that's how the team was able to get those things done back in those days."

During Grey Cup week, the Roughriders had a hospitality suite at Toronto's posh Royal York hotel. Dave Ash, a staunch Riders fan, was chatting with Roughriders executive members during one gathering, at which he suggested that the team have its own mascot. The idea quickly gained traction.

"The idea of our own mascot was then pursued by Ron Lamborn, Doug Alexander, and Pat Bugera at CKCK Radio through the following winter," Staseson said. "That resulted in the radio station conducting a 'name the mascot' mail-in campaign.

"The idea of a gopher came as a result of the mail-in suggestions. Gainer was not the first pick of the committee, but [he] was everybody's second choice."

The decision was also made to give Gainer a hometown (or hole town?) of Parkbeg, which is 130 kilometres west of Regina. But plenty of work remained to be done, beyond the conceptualization.

The eight-foot-tall costume was designed and created by Metromedia, which was owned by Merv Griffin. Metromedia then owned Ice Capades and, as such, was eminently qualified to produce the costume—but this time for a football team, instead of a skating event.

Gainer the Gopher made his regular season debut on July 20, 1977, when the Roughriders lost 34–14 to the B.C. Lions. Ash and Don Hewitt took turns as Gainer that evening at Taylor Field.

It was the dawn of a difficult run for the Roughriders, who did not make another playoff appearance until 1988—Gainer's 12th season as the mascot.

In fact, the Roughriders did not win a home playoff game with Gainer in attendance until his 30th anniversary season.

But he was far from a jinx. In some of the ugly years, Gainer provided much-needed comic relief.

In 1982, for example, the Roughriders had a power outage during a game against the Hamilton Tiger-Cats. To pass the time, Gainer was passed around—up and down the east-side stands.

Now a fixture for 40-plus years, Gainer's biography appears on the Roughriders' website (Riderville.com).

"Gainer was one of 38 children born to Dwayne and Agnes Gopher, owners of a small trenching and excavation company in Parkbeg, Saskatchewan," the biography begins. "Although his parents always knew Gainer was different from his siblings, they never in their wildest dreams ever expected one of their own to become a true Saskatchewan icon."

Paws for thought: The oversized gopher was not the Roughriders' first Gainer. Bruce Gainer, a linebacker, played for the team in 1969 and 1970.

43 Family Ties

The importance of being Urness was underlined at the 1989 Grey Cup.

Mark Urness, an offensive lineman, helped the Roughriders defeat the Hamilton Tiger-Cats 43–40 in a game that was witnessed by his father, Ted.

Twenty-three years earlier, to the very day, Ted Urness had played centre for Saskatchewan in its only previous Grey Cup victory.

Lineage aside, Ted also had a close tie to the 1989 Roughriders. He was on the team's management committee—in fact, it was Ted who suggested that Bill Baker be named the Roughriders' GM in December of 1986—so father and son were able to wear 1989 championship rings.

"It was awesome sharing that with my dad," Mark Urness reflected.

"We enjoyed that," Ted Urness said in 2006. "It was quite a thing. I've got an '89 Grey Cup ring. I bought one because they were available to us.

"There's quite a difference between the rings. One looks like a wedding band and the other one is like a billboard."

Al Urness, Ted's father, was never able to savour a championship celebration despite playing for the Regina Roughriders in five consecutive Grey Cup games (1928 to 1932). Al, who was born in Preeceville, played with the Roughriders for seven seasons.

Al's brother, Harold Urness, was a Roughrider in 1930 and 1931. His football career intersected with that of Fred Goodman, Ted's uncle, who was a member of the Roughriders from 1929 to 1933. The family connection to the team was re-established in 1958, when Jack Urness (Ted's twin brother) played quarterback in his first of two seasons with Saskatchewan.

Regina-born Ted Urness made his debut with the Roughriders in 1961. Beginning in 1965, he was the CFL's All-Star centre for six consecutive seasons before retiring at age 33.

"I played until 1970, when John Helton retired me," Urness quipped, referring to the Hall of Fame defensive lineman. "I got tired of lying on my back and yelling at Ronnie [Lancaster] to look out...I say that with the highest respect for Helton. He was an excellent football player. He was young and I was old. I wanted to leave the game on my terms. I didn't want people to say I was over the hill."

Fine Football Families

The final statistical tally of the final play of the 1966 Grey Cup game was partially correct.

Ottawa Rough Riders tailback Bo Scott was trapped for a loss of two by Shaw. That much is accurate. But the stop was actually made by Cliff Shaw—not his brother Wayne.

"That was probably the best game I ever played from '61 to '66," said Wayne, who was a defensive terror for Saskatchewan in its 29–14 victory over the eastern Riders.

"My brother went in for me at the end of the game and made the tackle, and I got credit for it."

That tackle concluded Cliff's first of five seasons with the Green and White, for which his older brother excelled at linebacker from 1961 to 1972—earning All-Star honours on six occasions.

The elder Shaw hardly took the conventional path to the CFL. In fact, he did not play organized football until he was in Grade 12 at Notre Dame College—a residential school in Wilcox, Saskatchewan.

Shaw had not planned to attend Notre Dame, but everything changed as the 1956–57 academic year loomed.

"They were not going to have a Grade 12 in Bladworth High School, because I was the only one in Grade 12," recalled Wayne, who grew up on a farm between the Saskatchewan communities of Davidson and Bladworth. "They said, 'We're not going to have Grade 12 here just for you. You've got to go to Davidson.'"

Instead, he went to Notre Dame, with ambitions of going places in hockey. He did not contemplate hitting the gridiron with the Notre Dame Hounds until he played touch football and found that he enjoyed the sport.

Shaw excelled in football and in the classroom at Notre Dame, boasting a 90-plus average. He opted to remain at the school after Grade 12, taking advantage of Notre Dame's affiliation with the University of Ottawa's arts program.

At the same time, Shaw played football for a travelling Hounds team that played exhibition games against junior squads such as the Regina Rams and Saskatoon Hilltops.

In 1959, Shaw enrolled at the University of Saskatchewan and joined the Hilltops. His play over two seasons with Saskatoon's junior squad impressed the Roughriders, even though he was a raw product in some ways.

Consider his tackling technique, which was not textbook material but effective all the time.

Shaw was nicknamed "Clamps" because of his powerful hands, which allowed him to routinely shed blockers and bring down ball-carriers (who were usually grabbed by the shoulders and flung to the ground). Once Clamps got his hand anywhere on a ball carrier, he was unshakeable—so much so that people simply expected him to make the tackle…even if it was actually his younger brother in the game.

The Shaws are among the notable families in Roughriders history. Some others:

Aldag: Barry (1967–72) and brother Roger (1976–92) were offensive linemen.

Anderson: Paul (lineman, 1953–59), brother Wayne (halfback, 1952), and Paul's son Mike (offensive lineman, 1984–95).

Hackney: Millar (halfback in 1920, 1922, and 1924) and grandson Campbell (linebacker, 1980–82).

Hendrickson: Offensive linemen Craig (1991–93) and brother Scott (1992–97); their father, Lefty, was a tight end with the B.C. Lions, 1968–74.

James: Eddie (halfback, 1928, 1929, 1931) and son Gerry (running back/kicker, 1964).

Molnar: Steve (outside wing, 1941) and son Steve Jr. (fullback, 1969–78).

Murphy/Garza: Cal Murphy (assistant coach, 1997–98; head coach, 1999) and son-in-law Sam Garza (receivers coach, 1998–99).

Pelling/Mahoney: Bob Pelling (receiver, 1947–53) and grandson Mike Mahoney (linebacker, 2005–06).

Pyne: Wayne (lineman 1946–53), brother Fran (offensive lineman, 1947), and son Rob (defensive back, 1972–73).

Rennebohm: Middle wings Howard (1916, 1919–26) and son Howard Jr. (1945–48); both Rennebohms were nicknamed Tare.

Ted was inducted into the Canadian Football Hall of Fame in 1989—an inevitable honour for a player of that calibre.

"Bud Grant said of Ted Urness that he was the best centre he had ever seen, regardless of what league he was in," said former Roughriders defensive back Dale West, referencing the legendary Winnipeg Blue Bombers and Minnesota Vikings head coach. "I really believe that."

Coincidentally, a field goal decided each of the final CFL games played by Ted and Mark. Ted signed off after the 1970 Western Conference final, which was decided by an improbable, 32-yard kick by the Calgary Stampeders' Larry Robinson. Dave Ridgway's three-pointer in Mark's last game gave Saskatchewan a title in 1989.

"I'm not that nostalgic," Mark, who joined the Roughriders in 1985, said in 2010. "All I know is we won the last game and I got cut the next year, and [Ted] went out on his own terms. I'm extremely proud of him.

"I've got one favourite team in the world and it's the Roughriders. To come home and actually have the opportunity to play for them, let alone play with the people I got to play with, I couldn't have planned it any better and I couldn't have asked for anything more."

Ted Urness was 81 when he died on December 29, 2018, following a lengthy illness.

44 The Pride of Gull Lake

As a youngster, Roger Aldag dreamed of being under the spotlight in Toronto when he celebrated his greatest athletic moment. The goal was attained, but not in the manner he initially envisioned.

"I wanted to be a defenceman for the Maple Leafs, but that dream died when I realized I couldn't skate backward," Aldag said.

He was, however, determined to move forward in football— playing at a level that was duly recognized in 2002 by enshrinement in the Canadian Football Hall of Fame.

His signature moment over 17 CFL seasons was on November 26, 1989, when the Roughriders defeated the Hamilton Tiger-Cats 43–40 in a Grey Cup classic at Toronto's SkyDome (now Rogers Centre).

Earlier that day, Roughriders fans had attended a pep rally at Maple Leaf Gardens, which rivalled Taylor Field in terms of a sporting mecca when Aldag was growing up on a farm near the southwestern Saskatchewan town of Gull Lake. Over time, pro football became more of a focus for the stocky Saskatchewanian.

"I probably thought about it for the first time when my brother Barry played for the Riders," Aldag recalled. "I started to see what it was all about then. I saw the games. I saw the training camps. I had a front-row seat to what was going on."

Barry Aldag was an offensive lineman with the Green and White from 1968 to 1971, having previously excelled for the Regina Rams.

Roger joined the Rams, who were then coached by the legendary Gordon Currie, in 1972. After spending most of the first two seasons as a defensive lineman, Roger moved to centre. His

The Polecat

Bob Poley was a Rider long before he became a Rider.

While attending Hudson Bay High School, Poley stood out for a team that carried the moniker of the home province's beloved professional club.

When the strapping lineman tried out for the Hudson Bay Riders, head coach Gord Brown could not contain his excitement.

"When you're a high school coach and in walks a guy of his size, your eyes light up," Brown recalled. "You can do so many things with a big, imposing person. I had him playing both sides of the ball."

Poley actually grew up in Prairie River, 50 kilometres west of Hudson Bay. In high school, he played nine-man football before joining the junior Regina Rams—with Brown providing a recommendation.

Poley played defensive line with the Rams for all but one season. In 1977, as a graduating junior, he was deployed as one of two tight ends in the team's offensive scheme.

From there, it was off to the Riders—the other version—with whom he spent most of his professional football career.

"The Polecat" was a Roughrider from 1978 to 1984 before being surprisingly traded to the Calgary Stampeders, for whom he played until 1988. After being cut by Calgary during the 1988 campaign, Poley rejoined the Roughriders and remained in green through the end of his playing career in 1992.

A popular personality and a productive player, Poley was known to entertain his teammates while playing the guitar and cracking jokes.

"There's lots of Bob Poley stories," reflected Hall of Fame guard Roger Aldag, a close friend and longtime teammate.

"One year, he broke his collarbone and guys were just amazed he went to training camp. Before that, he had a toe cut off in a mill in Hudson Bay. He's missing his middle toe—about three-quarters of 'er, anyhow. He's got that scar on his shoulder, and that toe that looks like it's blown off.

"Somebody said to him one time, 'What happened to your toe?' He said, 'Vietnam. I stepped on a grenade.'

"He was so good for the team. He was so relaxing. In training camp, we'd be hurting, and he'd always bring in that guitar and start singing. You could always tell when he was hurting, because he wasn't singing. He kept everybody going.

"He used to drive me nuts before games. He'd be pissing around with everybody. Of course, I'm the other way. He'd say, 'I can turn that switch on and off, just like that.' He could, too. He'd be smiling one minute, and the next minute he'd tend to business.

"He just enjoyed the game. He probably enjoyed his teammates more than anybody. He got along with everybody. He was a lot of fun."

The fun peaked on November 26, 1989, when the Roughriders won the second Grey Cup in franchise history. Poley was the snapper on the last-second, game-winning field goal, kicked by Dave Ridgway, against the Hamilton Tiger-Cats.

The following day, when the Roughriders returned to Regina and a raucous welcome, Aldag and Poley carried the trophy on to Taylor Field.

Not long after that, Poley was given some time with the Cup. One of his first stops was in Melville, at the residence of his former high school football coach.

"Gord was downstairs, watching TV," Poley said. "I walked down with the Cup and said, 'Hey, Gord, how's it goin'?' I put the Grey Cup right on the coffee table."

Once a Rider, always a Rider.

excellence at both positions was such that he was invited to three Roughriders training camps during his junior football years.

Roger became a Roughrider to stay in 1976, when he was quickly indoctrinated into the Canadian football wars. Veteran centre Larry Bird suffered a knee injury, so Aldag was quickly called up from the junior protected list and designated a starter by the Roughriders' head coach.

"I remember the words of John Payne the day I was to start against Calgary at Taylor Field," Aldag said. "What really got me fired up was John Payne looking at me and saying, 'You're our centre. We've got nobody else.'"

With Aldag snapping the ball to Ron Lancaster, the Roughriders downed the Calgary Stampeders 35–10, but victory came at a cost. The team's injury woes were exacerbated when Aldag was hurt. With the stricken ankle frozen, he played the following week in Winnipeg against the Blue Bombers but was then fitted with a cast. Season over.

Ironically, the player injured in his very first CFL game would become one of the league's all-time iron men. Beginning in 1977, he played in 255 consecutive regular season and playoff games.

Unfazed by a serious knee injury near the end of the 1991 season, he returned the following year for one more campaign and, of course, played in every game.

The conventional three-year waiting period for the Roughriders' Plaza of Honour was waived so Aldag could be inducted in 1993. He was also honoured by the retirement of his jersey (No. 44) and, eventually, his picture was affixed to the west-side facing of Taylor Field.

Always modest, Aldag sincerely believed he wasn't worthy of any of the accolades, which put him in a minority of one.

As a player, he was named a CFL All-Star guard on five occasions and, most notably, won the award for the league's most outstanding offensive lineman in 1986 and 1988.

On a less glamorous note, Aldag was a member of a Roughriders team that missed the playoffs for 11 consecutive seasons, beginning in 1977. He did not take part in a playoff game until age 35. The following year, at long last, he was a champion.

"Roger's determination to get to the Grey Cup became our determination," quarterback Tom Burgess said. "He was our link to the past. He had been with the team for so many years. That was a lot on our shoulders, but when we got there and won it, we were happier for Roger than we were for us."

After all those years of waiting, Aldag wasn't quite sure how to handle the championship celebration. He certainly wasn't well-versed in the protocol, so his actions after the final gun were the product of improvisation.

"I was going around hugging people and shaking hands," Aldag recalled. "I kind of wandered around the field. It was a Fantasyland type of thing."

Fantasy had become reality for Roger Aldag—except, of course, for the part about playing for the Leafs.

Attend a Roughriders Practice

The price is right to watch the Green and White.

Check them out on a weekday and admission is free.

Most Roughriders workouts are open to the general public. Fans can simply stroll into Mosaic Stadium, occupy the new seats, and watch their favourite football team as it is immersed in preparation.

Such accessibility is often unthinkable in the ultra-secretive world of professional football. In the NFL, for example, good luck to anyone who shows up at a practice facility and expects to get anywhere near the team. At that tier of football, the environment is hermetically sealed.

The CFL, by contrast, is welcoming to fans and media—except for the one session per week the teams have the option to close. Even then, it is tough to beat the access.

Want to meet your favourite player? Or the entire team? It's a snap. Simply make your way to the front row after practice and hang out near the northwest tunnel. All the players and coaches walk by en route to the dressing room. Rare is the occasion when anyone who seeks an autograph, a handshake, a selfie, or even a conversation is turned down.

Again, imagine that in the NFL, or even NCAA football. Many of the principal figures reside in a Secret Service–style bubble.

You may be Tom Brady's most ardent fan but, unless you have an "in" or the influence that only millions of dollars can buy, good luck approaching the New England Patriots quarterback…or even his backup.

The atmosphere is much more relaxed north of the border, where the stars of the game can mingle with the paying customers—even during Grey Cup week.

In 1996, for example, the Ron Lancaster–coached Edmonton Eskimos were preparing to meet the Toronto Argonauts for the CFL championship. A few days before the big game, following an Eskimos practice at Hamilton's Ivor Wynne Stadium, a fan attained what he described as a lifelong goal of meeting Lancaster. The Little General not only met the fan and signed an autograph (legibly!), but also chatted amicably with him for about 10 minutes before being summoned to the dressing room. The fan walked away, beaming.

Lancaster had previously coached the Roughriders in 1979 and 1980 during their first two seasons at an expanded Taylor Field. The improvements also included a practice field, located only a few first downs away from the stadium. Rider Priders typically lined the wire fence and watched practices—so faithfully, in fact, that they were dubbed "the railbirds."

The daily delegation became so familiar to coaches and players that friendships often developed. When Roy Shivers was the Roughriders' general manager, he knew most of the railbirds by name and often inquired about their well-being and their families. If one of them happened to be absent, Shivers would inquire as to why.

Before the railbirds, there was another form of onlookers at Roughriders practices—equine beings, athletes in their own right, who were not particularly conversant in the nuances of football. The Roughriders, you see, used to practise on the infield of a horse racing facility—Regina Exhibition Track.

"The sulkies were out there practising the same time as us, so you had to cross the track," said Jim Hopson, who was an offensive lineman with the team from 1973 to 1976. "If it was a dry day, it would be okay, but if it was muddy, you'd be walking in mud. I still remember [head coach] John Payne when we'd bring in two or three guys during the season because of injuries. He'd give us a little pregame talk and then he'd say, 'Okay, men, remember to watch for horses.' The young guys from Alabama would look at each other and say, 'Watch for horses? What is he talking about?' We'd just say, 'Watch the horses.' They went both ways sometimes, so the players would be dancing to try to get across."

Northern dancers, you might say.

Back in those days, the Roughriders' dressing room was located inside the grandstand at the horse track. On game days, the team would take a bus to and from Taylor Field. There was also a time when the team needed a ride to practice.

In 1977, the Roughriders got off to a bad start and, well, so did some cars. In a *Leader-Post* column headlined CAR WRECKS FORCE ROUGHRIDERS OFF PRACTICE FIELD, Bob Hughes described the scene:

"The Saskatchewan Roughriders have had their problems this season. Fumbles. Interceptions. Fake kicks. Big runbacks. Edmonton. Winnipeg. B.C. Injuries. Retirements. And now, a demolition derby.

"The Roughriders were turfed out of their regular practice area last week, which is the infield of the racetrack at the exhibition grounds, which was the site of tractor pulls, demolition derbies and chuckwagon races during Buffalo Days.

"They were supposed to report there Sunday, though, to work out. But the demolition derby left more than torn-up turf. It also left some of the wrecks. The Roughriders tried to get into Taylor Field, but couldn't, and ended up at Currie Field."

No railbird sightings were reported.

46 Bravo to Alex, Etc.

Jeff Fairholm pulled up lame while pulling away from members of the Winnipeg Blue Bombers' defence.

The date was September 2, 1990, and the speedy slotback had just caught a bomb from quarterback Kent Austin—who a few seconds later would be credited with the longest completion in Roughriders history.

"The 107-yarder was kind of funny because I pulled my hamstring halfway to the end zone," Fairholm said with a chuckle. "It's a good thing that the defensive backs gave up."

The touchdown, scored during the Roughriders' 55–11 home-field victory over the Winnipeg Blue Bombers, erased the previous distance standard of 104 yards—set in 1962 when Bob Ptacek found Ray Purdin.

Oddly enough, the Roughriders also had another touchdown pass exceeding 104 yards within a year of Fairholm's record-setting sprint. Rick Worman found Willis Jacox for a 106-yard score in 1991.

Over the years, Roughriders players have gone to several lengths to establish team records. For example:

Longest Run: 98 yards, by Alex Bravo in a 46–28 victory over the B.C. Lions at Taylor Field on September 29, 1956.

As the *Leader-Post*'s Hank Johnson put it, "The most spectacular scoring play of them all was executed by Alex Bravo. Frustrated all season in an effort to hit the scoring column, the fleet California Poly back finally made the grade on a run that fans will be talking about for a long time to come. Alex sprinted off tackle on a quick opener and ran 98 yards for his first touchdown since he joined the Riders."

Bravo, who had 126 yards on five carries for the day, played in only 13 games with Saskatchewan (all in 1956) and rushed for 399 yards overall. Nearly one-quarter of his regular season rushing yards as a Roughrider came on that long-distance touchdown.

Longest Punt Return: 109 yards, on a touchdown by Herb Johnson during a 19–17 loss to the host Edmonton Eskimos on August 31, 1953.

The *Leader-Post*'s Hank Johnson referred to a "jet-propelled Johnson" while describing his touchdown as such: "It was 109 yards as the crow flies but Herb covered a lot more ground than that as he danced along his own goal line before heading out for pay dirt along the sidelines." Johnson, playing in his first game of Canadian professional football, also scored on a four-yard run.

Saskatchewan has also had two 108-yard punt returns—by Jacox (1991) and Paul Williams (1976). The latter return actually followed a missed field goal, but for statistical purposes it was considered a punt return. (Now it would be categorized as a missed field goal return.)

And then there was a 107-yarder by Fran McDermott in 1982—the oddity being that he did not score on the play. He was tackled on the Hamilton Tiger-Cats' 5-yard line.

Longest Kickoff Return: 115 yards for a touchdown by Bobby Thompson in a 50–18 victory over the visiting Lions on October 24, 1971.

It was a spectacular day for the speedy halfback, who also scored on receptions of 97 and 14 yards. Thompson caught five passes for 163 yards and rushed eight times for 57 yards.

Longest Interception Return: 112 yards for a touchdown by Bruce Bennett in a 35–3 victory over the visiting Calgary Stampeders on August 27, 1972.

Bennett stepped in front of Hugh McKinnis, intercepted Jerry Keeling, and raced to the opposite end zone.

The *Leader-Post*'s Bob Hughes described the long-distance sprint as follows: "I was trying to figure out why Bennett ran so hard when there wasn't a Stampeder within mailing distance. 'I was running like that because I knew somebody was chasing me,' Bennett would explain later. 'I could hear him behind me. But when I did look back, I didn't see any Stampeders.' That was because the guy thundering behind Bennett was the referee. He almost caught him."

The Roughriders also got a 98-yard interception-return touchdown from Lewis Cook while routing the Stampeders. That afternoon, Saskatchewan registered 291 interception-return yards, still a league record as of this writing. Cook had two of the Riders' four picks. Bennett and Charlie Collins added singles.

Longest Fumble Return: 108 yards for a score, a CFL-record, courtesy of cornerback Omarr Morgan in a 31–27 loss to the visiting Eskimos on September 20, 2009.

Morgan scooped up the ball after Jerrell Freeman, a future NFL player, forced a fumble by running back Arkee Whitlock. It was a bittersweet day for Morgan, who was later beaten by Maurice Mann on a 68-yard, game-winning touchdown reception with 1:09 remaining in the fourth quarter.

47 The Magic of Kent Austin

Kent Austin went from being reviled to revered, in only a few short months.

Once a pariah in Rider Nation, Austin became a rock star in Saskatchewan while guiding the Roughriders to a Grey Cup championship in 2007—and then he left, again, under distinctly different circumstances from those of 13 years earlier.

Austin was Public Enemy No. 1, and perhaps Nos. 2 and 3, after demanding and receiving a trade following the 1993 CFL season. Then among the league's elite quarterbacks, he was part of a three-way deal and ended up with the B.C. Lions, with whom he received a vitriolic response in his return to Taylor Field.

He was, at that point, the unlikeliest candidate to become a repeat Roughrider. After all, some frustrated fans had taken a sledgehammer to an Austin Mini outside the stadium before the Lions' 1994 visit to Regina.

But never say never in the CFL.

Following the 2006 season, general manager Eric Tillman hired Austin as the Roughriders' head coach. A storybook season ensued, as Austin guided Saskatchewan to a Grey Cup title. The Green and White won the championship in Toronto, in the very complex where Austin had thrown for 474 yards and three touchdowns to lead the Roughriders to a 43–40 Grey Cup victory over the Hamilton Tiger-Cats on November 26, 1989.

However, that euphoria eventually soured, leading up to 1994, but the restoration of his reputation in Riderville eventually took place in 2007.

How to Get Re-Hired

Bill Baker was nicknamed The Undertaker during his CFL career as a ferocious defensive lineman but, early in his first stint as a general manager, The Terminator would have been more fitting.

Baker took over as the Roughriders' general manager late in 1986. One of his first moves after assuming control of the cash-strapped club was to terminate all the football-operations staff—a decision that left director of player personnel Dan Rambo in limbo.

Rambo had a card to play, however, and used it wisely to provide the Roughriders with someone who had a winning hand—quarterback Kent Austin.

"I had seen [Austin] at an NFL camp and we put him on our neg list," Rambo recalled. "On January 4, 1987, I had gone from Tucson, where my parents stayed for the winter, to San Diego to meet with Bill Baker and John Gregory. John had just been hired by the club [as head coach] and Bill had said it was his belief that the coach should be part of the hiring process when it comes to a personnel guy, which I completely agreed with. They wanted to meet with me and see if I was on the same path.

"One of the last questions John had for me in the interview was, 'We need a quarterback. Who do you recommend?' A bell went off in my head that this question was the key. I wasn't the best negotiator, but instincts told me he was asking a question reserved for the new director of player personnel to answer.

"I told them that if they [re]hired me, I'd tell them. They looked at one another and then looked at me and said, 'You're hired.' I said, 'Okay...Kent Austin.' That's how it went.

"The only reason I said it like that was that morning at about 2:00 AM, I got a phone call from my mother saying my dad had died a few hours earlier. When the guys were grilling me like that, I was in one of those take-it-or-leave-it moods. They took it and I didn't leave—they hired me. Whew!"

Austin, who spent the 1986 season with the St. Louis Cardinals, was released by that NFL team in the summer of 1987. He arrived in Saskatchewan that September and, after being thrust into front-line duty, won his first two starts.

"Kent didn't disappoint," Rambo said. "The first time he came up to Regina, he sat in the stands watching the game, because he was on what was called a 21-day tryout then. I swear, the first quarter wasn't even over and he looked at me and said, 'I can win in this league,' and that I had to find a way to get him on the roster.

"Of course, it was all Kent that got him on the roster. He was a natural-born leader. He had an aura that conveyed his confidence to his team. He also had some help from another quarterback named Tom Burgess—an equally impressive man.

"I negotiated many a contract with Kent—some in Saskatchewan and some at his home in Tennessee. It was always the same. He knew what he wanted and he was always fair about it. He was a good kid, from a good family growing up."

Austin and Burgess were key contributors to the growth of the Roughriders, as was Rambo.

Both quarterbacks received extensive playing time in 1988 and 1989. The latter season concluded when Austin threw for 474 yards and three touchdowns to guide Saskatchewan to a 43–40 Grey Cup victory over the Hamilton Tiger-Cats.

Burgess, who sought and deserved more playing time, was traded to the Winnipeg Blue Bombers the following spring. He was named the offensive MVP of the 1990 Grey Cup after throwing for 286 yards and three touchdowns in a 50–11 victory over the Edmonton Eskimos.

After another season in Winnipeg, Burgess was with the Ottawa Rough Riders for two years before being dealt back to Saskatchewan in 1994. He was part of a three-way swap that resulted in Austin, who had demanded a trade, joining the B.C Lions.

In 2009, Burgess joined Austin in the Plaza of Honour. Austin had been enshrined 10 years earlier.

"It was my most special year in football—of any year, as a player or a coach," Austin said in June of 2008, a few months after leaving the Roughriders for a second time—to become the offensive co-ordinator at his alma mater, the University of Mississippi. "If you weren't on the inside, it's hard to explain how magical it was."

The magic began before the opening workout of training camp, when Austin addressed the players—including veterans who had become accustomed to mediocrity—and instantly set the tone with an eye-opening address.

"Welcome, 2007 Saskatchewan Roughriders," Austin began. "We will win the Grey Cup this year. If anyone has any issue with that, there is the door. No hard feelings."

Those words were prescient. The Roughriders punctuated that season by defeating the Winnipeg Blue Bombers 23–19 at Rogers Centre, which was known as SkyDome in 1989 when Austin was named the Grey Cup's most valuable offensive player.

He went on to register stratospheric passing totals over the next four seasons, amassing 20,720 aerial yards and 125 touchdown passes. In 1992, he set franchise single-season records for passing yards (6,225) and touchdown throws (35).

Austin didn't possess the strongest arm, nor was he especially nimble, but his preparation and intellect were unparalleled.

"The team has you for four-and-a-half hours [on practice days], and some of the other quarterbacks I had a chance to play with in the mid-'90s were there for four hours and 35 minutes," recalled Dan Farthing, a Roughriders receiver from 1991 to 2001. "But Kent Austin was putting in eight to 10 hours, and he'd go home with a stack of VHS tapes. He was a coach, and it's pretty good to have a coach on the field."

"He was very smart," agreed Jeff Fairholm, a member of Saskatchewan's receiving corps from 1988 to 1993. "He would be in extremely early in the morning, working on game plans. I remember him coming into the locker room and being all excited about the new plays we had, and he'd tell us all about them before we went into meetings, so we'd get all excited."

The excitement reached a crescendo in 1989, and again, in 2007, when Austin was a catalyst for a rare Grey Cup championship in Saskatchewan.

And when he left the team a second time, the bricks were replaced by bouquets. There was no longer an Austin Mini outside

Taylor Field—but a giant picture of the Roughriders legend, wearing his No. 5 jersey, which was eventually affixed to the west-side exterior of the stadium.

48 The Forgotten Classic

One splendid Saturday afternoon in 1993, the Roughriders and Calgary Stampeders played the best CFL game that nobody remembers.

Hardly anybody, anyway.

A down-to-the-wire shootout, won 48–45 by the Roughriders at Taylor Field, was soon overshadowed by the events of that evening.

On October 23, 1993, Joe Carter hit a three-run, ninth-inning, World Series–winning home run for the Toronto Blue Jays against the Philadelphia Phillies.

Across Canada, fans spilled on to the streets—as did some of the revellers' beverages—to celebrate the Blue Jays' second successive championship. The party raged on Albert Street in Regina, only a few blocks away from the site of that day's Canadian football classic.

"When I looked up the original *Leader-Post* game report written by Darrell Davis, he had written in the first paragraph that the game in 1993 versus Calgary should be 'put in a time capsule,'" Hall of Fame kicker Dave Ridgway said. "It was that good."

That great, in fact. But the events of that afternoon have been expunged from some memory banks—including that of at least one of the participants.

"I honestly do not remember that game," said Jeff Fairholm, who was part of the Roughriders' formidable aerial arsenal during the Saturday matinee against the Stampeders.

The quarterbacks—Saskatchewan's Kent Austin and Calgary's Doug Flutie—combined for 1,093 aerial yards, still the most ever in a CFL game. Flutie threw for 547 yards, one more than Austin. Austin went 16-for-20 for 312 yards—over the first two quarters—to help Saskatchewan enjoy a 35–10 halftime lead. On the day, he was 33-for-42 while throwing touchdown passes to Fairholm, Ray Elgaard, and Bruce Boyko.

Flutie, who would soon win his third of an unprecedented six CFL most-outstanding-player awards, dominated the second half on his 31st birthday. He completed 24-of-33 passes for 377 yards, with four touchdowns, over the final 30 minutes.

Three of the touchdown passes were caught by Brian Wiggins, who had 16 catches for 225 yards. After Wiggins' third major, Flutie found Derrick Crawford for a two-point convert that created a 45–45 tie with 1:58 remaining.

Austin took it from there, moving Saskatchewan into range for a 34-yard field-goal attempt by Ridgway, who split the uprights with one second left.

Even then, the excitement was not over. Consider the frenetic final play—which began when Calgary scrimmaged the ball on its 35-yard line—as described on the normally by-the-book CFL statistical summary:

"Flutie to Wiggins, followed by a potpourri of pitchouts, laterals, fumbles, handoffs and such until everyone on the field except Gainer and two security guards touched the ball. Eventually a lateral to [Karl] Anthony brings an end to the play and the day. Amen!"

49 Striking Gold after a Fold

A question to ponder: Would the Roughriders have three fewer Grey Cup victories if not for other teams' demises?

Dispersal drafts, held after the Montreal Alouettes and Ottawa Renegades folded, helped to stock Saskatchewan teams that won CFL championships in 1989, 2007, and 2013.

The Alouettes (not to be confused with the current version) ceased operations as the 1987 regular season loomed. In short order, a draft was arranged to allow refugees from the Alouettes to find new CFL homes—an arrangement that unquestionably benefited the Roughriders.

Placekicker Dave Ridgway had been ill-advisedly dealt away by the Roughriders following the 1986 season, but thanks to the disappearance of the Alouettes, he was once again available to Saskatchewan.

"We were going to make sure we got Dave Ridgway," head coach John Gregory said at the time.

Upon rejoining the Roughriders in time for their second game of the 1987 regular season, Ridgway ascended to a new tier, accuracy-wise, and began kicking at a level that would ultimately result in his enshrinement in the Canadian Football Hall of Fame.

Ridgway's defining moment was a game-winning, 35-yard field goal with two seconds remaining in the 1989 Grey Cup game.

Saskatchewan's first-round choice in the 1987 dispersal draft had been defensive lineman Brett "The Toaster" Williams, whose rights were promptly traded to the B.C. Lions for its second-rounder in the Montreal fire sale.

The Roughriders wisely spent their two second-rounders on Ridgway and linebacker/special-teams ace Dan Rashovich. Thus began a 13-year stint in Saskatchewan for Rashovich, who eventually joined Ridgway in the Roughriders' Plaza of Honour.

Although Terry Baker was bypassed in the dispersal draft, he was quickly brought to Regina, where he participated in a punting derby with Paul Hickie and Mike Lazecki.

Baker won the contest and never looked back, spending the next 16 seasons as a full-time CFLer. In his final game as a Roughrider—the 1989 Grey Cup—he punted six times for an average of 46.5 yards in a 43–40 victory over the Hamilton Tiger-Cats. Baker's precise directional punts, including one that went out of bounds at the 3-yard line, repeatedly forced the Tiger-Cats to begin possessions deep in their own zone.

When the Roughriders next won a Grey Cup, green-and-white confetti flew once again in Toronto. Saskatchewan defeated the Winnipeg Blue Bombers 23–19 to win the third championship in franchise history.

The victorious quarterback was Kerry Joseph, who was also named the CFL's most outstanding player in 2007. Joseph had been added in an April 12, 2006, dispersal draft that followed the loss of the Renegades (2002–05).

Hamilton owned the first overall pick but traded it to Saskatchewan when general manager Roy Shivers surrendered tailback/returner Corey Holmes (the league's special teams player of the year in 2002 and 2005), safety Scott Gordon, and a first-round pick in the 2007 CFL draft. As part of that transaction, the Roughriders and Tiger-Cats exchanged negotiation-list quarterbacks. Saskatchewan added the rights to Darian Durant, while Reggie Ball was transferred to the Tiger-Cats' negotiation list. Durant had been the property of the Renegades, but his rights were obtained by Hamilton in a negotiation-list dispersal draft.

In the primary dispersal draft, Saskatchewan used its own first-rounder (third overall) to select receiver-returner Jason Armstead.

One important free agent at the time was Eric Tillman, who had been the Renegades' GM for their first three years of operation. Due to the dysfunction in the Renegades' front office, Tillman spent the 2005 season and part of 2006 as a football analyst with CBC and Sportsnet.

When Shivers was fired by Saskatchewan in August of 2006, Tillman was quickly installed as the Roughriders' GM and began the process of transforming the team into a consistent winner.

Tillman consummated two larcenous trades in 2007, with ex-Renegades figuring in both deals with Hamilton.

On January 31, Tillman obtained receiver D.J. Flick (who had played for Ottawa in 2002 and 2003), offensive lineman Wayne Smith, a second-round draft pick in 2007, and the negotiating rights to quarterback Dalton Bell in exchange for quarterback Rocky Butler, second- and fifth-round picks in 2007, and the negotiating rights to quarterback Bret Meyer.

On August 19, Tillman shipped Armstead to the Tiger-Cats for Holmes and Regina-born rookie receiver Chris Getzlaf, whom Hamilton had selected in the fifth round of the 2007 draft.

The Roughriders' roster in 2007 also included ex-Renegades such as offensive linemen Mike Abou-Mechrek and Marc Parenteau, running back Josh Ranek, and receiver Yo Murphy.

Six years later, the Roughriders were still deriving immense benefits from the Renegades' demise.

Durant, who guided Saskatchewan to Grey Cup berths in 2009 and 2010, was the triumphant quarterback in 2013. He threw three touchdown passes as Saskatchewan downed Hamilton 45–23 on Taylor Field. (Tillman, while in Ottawa, had placed Durant, then of the University of North Carolina Tar Heels, on the Renegades' negotiation list.)

After the game, Getzlaf—a seeming throw-in in the Armstead/Holmes trade—was named the 101st Grey Cup's most outstanding Canadian. A two-time 1,000-yard receiver with Saskatchewan,

Getzlaf caught three passes for 78 yards in the 2013 Grey Cup, with two of the receptions setting up short touchdown runs.

Rewind even further to the folding of the Alouettes and marvel at all the key players Saskatchewan added to the fold, as it were, en route to Grey Cup glory.

50 A Quarterback Who Gave Back

Kerry Joseph is the rare ex-quarterback who has fond recollections of interceptions—three of them, to be precise.

Joseph, who was a starting safety in the NFL before venturing north of the border and returning to his natural position of quarterback, registered all three of his picks with the 1999 Seattle Seahawks.

In fact, one of those interceptions was at the expense of Doug Flutie, a six-time winner of the CFL's most-outstanding-player award.

Joseph, for his part, received the CFL's most prestigious individual prize three days before he quarterbacked Saskatchewan to the 2007 Grey Cup championship.

"It has been quite a journey," Joseph, then 34, said with a smile while holding the MOP trophy.

A star quarterback with the McNeese State Cowboys, Joseph was introduced to the pro ranks in 1996 when he signed with the Cincinnati Bengals as an undrafted free agent. He was Cincinnati's third-string quarterback for most of that season.

In 1997, he quarterbacked NFL Europe's London Monarchs before returning to the NFL—but as a tailback, with the Washington Redskins.

Another position change followed in 1998, when he played safety for NFL Europe's Rhein Fire. He remained at safety for the next four seasons, spent with Seattle.

Having exhausted his NFL options, Joseph joined the Ottawa Renegades in 2003 and finally returned to playing quarterback.

Joseph starred with Ottawa for three seasons, with 2005 being especially noteworthy. In addition to passing for 4,466 yards and 25 touchdowns, he rushed for 1,006 yards and nine scores.

That turned out to be the last of four seasons for the Renegades (2002–05). On April 12, 2006, Saskatchewan traded for the first overall pick in a dispersal draft of Renegades players, and then spent that choice on Joseph.

Very quickly, Joseph immersed himself in the Roughriders' playbook and in the community. He became the face of "Kerry's Catch for KidSport," a program that raised money to help under-privileged kids take part in sports programs, and was accessible to any fan who wanted an autograph, a handshake, or a chat.

"It's a blessing to be able to play a game that you love to play and get paid to do it," Joseph, from New Iberia, Louisiana, said in 2006. "A lot of athletes don't want to be role models but, in truth, we are. A lot of kids look up to us.

"I remember growing up and looking up to professional and college athletes. I wanted to do that as a dream, so I know kids have that same admiration. To give them an opportunity and just to let them know that, 'Hey, you have goals and you have dreams and you can accomplish them,' that's what drives me to do it.

"My parents have always taught me to never forget where you come from and never forget about other people. That's just the caring and love in my heart that I have for others."

The 2007 campaign, in particular, was a love-in. Joseph enjoyed his finest CFL season, throwing for 4,002 yards and 24 touchdowns, with only eight interceptions, in addition to rushing for 737 yards (averaging 8.2 yards per carry) and 13 majors.

A sterling season was unquestionably validated when Joseph became part of an ultra-exclusive fraternity—members of the Roughriders who have been named the league's top player.

George Reed, in 1965, was the first Roughrider to receive the award. Ron Lancaster followed in 1970 and 1976. Thirty-one years elapsed before another Roughrider—Joseph—would be recognized in that fashion.

Joseph proceeded to pilot the Roughriders to a 23–19 Grey Cup victory over the Winnipeg Blue Bombers. Although his passing stats were below average—13-for-34 for 181 yards, with one touchdown and one interception—he did rush for a game-high 101 yards on 10 carries.

His 11th carry of the day—the act of triumphantly lifting the Grey Cup over his head—was not reflected in the statistics.

"Even with my years in the NFL and my years in the CFL, 2007 has to rank at the top," Joseph said 10 years later when asked about career highlights. "Every time I look up at my TV at home, my MVP trophy is sitting right there. I still wear the Grey Cup ring.

"So, 2007 is at the top—definitely at the top."

51 Wear a Watermelon on Your Head

The Roughriders and Phoenix Group were using their melons during a brainstorming session that contributed to a lasting tradition.

Leading up to the 2002 CFL season, the Roughriders and their advertising partner were developing a theme for a marketing campaign. The objective was to convey the fun that could be derived from game day, irrespective of the score.

In timely fashion, great minds would rewind to 2001, when Trent Fraser (then the Roughriders' vice-president of marketing) and Phoenix Group's Darren Mitchell attended a Saskatchewan game in Winnipeg.

"We were looking to see what they were doing well," recalled Mitchell, Phoenix Group's vice-president of strategic development. "We had toured the facility, watched the in-game presentation, the signage, et cetera, and met with the production team."

Fraser and Mitchell were sitting in upper-level seats, near the student section. All of a sudden, they saw two shirtless young men, each with an "S" painted on his chest and a watermelon—which had been cut into a football helmet of sorts—on his head.

"We actually turned to each other and said, 'That's it,'" Fraser recalled of the "Eureka!" moment.

"Everyone was high-fiving him and booing him," Mitchell added, "and we thought he was a fun character."

The melon-headed fans were in keeping with the club's growing emphasis on appealing to a younger demographic. The Roughriders had already established an e-commerce website and incorporated live bands into pregame festivities. A natural next step was to have a little fun with the melon-head concept.

Early in 2002, Fraser approached the Roughriders' board of directors and asked for more money than had ever been allocated for a marketing campaign. The marketing team planned to shoot two commercials—one showing a face-painting fan, and another featuring the melon-head.

The additional expenditure was approved and the Roughriders, in conjunction with Phoenix Group's creative team, went to work.

"Melon-head took off," Fraser said. "We jumped on it. I arranged watermelon-carving contests in the pregame festivities on the practice field and we even had one of our partners, Safeway, put the Riders' 'S' logo stickers on watermelons in their large crates in their Regina stores.

"I knew we hit it right when a friend of mine was taking his then-five-year-old son to his first game and the young man exclaimed, 'We have to go to the grocery store!' The dad asked why. 'You can't go to a Rider game without wearing a watermelon on your head,' the son replied.

"The TV, radio, print, and billboard ads had worked. Wearing a carved-out melon on your head was somehow cool."

It still is. The tradition has endured through good years and bad—seasons in which the Roughriders have been successful, and ones in which the fans have been, well, melon-choly.

52 "Hoppy" Days

Rider Nation enjoyed a transformation under president-CEO Jim Hopson.

The community-owned team's increasing solvency was especially pronounced in 2007, when the thinnest of profit margins became a thing of the past.

In the spring of that year, the Roughriders announced a net profit of $455 on their 2006 operations. The difference between a surplus and a deficit was so minute that a cancelled season ticket or two could have tipped the balance toward a negative outcome.

By the end of 2007, however, the Roughriders were suddenly adjusting to revenues that were in the millions—all because of a game-changing season in franchise history.

The template for success had actually been established three years earlier, when the club's board of directors decided to hire a paid president-CEO—who turned out to be Hopson—for the first time.

One of Hopson's earliest key hirings was former Roughriders and Regina Rams teammate Steve Mazurak, whose second stint with the Green and White lasted 13 years before he retired as the vice-president of sales and partnerships. Mazurak was an important difference-maker during and after the Hopson regime.

"The credit has to be given to the board that envisioned that things could be different," reflected Hopson, a 2019 inductee into the Canadian Football Hall of Fame. "People like Tom Robinson, Garry Huntington, Graham Barker, Paul Hill, and others said, 'We've been doing this for nearly 100 years and we've got the best fans in the world, but we can only turn a profit of $400. We need to look at this differently. We need to start thinking of this as a business, and a business that can be profitable, rather than as a charity or social club or something.'

"It was a real shift in thinking—a real shift in culture."

Until Hopson was appointed to the position in October of 2004, members of the all-volunteer board had designated a president to run the franchise. Barker was the volunteer president when Hopson assumed the paid post.

Although the chair of the Roughriders' board of directors remains an important position, the buck stops primarily at the desk of the president-CEO. He reports to a board that generally operates behind the scenes, although the commitment of the volunteers who serve remains strong and commendable.

The club's fortunes skyrocketed during Hopson's 10-year tenure.

Seven-figure profits became the norm during a decade in which Saskatchewan won two Grey Cups (in 2007 and 2013) and became the financial envy of the league. Gone were the days of eking out a $455 profit or, infinitely worse, requiring a telethon to remain alive.

"Jim was absolutely the right person at the right time," said Craig Reynolds, who took over as president-CEO after Hopson stepped down in 2015. "He just brought an attitude and a belief and he focused in on the right things."

Some changes were highly visible, such as the installation of Mosaic Stadium's first video board in time for the 2005 season. Other improvements were more subtle, but important nonetheless.

"He focused in on the team and the facilities and made changes to little things that meant a lot, like investing into the locker room and investing a little bit into the stadium and investing into the fan experience and investing into marketing," Reynolds said. "Those are things that just hadn't been done before, for lots of good reasons.

"Jim just brought a different attitude and he brought a belief to the organization that we can have success here. Prior to that, every once in a while you'd believe that, but there wasn't a consistent belief. He brought an attitude-change here, which was exactly what this organization needed."

The Roughriders were the last CFL team to appoint a paid president-CEO. The decision was made shortly after the club had become debt-free for the first time in 20 years.

Hopson was a natural in so many respects. He was an offensive lineman with the team from 1973 to 1976 and was later appointed to the board of directors as a special advisor. He was the CEO and director of education of the Qu'Appelle Valley School Division before being hired by the Roughriders.

As someone who was equally comfortable in the boardroom or at a barbecue, Hopson made a seamless transition into the role of president-CEO while running the organization during a period of unprecedented success.

"I won't tell you that it was easy," Hopson noted. "It was hard, because it was such a shift in thinking from volunteers sort of running game day and running the board and running the team. All of a sudden, we now have paid employees who are responsible for this and we depend heavily on volunteers, but now the volunteers have to step back.

"We always said internally that we were going from being a volunteer-run to a staff-run organization, and that was quite a shift."

Once that shift was made, the Roughriders never looked back—except to marvel at the days when any profit, even one as small as $455, was noteworthy.

53 Shivers Delivers

Roy Shivers' introduction to life as the Roughriders' general manager could have been sponsored by Gravol.

"I was feeling okay today," he said early in his tenure, "but then I looked at our team's depth chart and I got sick."

Hired just before Christmas in 1999, Shivers inherited a team that was coming off a 3–15 season while playing home games on a worn, patched-up artificial surface (while, in many cases, also fielding a worn, patched-up collection of players). The Roughriders' financial challenges made it difficult to recruit or retain top-calibre players, as did the overall state of the club and its facilities.

Considering all those factors, Shivers was the right man at the right time—someone who improved the perception and performance of the on-field product.

As the team became more competitive, the financial picture brightened and expectations soared—ultimately to a point where they couldn't quite be met under Shivers and head coach Danny Barrett.

Although Shivers was fired on August 21, 2006, nobody could say at that point that the roster induced nausea. The foundation

"We Want Jackson!"

The debut of Robert Ellis "Stonewall" Jackson—the Regina Roughriders' first black player—constituted an advancement in one sense.

But a media account of his introductory game, while complimentary in many ways, is a discomforting reminder of the times.

"The performance of 'Stonewall' Jackson was a revelation," the *Leader-Post* reported on September 22, 1930, two days after the Roughriders' 22–0 victory over the Moose Jaw Maroons at Regina's exhibition grounds. "Only twice did the dusky athlete touch the pigskin—but how he made those occasions count. Players, water boys and coaches alike looked on dumbfounded when the ebony-hued boy sped through the Moose Jaw line for 45 yards in the last quarter but the ball carrier did not seem in the least excited and took everything in a matter-of-fact way."

In *Saskatchewan Roughriders: First 100 Years*, Bob Calder noted that Jackson was employed in Regina as a porter with the Canadian National Railway, and that he "soon became a favourite of the Regina fans."

That was evident on November 1, 1930, when the Roughriders posted a 23–0 first-round playoff victory over the St. John's College team from Winnipeg. A "We Want Jackson!" chant was audible from a crowd of 2,000 spectators at the exhibition grounds.

"Every move he made was cheered," the *Leader-Post* reported, "and when he brought Eddie James down on an end run, howls of joy emanated from the grandstand."

Jackson scored one touchdown in his single season with the Roughriders, which included an 11–6 loss to Toronto Balmy Beach in the 1930 Grey Cup. It remains unclear why he never returned to the Regina team.

Another 17 years elapsed before the Roughriders dressed another black player—Gabe Patterson.

A running back who had played college football at Kentucky State before joining the Montreal Alouettes, Patterson was an all-star in both of his seasons with the Roughriders.

In 1947, Patterson was by far the team's leading scorer, registering 36 points (three five-point touchdowns, three converts, five field goals, and three singles). As well as excelling along the ground, he made eight receptions for 206 yards—an average of 25.8 yards per catch—and one touchdown. His list of big plays included a 62-yard run, a 70-yard reception, a 57-yard fumble return, and a 76-yard kickoff return. He also tied Stan Stasica for the team lead in interceptions, with two.

Patterson followed up in 1948 with 32 points (two touchdowns, 14 converts, two field goals, and two singles). In addition to being an explosive runner and receiver, he saw some duty at quarterback in relief of starter Johnny Cook. Patterson and Cook also played defence, tying for the team lead with three interceptions.

Although Patterson was an elite player, there were some off-field issues due to the societal mindset of the time.

Calder and Garry Andrews, in *Rider Pride*, wrote that "some of the executive members were slow to accept integration."

Longtime Roughriders halfback Sully Glasser, interviewed for the Calder/Andrews book, said, "It is a story somewhat similar to Jackie Robinson's. The ice had to be broken with Gabe."

Calder and Andrews added, "Patterson ran into some personal problems in 1948 and was not invited back even though he had just earned All-Star honours."

of talent was such that, with some key additions in the year that followed, the Roughriders were able to win the Grey Cup title that eluded Shivers and Barrett during their time in Saskatchewan.

"They absolutely righted the ship," former Roughriders president-CEO Jim Hopson said. "We were sinking. I give Roy the lion's share of the credit, because it was Roy who drove the bus. It was Roy's vision and Roy's decisions and so on. The team didn't turn around overnight, but they had patience. They brought in good players and they started to develop a different attitude around the team."

Shivers and Barrett established a milestone by sheer virtue of their presence with the Roughriders. They were the first black GM–head coach combination in pro football history, albeit a duo that was different in a multitude of ways.

Whereas Shivers was outspoken, often using some choice words in the process, Barrett was more cautious and loath to utter an expletive. Barrett was guarded with the media, while Shivers loved to hold court and chat extensively about virtually any topic—the civil-rights movement (during which he grew up), music (he loves jazz), family (any conversation about his father was fascinating) and, yes, even football.

Football-wise, Shivers and Barrett guided the team to victory totals of five, six, and eight before enjoying an 11-7 breakthrough and a long-awaited playoff win in 2003.

Three consecutive 9–9 seasons followed. Shivers wasn't around for the conclusion of the third one, having been succeeded by Eric Tillman during the 2006 campaign. Tillman hired Kent Austin as the head coach after it was announced, unsurprisingly, following the 2006 season that Barrett's contract would not be renewed.

"Roy and Danny took the team from a laughingstock to respectability," said Rod Pedersen, the radio voice of the Roughriders from 1999 to 2018. "The sad thing, because I have a lot of affection for Roy and Danny, is that they only took it so far and it got to a point where they weren't going to get over that hump."

Tillman and Austin cleared that hurdle, producing a Grey Cup in their one full season together in Saskatchewan. At every opportunity, Tillman made a point of commending Shivers for having left such a strong nucleus, which was augmented by the likes of running back Wes Cates; offensive linemen Mike Abou-Mechrek, Wayne Smith, and Jermese Jones; receiver D.J. Flick; and running back/returner Corey Holmes.

Austin and offensive co-ordinator Ken Miller also extracted a career season from quarterback Kerry Joseph, whom Shivers had selected first overall in the Ottawa Renegades dispersal draft of April 12, 2006. Shivers traded up to obtain the No. 1 pick from the Hamilton Tiger-Cats. As part of that deal, Saskatchewan also received the rights to Darian Durant, who had been on the Tiger-Cats' negotiation list.

In one transaction, Shivers added two quarterbacks who eventually led Saskatchewan to a combined four Grey Cup appearances (Joseph in 2007; Durant in 2009, 2010, and 2013). Joseph was also named the league's most outstanding player in 2007. One of his understudies at the time, Durant, went on to become a franchise icon and, in 2013, a Cup-winning quarterback in his own right.

"I don't think Roy gets as much credit as he deserves," Durant said. "He has a great eye for talent. A lot of people get caught up in him and his personality, but it's about results with him. You look at the success he had with [Hall of Fame coach] Wally Buono in every stop they've had together.

"Roy brought some great talent to Saskatchewan. You've got to thank him for that."

54 "Good Morning, Riders!"

A latecomer to the pro football head-coaching fraternity was known for his early-in-the-day repartee with his players.

"Good morning, Riders!" Ken Miller typically exclaimed in the team's dressing room, signalling the commencement of pre-practice meetings.

That became a signature phrase for the genial, avuncular Miller, who was 66 when he was promoted to the role of head coach by general manager Eric Tillman in 2008.

"Who would have thought that Ken Miller, when he was hired here, would one day be one of our most beloved and successful coaches?" former Roughriders president-CEO Jim Hopson said. "Players would walk on glass for him."

Miller's predecessor, Kent Austin, walked on water. In one storybook season as the head coach, Austin guided the Roughriders to a Grey Cup championship, in 2007, before leaving to become the offensive co-ordinator at his alma mater, the University of Mississippi.

As a parting recommendation, Austin touted the talents of Miller, who was the oft-unheralded co-ordinator of a potent Saskatchewan offence in 2007.

"I didn't try to copy everything that Kent did, but certainly he was a tremendous role model," Miller reflected. "And when we went there in 2007, there was a concerted effort by Kent and Eric, and I feel like I contributed to it to some degree, of really changing the philosophy. I think the previous regime was a player-centred organization, but maybe it didn't have the accountability that we put in place.

"I really wanted players to contribute and be part of the process, but I wanted there to be accountability, too. The accountability that I tried to foster was different than the accountability that came before. The accountability I wanted was self-accountability. I wanted the players to be self-policing—for themselves, first of all, and then for each other. It was not so much of a coach-imposed or an organizationally imposed kind of discipline, but a self-discipline."

The formula worked wonderfully for Miller, who guided an injury-riddled Saskatchewan team to a 12–6 record (including a 6–0 start) in 2008. Saskatchewan reached the Grey Cup game in each of the following two seasons, losing a heartbreaker to the Montreal Alouettes both times.

In 2009, Miller became the first—and only, as of this writing—head coach since John Payne in 1976 to lead Saskatchewan to first place in the West.

Despite the ensuing "13th-man" meltdown (see Chapter 13) in the 2009 Grey Cup—a situation that would have led to the vilification and termination of many head coaches—Roughriders fans largely sympathized with and ached for Miller and the players. The "13th man" became a rallying cry, as much as anything, and Miller emerged with his popularity intact.

It was an impressive accomplishment from a self-described "journeyman assistant," who had coached football and baseball at the high school and college levels.

At the University of Redlands in California, Miller adopted a different persona while serving as the offensive line coach. He liked to joke afterward that one of his players labelled the erstwhile taskmaster "the meanest man in America."

That cranky coach was never seen in Saskatchewan, a province that Miller and his wife, Maureen, embraced during their residency in Regina from 2007 to 2011.

Miller, as much as anyone who has been the Roughriders' head coach, loved a good laugh. He was known to quietly plant a question with a member of the media in order to set up a one-liner during a group interview.

Or, if there was a message he wanted to convey, a subtle "a smart reporter might want to ask me about…" would suffice.

In the often-secretive world of professional football, Miller was an open book during his tenure with the Roughriders—a chapter that ended after five years.

"Maureen's and my time in Saskatchewan was really the high point of our lives up to that point, and certainly has provided a lot of memories that we're able to reflect on," Miller said from Asheville, North Carolina. "Our association with the people from there and the fact that she goes back and does the dragon-boat races, and the relationship with the players and the people while being part of that community is just a phenomenal experience for the two of us."

He then paused—of course, to set up another punch line.

"And," he concluded, "there was the fact that we were able to survive the media there."

55 Meet Maureen Miller

Every Roughriders fan should—and probably can—meet Maureen Miller.

The affable wife of former head coach Ken Miller doesn't live anywhere near Regina or Saskatchewan, but that is a technicality.

"Look at Facebook and my address is still Saskatchewan," Maureen said with a chuckle from her home in Asheville, North Carolina. "I belonged there. I was very sad when I left. I didn't want to go. I was very upset. The toughest part of being in Saskatchewan was being away from my family, but it was home."

Because of that, the Millers return "home" at every opportunity, such as when Ken is invited back to Saskatchewan—where many Americans stay after their playing careers—for speaking engagements.

Northward treks are also made to visit friends, or so that Maureen can take part in the annual dragon-boat festival on Regina's Wascana Lake.

At all times, Maureen embraced Saskatchewan but, as she noted, "I was embraced, too. I got so much more back."

So she keeps coming back. A dragon-boat-related trip can last as long as a fortnight. One of her bike rides through Regina, or a walk around the parks, also provides friends and Roughriders fans with an opportunity to renew acquaintances.

"When I first got there, I had no idea what to expect," Maureen recalled. "I got there in February of 2007. There was lots of snow. But the first week that I was there, I had friends."

The couple moved to Regina when head coach Kent Austin hired Ken Miller as the offensive co-ordinator—an arrangement that paid off with a championship in 2007.

Early the following year, Austin left to become the offensive co-ordinator at the University of Mississippi, and Ken was promoted to head coach. He held that position from 2008 to 2010, and for the second half of the 2011 season. In the latter year, he was also the vice-president of football operations.

Rare was the practice that was not attended by both Millers. Maureen typically sat in the stands at Mosaic Stadium and chatted with fans, friends, and members of the media. The conversations generally pertained to life more than football. And if anyone wanted to discuss her beloved New York Yankees, that topic was certainly fair ball.

But her presence in Regina was about more than just football. She volunteered everywhere, or so it seemed, helping assorted good causes and cherishing time spent as the librarian at the Royal Saskatchewan Museum.

"I grew when I was in Saskatchewan," Maureen said. "I think we both did. I think we both left there as better people."

And you won't find better people than either of them.

56 The Marshall Plan

Jim Marshall, who is remembered for his wrong-way run as a member of the 1964 Minnesota Vikings, also went in another direction that people might not have expected.

Before becoming a standout defensive lineman in the NFL, Marshall spent the 1959 season with the Roughriders. He left Ohio State University prior to his senior year and journeyed north to Canada, playing in nine games with a Saskatchewan team that posted a 1–15 record—the worst in franchise history.

Upon becoming eligible for the NFL draft in 1960, Marshall was chosen in the fourth round (44th overall) by the Cleveland Browns. Cleveland then acquired his playing rights from Saskatchewan in a rare NFL-CFL deal, with the Roughriders receiving quarterback/linebacker/defensive back Bob Ptacek (a future Plaza of Honour inductee).

After one season in Cleveland, Marshall was part of a multi-player trade with Minnesota. So began a 19-year association with the Vikings, in whose employ he set a since-eclipsed NFL record by playing in 282 consecutive games—many of them as a member of the famed "Purple People Eaters," as Minnesota's defensive line was dubbed in its heyday.

The Vikings eventually celebrated his career with induction into their Ring of Honor, in addition to retiring his No. 70.

Quite emphatically, he overcame the ignominy of the Wrong Way Run—one of football's all-time gaffes.

Against the San Francisco 49ers on October 25, 1964, Marshall scooped up a fumble (good idea) and ran 66 yards (great exercise and athleticism!) into his own end zone (inadvisable).

Thinking he had scored a touchdown, he discarded the football, which landed out of bounds. The 49ers received a gift-wrapped safety touch.

On a brighter note, Marshall does hold the NFL record for defensive fumbles recovered (29).

He leads our list of NFL players who have had an association with Saskatchewan. Also consider the following:

Michael Bishop: After starring at Kansas State, Bishop was a member of the New England Patriots in 1999 and 2000. During the latter season, he was an understudy to starting quarterback Drew Bledsoe—as was a rookie named Tom Brady.

Gino Cappelletti: Cut in training camp by the Roughriders in 1958, he went on to star for the old Boston Patriots from 1960 to 1970. He was one of only three people to play in every American Football League game—the others being George Blanda and Jim Otto. Cappelletti, a wide receiver and placekicker, was the AFL's all-time leading scorer (1,130 points, courtesy of 42 touchdowns, 176 field goals, and 342 extra points). He was named the 1964 AFL MVP after scoring 155 points in 14 games.

Thomas Dimitroff: Now the Atlanta Falcons' general manager, Dimitroff was the Roughriders' Canadian scouting co-ordinator in 1990 and 1991.

Frank Filchock: With the 1939 Washington Redskins, Filchock threw the first 99-yard touchdown pass in NFL history. He spent seven seasons in the NFL before being suspended indefinitely by commissioner Bert Bell. Filchock and New York Giants teammate Merle Hapes were punished for failing to report bribes offered by, but not accepted from, a gambler who had hoped to fix the 1946 NFL championship game. Filchock played for seven more seasons, almost entirely in Canada, even though the NFL lifted his suspension in 1950. He joined the Roughriders as a quarterback/coach in 1953, the first of his five seasons as the team's field boss. He later became the first head coach of the AFL's Denver Broncos—whose

From Saskatchewan to Montana

Two of Bob Bruer's first three touchdown catches as a pro football player were the result of an aerial collaboration with an established or future legend.

Bruer hauled in a scoring pass from Ron Lancaster with the 1978 Roughriders. The following season, the first-year NFL tight end caught the first of Joe Montana's 273 touchdown tosses.

On November 18, 1979, Bruer snared a 16-yarder from Montana, then a rookie with the San Francisco 49ers, for the only fourth-quarter score in a 38–28 loss to the visiting Denver Broncos.

"With perfect pass protection, [Montana] looked left first, then peeked right and fired a dart over the middle into the end zone," Chris Willis of *Pro Football Journal* wrote. "The pass looked to be too high. But not for the 6-foot–5 Bruer, who put his right hand up as high as he could to grab the ball with one hand. He then brought the ball into his body in the end zone for a touchdown."

The following summer, Joey Walters—who caught Lancaster's 333rd and final touchdown pass—tried out for the 49ers but was among the final cuts.

Walters and Dwight Clark had been teammates in 1976 with the University of Clemson Tigers. Clark, who debuted with the 49ers in 1979, became a favoured target of Montana and was the recipient of one of the most famous passes in NFL history.

"The Catch" was made by Clark for a six-yard touchdown on January 10, 1982, in the NFC championship game against the Dallas Cowboys.

On third-and-three with 58 seconds left in the game, Montana rolled to his right and, just before being forced out of bounds, threw a high pass to Clark in the back of the end zone. Clark made a leaping grab, after which Ray Wersching kicked what proved to be the game-winning convert to put San Francisco ahead 28–27.

Two weeks later, Montana celebrated the first of his four Super Bowl victories as the 49ers' starting quarterback.

Bruer played in 17 games with San Francisco (16 in 1979 and one in 1980) before spending the better part of four seasons with the Minnesota Vikings. In 68 career NFL regular season games, he caught 72 passes for 709 yards and eight touchdowns.

first starting quarterback was ex-Roughrider Frank Tripucka. Moreover, the Broncos' founding general manager was Dean Griffing, who played for and coached the Roughriders between 1936 and 1943.

Lee Grosscup: Well-known as a football broadcaster, Grosscup was drafted 10th overall by the Giants in 1959. He was part of the Roughriders' 1963 quarterback carousel, one that also included Tripucka and Ron Lancaster.

Joe McKnight: After starring for the USC Trojans and excelling as a kickoff returner with the New York Jets, McKnight bounced around the pro ranks. He enjoyed an auspicious CFL regular season debut with Saskatchewan, rushing for 150 yards on 17 carries on October 15, 2016, against the host Toronto Argonauts. Tragically, he was shot and killed in a road-range incident six weeks later in Terrytown, Louisiana.

Steve Owen: A legendary Giants head coach and a Pro Football Hall of Famer, "Stout Steve" was the Roughriders' head coach in 1961 and 1962, winning the CFL's coach-of-the-year award in the latter year.

Sherman Lewis: Long before becoming a successful assistant coach in the NFL, Lewis played one game with Saskatchewan in 1965. He had a 14-yard carry and a two-yard reception.

Terrell Owens: One day after being inducted into the Pro Football Hall of Fame in 2018, Owens—at age 44—worked out informally for Roughriders head coach Chris Jones. Nothing came of the look-see, although it did make major news.

Trent Richardson: After starring at the University of Alabama, Richardson was a first-round draft choice of the Browns but never panned out in the NFL. He played in four games with the 2017 Roughriders, rushing for 259 yards and two touchdowns.

Jon Ryan: See Chapter 90.

Steve Sarkisian: The former BYU star spent all three of his seasons as a pro football quarterback with Saskatchewan. He was an NCAA head coach at USC and Washington before becoming the Falcons' offensive co-ordinator in 2017 and holding that job for two years.

Phil Simms: While playing at obscure Moorhead State, Simms caught the eye of the Roughriders' brass and was, in fact, very interested in signing with Saskatchewan after his graduating season. There was only one snag: the Giants surprisingly drafted him seventh overall in 1979. He quarterbacked New York to a Super Bowl title in 1987.

Mac Speedie: A six-time all-pro receiver with Cleveland, Speedie completed his playing career in the CFL with Saskatchewan (1953 and 1954) and the B.C. Lions (1955). He was an All-Star in both of his seasons with Saskatchewan.

Mike Vanderjagt: One of the most accurate placekickers in NFL history, Vanderjagt never actually attempted a field goal during his two-game stint with the 1993 Roughriders (the presence of future Hall of Famer Dave Ridgway being an impediment). Vanderjagt, chosen by the Roughriders in the 1993 CFL draft, punted 17 times for an average of 39.5 yards.

Steve Walsh: An NFL signal-caller from 1989 to 1999, Walsh was hired as the Roughriders' quarterbacks coach in 2018.

57 Line of Succession

Prosperity certainly begins at home when the CFL's beefiest contributors are assessed.

Since the CFL first awarded a trophy to the league's top offensive lineman in 1974, a Roughrider has been honoured six times. The winner has been Saskatchewan-born on five of those occasions.

Roger Aldag, from Gull Lake, received the DeMarco-Becket Memorial Trophy in 1986 and 1988. Gene Makowsky (Saskatoon) was also a two-time winner (2004 and 2005), in addition to being the runner-up in 2008. (The Montreal Alouettes' Scott Flory, from Regina, got the nod over Makowsky in 2008 and repeated as the winner in 2009. Aldag, Makowsky, and Flory are in the Canadian Football Hall of Fame.)

Weyburn-born Brendon LaBatte emulated all of the above by being called to the podium in 2013.

"All those guys are legends," LaBatte said. "If you're an offensive lineman coming up through the ranks in this province, those are household names and that's the upper echelon that you strive to one day attain. That's a lot of really good football players. Their impact went long past their days playing."

LaBatte was succeeded by another lineman from Weyburn—then–Calgary Stampeders centre and fellow University of Regina Rams alumnus Brett Jones—when the coveted trophy was handed out in 2014.

Through 1973, the league presented an all-encompassing lineman-of-the-year award, covering offence and defence. Roughriders centre Ted Urness, a Regina-born Hall of Famer, was the runner-up in 1968.

Over the years, the Roughriders' roster has also included Saskatchewan-born offensive linemen such as Bob Poley, Mike Anderson, Ben Heenan, Dan Clark, Gary Brandt, Bryan Illerbrun, and Patrick Neufeld.

"It's really a testament to the calibre of football players we have in this province," LaBatte said. "I also think it comes with the work ethic that almost comes with being raised here. You've got to be humble, check your ego, and just take the coaching.

"I think that's one of the strengths that allows the offensive linemen from the prairies to excel. They take the coaching and they're just going to do what they're told and try to get it done the way the boss wants it. That probably has a lot to do with the upbringing around here."

As part of LaBatte's upbringing, he paid close attention to the Roughriders and, naturally, the "Hoggies" up front. With all due admiration for all the fine linemen who have played for the Green and White over the years, one name stands out for LaBatte.

"To this day, I've never seen an offensive lineman do it the way Gene Makowsky did," LaBatte said. "I think he's the best to ever do it. I think he revolutionized the game. He brought in technique before technique was really popular."

Makowsky refined his craft over a 17-year playing career that concluded in 2011, by which time he had performed effectively at centre, guard, and tackle.

"Growing up, and when I came into the league in 2008, Gene Makowsky was the guy who you wanted to watch every down and just try to emulate everything he did," said LaBatte, who debuted with the Winnipeg Blue Bombers before signing as a free agent with Saskatchewan in 2012.

"I think Gene was the guy who showed just how important technique was. He played in an era when everybody wanted to be bigger, stronger, faster, and the thought process was, 'The bigger you were, the harder you were going to hit.' I think he really showed that it's not about size. It's about technique. There used to be some big guys who used to just go out there and play on just size and aggression, but that won't get it done anymore."

Makowsky, by the way, typically played tackle alongside guard Andrew Greene—the league's most outstanding offensive lineman in 2003. Greene, who grew up in Ontario, was also the West Division finalist in 2000.

58 Rough Welcome

Al Benecick's debut with the Roughriders did not portend great things to come for himself or the team.

After attending NFL training camp with the Philadelphia Eagles in 1959, Benecick arrived in Saskatchewan just in time to make a road trip to Edmonton, where the Eskimos won 44–15, leaving the losing side with an 0–10 record.

"Afterward, we were at the airport," Benecick recalled. "It was embarrassing. The president back then [Sam Taylor] said, 'Ah, let's have a drink,' and he bought us drinks. I felt like a little kid. I was crying. I was so pissed off. I said, 'What the hell did I do?' And I had signed for a year. I said, 'Holy Christmas, what did I get into here?'"

Benecick ended up being part of an ignominious chapter in franchise history, having played for a team that set the Roughriders' all-time low-water mark of 1–15.

The Roughriders summoned Benecick after two-way lineman Jim Marshall, who went on to star for the Minnesota Vikings, strained his back. As much as Benecick welcomed the playing time, the rewards of his toil were few.

"It was awful," Benecick lamented. "Instead of drinking one beer after the game, you drank three or four. Sad to say…and they weren't victory beers, you know? It was, 'Dear Lord, please help us. Something's got to give.'"

Eventually, it did.

Benecick was a member of an offensive line that helped George Reed rush for a team-record 1,768 yards in 1965. It was a notable feat for Benecick, who had blocked for another legendary running back—Jim Brown—at the University of Syracuse.

"They had the same qualities, and the desire," Benecick said. "The biggest thing I would say between the both of them was they didn't get hurt. They were able to show up for every battle, every game. Even when they were hurt, they played. I saw that in George and Jim."

Reed rushed for 133 yards to help Saskatchewan defeat the Ottawa Rough Riders 29–14 in the 1966 Grey Cup game. Benecick made a key block to help Reed score a 31-yard touchdown that effectively salted away Saskatchewan's first championship.

The 1966 season was the third straight in which Benecick, a Roughrider from 1959 to 1968, was named a CFL All-Star. He was later enshrined in the Plaza of Honour (in 1991) and the Canadian Football Hall of Fame (1996).

"What made him good was that he loved the game and he loved hitting people," Reed recalled. "I think he got the biggest joy when he would pull out and go around and look for somebody to hit. I think he would be very disappointed when he couldn't find anybody to hit. He was a competitor and the one thing a running back like me always appreciated was that you knew he was going to hit somebody. It could be the wrong guy once in a while, but you knew that he was going to hit somebody.

"That's what I put the stock in. You knew that he was going to play and he was going to play hard. The tougher the game was, the more he enjoyed it."

Benecick, who spent a considerable portion of his post-football years in Regina, was 78 when he died in Tallahassee, Florida, in 2015.

59 The Decline of '59

Even when the Roughriders won, they lost.

Such was the plight of the Green and White on October 26, 1959, when Saskatchewan defeated the host Winnipeg Blue Bombers 37–30, but nonetheless forfeited due to the pre-arranged utilization of an ineligible player.

That was the final blow for the 1959 Roughriders, whose 1–15 record is the worst in franchise history.

Frank Tripucka, who had just taken over as the Roughriders' head coach, was forced to suit up as a quarterback due to an injury-related scarcity of signal-callers.

Tripucka, who had been a star quarterback for Saskatchewan for much of the 1950s, had been dealt to the Ottawa Rough Riders before the 1959 season. He was reacquired, but strictly as a head coach (or so it was thought), after the Roughriders fired George Terlep when their record fell to 0–9.

Under Tripucka, Saskatchewan registered its only official victory of the 1959 season—a 15–14 squeaker over the B.C. Lions on October 5. From there, though, the circumstances worsened.

Having released Bob Brodhead, the Roughriders elevated Don Allard to the role of starting quarterback. However, Allard suffered a shoulder separation in the Roughriders' 14th game, during which backup quarterback Ron Adam aggravated an ankle injury. Jack Urness, another quarterback, was on the shelf due to a nasty cut on his leg. Therefore, the Roughriders were forced to use a receiver, Jack Hill, at quarterback. Both his passes were intercepted in a 45–6 home-field loss to B.C.—a game in which Saskatchewan surrendered five fourth-quarter touchdowns. The implosion left Saskatchewan at 1–13 and without enough quarterbacks.

The Roughriders then sought permission from the league to use Tripucka, only to be informed that he was ineligible. Teams could not add American players to the roster beyond October 1, a date which came and went shortly before Tripucka arrived as the head coach.

The bright spot, as it turned out, was the lack of bright spots. The Roughriders were such a mess that their final two regular season games did not have any impact on the Western Interprovincial Football Union standings. Therefore, the decision was made to permit the Roughriders to use Tripucka.

"We agreed on allowing Tripucka to play," Edmonton Eskimos head coach Eagle Keys said in advance of an October 24 game in Regina. "This being what you might call a nothing game, we gave our consent because we want to see the Riders make a game of it. Any team would be seriously handicapped if it didn't have a top-notch quarterback to call upon."

The Roughriders were able to start Adam, with Tripucka backing up. Tripucka did enter the game in the second quarter, and it was he who threw an interception in the final minute to dash any hopes of Saskatchewan winning (yet losing by forfeit).

Edmonton proceeded to win 20–19 at Taylor Field. "Who should take the blame—the coach or the quarterback?" Tripucka asked the *Leader-Post* after Saskatchewan's penultimate game of a lost season.

Next up: a season-ending, misery-ending game in Winnipeg.

The result went in the books as "Saskatchewan 37, Winnipeg 30," but with an asterisk appended. Although the Roughriders' victory did not count, the game statistics had been declared official by league commissioner Sydney Halter.

As a result, the four touchdown runs and one scoring reception by Ferd Burket were part of the record—and a record, period.

Entering the 2019 season, Burket's five touchdowns remained a Roughriders single-game standard.

60 Genial Gene

Gene Makowsky finished what would be a Hall of Fame career with one Grey Cup ring—long after hearing a ring that he had impulsively dreaded.

"I remember the phone call, early in the morning at Luther College," Makowsky said while recounting the aftermath of his first preseason with the Roughriders. "It was, 'Call the GM.' I said, 'Okay, I'll get my playbook.' And I was told, 'No, you've made the team. Congratulations.' I was expecting a call, but a little different conversation."

Makowsky had been drafted with the 23rd overall pick in 1995 after playing for the University of Saskatchewan Huskies in his hometown of Saskatoon.

"I don't think that coming into camp I was a blue-chip prospect, that I was expected to make the team or anything like that," Makowsky recalled. "The day you're told that you're a Saskatchewan Roughrider for real is pretty special. I remember it pretty clearly. It's almost a surreal feeling. It was, 'I guess I've got to find a place to live. I'm becoming an adult.' You get a paycheque for doing something that you did just the year before for free. Of course, that's not the motivation in the CFL by any means. It's just a surreal feeling to have a dream and to realize it. The hard work all paid off."

Makowsky spent 17 seasons with Saskatchewan before retiring as the team's all-time games-played leader (284) in February of 2012. He overtook another venerable home-grown offensive lineman, 271-game man Roger Aldag, in 2011.

"I always took pride in being prepared and being available and just wanting to play the game," said Makowsky, who helped Saskatchewan win the 2007 Grey Cup. "I just wanted to be there

Gene Makowsky at Roughriders training camp in 2010. (Don Healy, *Regina Leader-Post*)

for my teammates and for the team and to be a reliable guy. Over time, that adds up."

The same can be said of the accolades. Makowsky was named the CFL's outstanding offensive lineman in 2004 and 2005, and was the runner-up for that award in 2008. He was a five-time CFL All-Star who made the West Division's dream team for seven successive seasons, beginning in 2004.

Those credentials made him an automatic selection for the Canadian Football Hall of Fame, into which he was enshrined in 2015.

"In those situations, you have to talk about yourself a little bit, but it's not about that," the soft-spoken Makowsky said. "It's about your teammates and your coaches and your family and everyone who helped you along the way. It's certainly not about me at all. I was a product of a lot of people.

"It's not the 'me' show, that's for sure. I was very lucky to play for a great franchise with a lot of great guys. I had a lot of fun and a lot of interesting experiences. I'm very grateful for that and for the fans who have supported the Riders like nothing else I've seen. I was very lucky to be a small part of it."

61 Welcome Back, Ed

The game, it seemed, was won during the player introductions.

A crowd of 16,980 erupted on August 27, 1971, when defensive lineman Ed McQuarters, No. 61, trotted on to Taylor Field shortly before a game against the Ottawa Rough Riders. He was back in the lineup just 72 days after having his left eye removed due to a carpentry accident.

McQuarters proceeded to help Saskatchewan win his comeback game 42–21 while being a handful, as usual, for rival offensive linemen.

"It was a humbling experience," he said. "After my first defensive play I knew that I could still play the game."

And play he did, through 1974, at a calibre that led to his enshrinement in the Canadian Football Hall of Fame in 1988.

McQuarters was an impactful player from the moment he arrived in Regina during the 1966 season, shortly after being released by the NFL's St. Louis Cardinals.

From the aircraft, he saw the Roughriders' home stadium and said, "*That's* Taylor Field?" The surroundings took some getting used to for someone who had starred for the University of Oklahoma Sooners before spending one season in the NFL.

"I landed and got my bag," McQuarters recalled. "I was looking around the airport and thinking, 'You know what? This is not as big as I thought,' but the people were so nice. Every time you mentioned the Roughriders, everybody would just go crazy. That made everything all okay. I kind of forgot about how small things were compared to what I was used to."

McQuarters quickly made a big difference during what would be the Roughriders' first championship season. He was the rare lineman who possessed the speed and athleticism of a running back. In fact, he once went head-to-head in a sprint with Saskatchewan's fleet halfback, Ed Buchanan, and held his own.

The open-field wheels were on display in Game 2 of the 1966 Western Conference final against the Winnipeg Blue Bombers. Saskatchewan was clinging to a 14–12 lead midway through the fourth quarter, at which point Blue Bombers quarterback Ken Ploen was smartly moving his team.

Everything changed, though, after Winnipeg advanced to Saskatchewan's 47-yard line. On first down, Ploen was met in the pocket by Ken Reed and Don Gerhardt, the latter of whom knocked the ball out of the quarterback's right hand. McQuarters then scooped up the ball near midfield at Winnipeg Stadium.

"When I saw Ed McQuarters with the ball, I thought, 'This is the fastest guy on the defence—as a lineman. It's in the right hands,'" Reed remembered.

McQuarters' fumble-return touchdown was followed by a Jack Abendschan convert that gave Saskatchewan a 21–12 lead with 3:59 left in the fourth quarter. The defensive touchdown became especially important after Winnipeg scored to reduce its deficit to 21–19, which held up for the duration.

The victory gave Saskatchewan a sweep of the best-of-three series and a berth in the Grey Cup game, won by the Roughriders.

According to several members of the 1966 team, McQuarters was the final piece in the puzzle.

"Ed McQuarters made our team, you know," trainer Sandy Archer said. "He was the guy who really put it all together."

McQuarters put together quite a resume as a Roughrider. He was named a CFL All-Star in each of the three seasons that followed the ground-breaking Grey Cup victory, in addition to being named the CFL's most outstanding lineman in 1967. He was only the second Roughrider to win a major CFL individual award, following George Reed—the league's most outstanding player in 1965.

"Ed McQuarters, I think, was probably the best thing that ever happened to our team, and especially to me because I played next to him," said Hall of Fame defensive tackle Ron Atchison, a Rider from 1952 to 1968. "Ed cleared the path and then I made the tackles lots of times.

"Ed McQuarters was probably the best player that our team ever had."

That is a subjective assessment, of course, but McQuarters' brilliance on the field was beyond dispute.

"You knew he was something special," Ron Lancaster said in 2006. "There's a lot of people who think there might not have been a better defensive lineman to ever play the game than him, and I'm not so sure I disagree with them."

62 The Miracle Major

The brave gentlemen who fielded punts in Gene Wlasiuk's day weren't liable to enjoy many happy returns.

A ridiculous rule at the time, prohibiting blocking on punt returns, rendered a long-distance, one-versus-12 jaunt virtually impossible. But one fine day—August 9, 1962—Wlasiuk defied the odds by returning a punt 67 yards for a Roughriders touchdown against the B.C. Lions.

"I can tell you exactly how it happened," Wlasiuk recounted. "Two guys converged on me. Everybody expected them to make the tackle. I managed to avoid them. A big hole opened. I went down the sidelines with everyone chasing me. The kicker was Bob Schloredt. He was chasing me. So was a fast receiver named Mack Burton. I went down the left sideline and literally stutter-stepped them. I hesitated and they kept running. I think Burton went by me three times. I'd slow down, they'd fly past me, and then I'd keep running.

"Nobody touched me. When I got to the end zone, I wasn't tired at all. It was a nice, slow jaunt."

It was also the unquestioned highlight of a slow day for the Roughriders, who lost 33–7.

"I was named star of the game," Wlasiuk noted. "That's how badly we played."

What motivated Wlasiuk to return punts with a mass of snorting humanity eager to squash him?

"Stupidity," he replied, chuckling. "The truth is, I never gave it any special consideration. It was harder to be a running back because you had to follow your blocks. I never had to worry about blockers. They never got in your way.

"I had a different approach to returning punts. My approach was this: catch the ball and look for a soft stomach. Everyone thought I was looking for a hole."

Wlasiuk was looking for a home after spending his first two CFL seasons with the Winnipeg Blue Bombers. He joined the Roughriders as a diminutive defensive back during the 1–15 season of 1959.

"I got traded for a helmet and a jockstrap," the fun-loving, cigar-chomping Wlasiuk quipped. "I'll be honest. I wasn't sure if it was waivers or a trade. It must have been a trade, because waivers in those days were $50. They couldn't afford that, so they traded for me."

Wisely so. Wlasiuk spent nine seasons with Saskatchewan, returning 549 punts during that time. He added 27 interceptions, including five in each of the 1962 and 1964 seasons, and was a member of the 1966 Grey Cup champions. In 1995, he was inducted into the Plaza of Honour.

"Geno was one of those true Roughriders," former *Leader-Post* sports editor Bob Hughes said in 2011, following Wlasiuk's death at age 75.

63 The Silver Fox

Al Ritchie was a true original. So, fittingly, he was among the original inductees into the Canadian Football Hall of Fame, back in 1963.

But he was equally accomplished and beloved in hockey circles, to the extent that a Regina arena—the Al Ritchie Memorial Centre—is named in his honour.

Ritchie was synonymous with sports in the Queen City, as evidenced by the fact that he is the only coach who has won Canadian junior championships in hockey and football.

His contributions to the Regina Roughriders are also legendary. He coached them to eight Western Canadian championships—winning 56 games in a row at one point—and in three consecutive Grey Cup games, beginning in 1930.

Ritchie had also been pressed into service as head coach for the 1928 Grey Cup when Howie Milne, normally the field boss, was unable to travel east.

Ritchie's involvement with the team began when it was known as the Regina Rugby Club. He joined the club's executive in 1919 and managed the RRC/Roughriders until the mid-1920s before coaching the club full-time from 1929 to 1932, with subsequent stints in 1933 (as an emergency replacement), 1935, and 1942.

"We have had many greats who were giants in sport, but Al Ritchie was their peer," Monsignor Athol Murray, founder of Notre Dame College in Wilcox, said after The Silver Fox died at age 75 in 1966, mere months before his beloved Roughriders won their first Grey Cup title.

Msgr. Murray also referred to Ritchie as the "Knute Rockne of Canada."

Born in Cobden, Ontario, in 1890, Ritchie moved to Regina with his family before the First World War—during which he was based in France while serving as an artilleryman.

Upon returning to Regina, he immersed himself in sports of all sorts—baseball and lacrosse also being among his pastimes—and helped his teams enjoy a string of successes.

The Regina Pats junior hockey team won Memorial Cups in 1925 and 1930 with Ritchie behind the bench. He also coached the Pats junior football team to a national championship—the first by a Western Canadian squad—in 1928.

During the same period, Ritchie was working tirelessly for the betterment of the senior Roughriders.

"He gave Regina its Roughriders," Hal Pawson of the *Edmonton Journal* wrote after Ritchie's death. "So he didn't invent, or even start them. But they flowered in his care."

Ritchie, who also scouted for the NHL's New York Rangers, was inducted into the Canadian Sports Hall of Fame in 1964. He entered the Saskatchewan Sports Hall of Fame in 1966 and the Plaza of Honour (as an original member, of course) in 1987.

"He had a heart of gold and I don't know a shadow of reproach that can be thrown at him," said Msgr. Murray, Ritchie's closest friend and himself a Canadian sporting legend. "He was one of the most genuine human beings I have ever known. In addition to being a great sportsman, Al Ritchie was a great Canadian."

64 Tale of the Tape

Ivan Gutfriend, Norm Fong, and Sandy Archer combined for nearly 100 years of service to the Roughriders—exemplary careers that were all recognized with inductions into the Plaza of Honour.

Not one of them played a down, or spent even a millisecond coaching the team, but their contributions were as valuable as they were memorable.

In a span of 65 seasons, beginning in 1951, Archer and Gutfriend were the Roughriders' only athletic therapists. Archer—the Wizard of Gauze—held the position through the 1980 season before Gutfriend took over on a full-time basis. They had worked together in 1978, 1979, and 1980.

Fong succeeded Dale Laird in 1979 and continued as the equipment manager through 2008, after which Gordon Gilroy took over. Laird had debuted in the championship season of 1966.

For a span of 50 seasons, only five people—Archer, Gutfriend, Laird, Fong, and Gilroy—worked with the Roughriders in the capacities of athletic therapist or equipment manager.

"It really is amazing when you think about it," Fong marvelled.

Hall of Fame offensive lineman Gene Makowsky was associated with Fong and Gutfriend for the first 14 seasons of a 17-year career.

"In a change business, they were two of the constants," Makowsky noted. "They were always there. They were cornerstones of the franchise."

In the cases of Fong and Gutfriend, the customary three-year waiting period was waived so they could be inducted into the Plaza the year after leaving the organization. Archer was a member of the Plaza's second group of inductees.

"Sandy was a guy who enjoyed life," Gutfriend said. "He had a good time dealing with the players, and that's what I learned from him.

"The thing I enjoyed the most was dealing with the players. You have to have fun with the players, and I did. You have to be able to relate to them. It's as simple as that."

Simple, but effective.

"I don't think the general public realizes how important that job is," Makowsky said. "In Ivan's case, you're dealing with people likely in their worst time, when they have an injury and they can't play anymore and they can't perform like they want.

"Ivan was such a good guy. He cared about the guys. He would ask how the family was doing, et cetera. He was just a lot of fun. He was like a 50-year-old kid in there. He liked to have fun with you and joke around. I just love the guy. He's just awesome."

Gutfriend's association with the Roughriders dates back to 1970, when he started helping Archer at training camp. Like Gutfriend, Fong debuted with the Roughriders long before becoming a full-timer, assisting the team as far back as 1975.

"Fongo was a lot of fun, like Ivan," Makowsky said. "He was the gatekeeper of all Rider merchandise. He was always there and he was always joking around with the guys. He was a pillar of the franchise—a guy you could rely on."

As was Archer, who entered the Saskatchewan Sports Hall of Fame (in 1984) and the Plaza of Honour (1988). He died in 2007 at age 86.

65 The Undertaker

According to Roughriders lore, defensive lineman Bill Baker—a.k.a. The Undertaker—knocked three Edmonton Eskimos quarterbacks out of the same game.

It makes for a good tale, but it isn't quite true.

Baker did sideline three Eskimos passers in 1972, but over the course of two games.

Baker levelled Bruce Lemmerman in a mid-August CFL contest and sidelined him with a broken collarbone. For good measure, Baker knocked Eskimos tailback Gene Foster (who suffered a knee injury) out of the game.

A month later at Taylor Field, Baker twice flattened Tom Wilkinson, who emerged with a concussion, before leaving Eskimos backup pivot Dave Syme in a bloodied state and with broken cartilage in his nose.

"That's the third quarterback of ours he's put out of a game," an outraged Norm Kimball, the Eskimos' general manager, complained to reporters. "We try to run a professional football league and we've got an animal running around and trying to take it away from us. You keep letting that b------t go on and you're going to have a riot. He's got to be controlled. Who's got to control him? The officials! We've got hundreds of thousands of dollars invested and we let a cheap-shot s--- like him take it away. If they're going to let that happen, it's going to be open season."

The Roughriders, for their part, countered that their own quarterback was the victim of foul play. The *Leader-Post*'s Bob Hughes wrote that Ron Lancaster "came out of the game with a black eye, an aching body, and little chunks of skin missing from around his eye. Somebody was scratching him on the last play of the game."

Bye-Bye, Bill Baker

Bill Baker wrapped up his pro football career by wrapping up another future Hall of Famer—Warren Moon.

Moon, then a CFL rookie, was quarterbacking the Edmonton Eskimos during an October 29, 1978, game when he was sacked by Baker for a safety touch late in the fourth quarter at Commonwealth Stadium.

That game, won 36–26 by Saskatchewan, is well-remembered for a Ron Lancaster–led comeback that allowed the Little General to conclude his playing career in style. Although Lancaster generated back-to-back touchdowns after entering the game in the fourth quarter, the final points were produced by Baker's safety.

"I had a pair of old natural-turf spikes," Baker recalled. "After the game, I threw them in the garbage can. [Roughriders defensive back] Kenny McEachern pulled them out and brought them back to me and said, 'Bill, you're still going to play, aren't you?' I said, 'Kenny, it's over. I'm through. I'm retiring.' I was 33.

"It was the only time I ever played a regular season game with a fierce hangover. I was standing on the sidelines, not feeling good at all, quite frankly. For the first part of the game, every time I stopped sweating a little bit, I'd feel sort of queasy—and I had a hell of a game.

"After, I said, 'I played 11 years and never had a hangover, and here I am in the last game of my life and I think I had three quarterback sacks.' I should have played with a hangover my whole career. I may have found something too late.

"We all knew it was the last game, so there were some people in town and we had a big goodbye party with a bunch of friends. We reminisced and sat around. You know it's the last night. The next day, the party is over. So you go out that night and you don't really feel like sleeping—at least I didn't. You'd drink too much with a bunch of people and celebrate the fact that it's going to end.

"The career was over. I knew I was going to retire. I was way too busy working [at the IPSCO steel company]. It was an end-of-the-career party. It was over."

But not for Moon, who four weeks later was part of an Eskimos team that won its first of an unprecedented five consecutive Grey Cup championships.

Moon played for Edmonton through the 1983 season, after which he began a 17-year NFL career.

In 2001, Moon joined Baker in the Canadian Football Hall of Fame, and five years later entered the Pro Football Hall of Fame.

Following the turbulent tilt, Baker maintained his innocence when asked about the collisions with Syme.

"I didn't mean to hurt the kid," Baker told the *Leader-Post*. "I didn't deliberately try to hurt him, or anybody. I've passed up a lot of shots at guys' knees on interceptions and things like that. The thing is, you're coming so hard...you hit him...the idea is to hit the quarterback. I've been clotheslining quarterbacks all my career. This year, everybody is making a big deal out of it. All of a sudden, I'm Godzilla turned loose."

If so, his tactics escaped the attention of the officials. Baker was not penalized during the game, although the CFL levied an after-the-fact $100 fine for excessive roughness. The CFL soon banned the clothesline.

"It was probably my major achievement in football," Baker said. "All the quarterbacks from that time forward should be thankful to me for getting the clothesline outlawed."

Baker's achievements were many, as shown by his induction into the Canadian Football Hall of Fame in 1994. A four-time CFL All-Star, he was named the league's top defensive player in 1976. Attending the awards ceremony that year was among his final acts as a member of the Lions, who traded him back to Saskatchewan—where he had played from 1968 to 1973—before the 1977 season. His final two seasons as a player were spent with the Roughriders.

Baker would again assume a prominent position with the team late in 1986, when he was hired as the general manager. One of his first initiatives was to rescue the team from near-bankruptcy. Having done that, he celebrated the resurgence of 1988, when the Green and White snapped an 11-year playoff drought.

The stage was set for the 1989 season, which culminated with the second Grey Cup championship in franchise history. Baker shared in the merriment even though he was no longer formally affiliated with the Roughriders. To punctuate his first and only year as the CFL's president and chief operating officer, it fell within his purview to present the Grey Cup to the West Division representative—and he did so on-stage at Toronto's SkyDome, while visibly and audibly elated.

"I was very, very proud of that team," said Baker, who was succeeded as the Roughriders' GM by Alan Ford. "Al and all of the guys had a hell of a team even though they only won nine games during the regular season.

"What was so great was the players we had brought in had made a contribution—guys like Kent Austin and Dave Ridgway. They were a bunch of high-quality people and you're very proud for the people like the volunteers whose efforts are so often ignored.

"When you look at the day and the amount of people we had in Toronto that day, it was a celebration of what Saskatchewan had become to the CFL."

Mr. Versatility

Alan Ford sat back as the checklist was read to him.

"Tight end, wide receiver, running back, punter, linebacker, defensive back, kickoff returner," an interviewer said to the Roughriders' Mr. Versatility. "Have I missed anything?"

"Oh," Ford added, "I returned a couple of punts."

"So," he was told, "the only positions you didn't play were quarterback, offensive line, and defensive line?"

"That's pretty much it," Ford replied.

The discussion then turned to his off-the-field capacities with the Green and White—assistant coach, administrative assistant, assistant general manager, general manager...

Oh. One more. Radio announcer. He was part of the Roughriders' radio crew in addition to describing some junior football games.

"I remember doing a broadcast from Saskatoon," Ford said with a laugh, referencing a Prairie Football Conference game between the Regina Rams and the arch-rival Saskatoon Hilltops. "I forget who the announcer was, but I'm pretty sure it was CKCK Radio. The press box was right behind the fans and some of them were really obnoxious, and they would turn and yell stuff at the play-by-play guy.

"About halfway through the third quarter, he went, 'Al, take the mic.' The play's on. He goes out, comes around, hammers the guy, comes back and says, 'Thank you,' and returns to the broadcast. For about five minutes, I was the play-by-play guy *and* the colour guy."

Even in the broadcast booth, he was versatile.

Ford demonstrated his skills in myriad capacities while playing for the Roughriders from 1965 to 1976. A graduate of Regina's Central Collegiate, he became a CFLer after being a running back, defensive back, and punter at the University of the Pacific in San Francisco, California.

"I started off in football learning both sides, so I just kept doing it that way," said Ford, a 1992 Plaza of Honour inductee.

"It wasn't hard for me. I think I could have played quarterback. I couldn't throw, but I could call the formation and the play correctly and know which way to hand it off and know which player I'm supposed to throw to, because no matter what position I was playing, I wanted to learn the whole offence and the whole defence. I didn't even think anything of it. I didn't think it was that hard at all."

Ford's multi-tasking was even evident outside the football environment. He also played hockey, basketball, baseball, and fastball.

During the Roughriders' off-season, he used to play senior hockey with the Regina Caps.

"I love sports and, of all the sports, I love football the most," he said. "So what better job than to be involved with the local professional football team that everybody loves? I never thought when I was playing that I would ever want to be a general manager, let alone have a chance to be, but things worked out. It was a fun time to be around."

That was especially true in 1966 and 1989—the Roughriders' first two championship seasons. Ford caught a touchdown pass in the 1966 Grey Cup and 23 years later, to the very day, celebrated a second CFL title—in the capacity of GM.

True to form, Ford scored two different ways as the Riders beat the Ottawa Rough Riders in the 1966 final. He registered Saskatchewan's second touchdown and concluded the scoring with a fourth-quarter punt single.

The touchdown, from 19 yards away, was scored when a Ron Lancaster pass was deflected by Ottawa defensive back Bob O'Billovich—right into the hands of Ford. With great concentration, and an element of luck due to the near-interception, Ford made the catch while falling down in the end zone.

"It got deflected, so you make the catch," Ford said matter-of-factly. "You're in the middle of a game. You don't really realize [what it means] until very close to the end.

"I remember George Reed running for a touchdown that put us in a situation where they weren't going to come back. Then, all of a sudden, you feel this, 'Wow! We're going to win!' But throughout the whole game, you're not thinking that, so it was another play in the game. There were lots of really good ones. I just seemed to be in the right place at the right time."

Or in many places, if need be.

67 Visit the Fan Cairn

Roughriders fans can check out their name while attending a game.

The CFL team's three fan walls were unveiled, along with a statue honouring the legion of ardent supporters, outside Mosaic Stadium on June 29, 2017—only two days before the Roughriders' first regular season game in the new facility.

Each wall is 20 feet long, with a different theme. The cairns pay tribute to the community, recognize the area's indigenous heritage, and look ahead to future achievements. As part of the "Build the Pride" campaign, the names of approximately 2,000 fans were engraved on the walls, having paid a minimum of $300 each for the privilege. Proceeds helped the Roughriders pay off their share of funding for the $278 million stadium.

"I see people all the time there [at the fan walls], just looking for their name and taking pictures," president-CEO Craig Reynolds said.

Also conspicuous outside the stadium, on the northeast side, is an 18-foot-tall white bronze statue that pays tribute to the fans and the community.

The Fine Art Studio of Rotblatt-Amrany created and designed the statue, having previously sculpted sporting icons such as Michael Jordan, Vince Lombardi, Gordie Howe, and Magic Johnson. The artist, Omri Amrany, spent time in Regina while conceptualizing the statue.

"Even with the design, where it's basically the fan lifting the team up to catch the ball, there's a symbolism that's kind of cool that the artist brought to us," Reynolds said.

"That artist is from Chicago and, really, it was just a series of two or three meetings where he talked to us about the team and what the fans meant. He came back with that concept.

"It really spoke to the fact that this guy who is not from here really got the essence of what this place is all about and how much the fans mean to the team, and he came up with the concept of the fan lifting up the player and, without the fans, the player doesn't catch the pass.

"I found that to be really neat symbolism, and it was clear to an outsider what this team is all about. He really got it, and I think it resonates with our fans."

68 King of Queen's

Rob Bagg was undrafted and undaunted.

Despite being bypassed in the 2007 CFL draft, he developed into a mainstay with the Roughriders—a popular and productive player for a decade. As such, he is a natural to be profiled in these pages.

"How many chapters are you doing on him?" Weston Dressler, Bagg's close friend and a former Roughriders receiving cohort, asked with a chuckle.

In fact, Bagg's football journey—with its many paths—is likely a book on its own.

This is someone who cracked the Roughriders roster in 2007 as an undrafted player, only to decide to rejoin the Queen's University Golden Gaels for a fifth season of Canadian college football.

Bagg returned to Saskatchewan in 2008 and again made the team. In 2009, by then a starter, he helped the Roughriders finish first in the West for the first time since 1976.

Underdogs Have Their Day

Brett Lauther spent several years kicking around the CFL without doing much kicking at all.

Then came the 2018 season, when a virtual unknown was virtually unerring.

Lauther's first regular season field-goal attempt as a Roughrider was the rare exception. He was wide from 32 yards away, leading to some shaking of heads, but soon came to be regarded as automatic.

As it turned out, Lauther was named the West Division's All-Star placekicker after hitting 54-of-60 field-goal attempts—a 90 per cent success rate. He flirted with the team's single-season accuracy rate of 90.6 per cent, set by Hall of Famer Dave Ridgway in 1993, and was thus in esteemed company.

A la Ridgway, Lauther got his chance with the Roughriders after the team's incumbent kicker suffered a serious injury. Ridgway took over in 1982 as the replacement for Paul Watson, who tore an Achilles' tendon while playing volleyball in the off-season. Lauther filled a void that was created when Tyler Crapigna, who had made an impressive 86.4 per cent of his field-goal attempts in two-plus seasons as a Roughrider, sustained a hip injury that necessitated surgery.

Lauther to the rescue!

And to think that, prior to 2018, he had not attempted a regular-season field goal since 2013—when he was 6-for-10 in a four-game stint with Hamilton. The Tiger-Cats had chosen Lauther, a product of the Saint Mary's Huskies university program, in the seventh round (53rd overall) of the 2013 CFL draft.

Lauther spent the 2014 season on the Tiger-Cats' practice roster before having look-sees with Saskatchewan (in 2015 and 2017), the Toronto Argonauts (2015), and the Edmonton Eskimos (2017).

Ultimately, he was third-time lucky with the Roughriders, who were equally fortunate to have him.

Lauther became the latest Roughrider to overcome the odds, some other examples being:

Danny Banda: The 5-foot-9, 165-pound Reginan played for the Roughriders from 1958 to 1962 as a defensive back, punt returner, and—get this—linebacker. At 165 pounds!

Jeff Bentrim: In 1987, Bentrim joined the Roughriders as a highly touted quarterback out of North Dakota State University. He started at quarterback in the season opener, but spent most of his four years with Saskatchewan as a backup. Even so, he contributed integrally in 1989 when the Roughriders ran into injury trouble. A superb athlete, he saw duty as a receiver and a kickoff returner—unaccustomed roles for a quarterback—for a Saskatchewan side that won the 77th Grey Cup. His quarterbacking prowess at NDSU was acknowledged in 1998 with induction into the College Football Hall of Fame.

Weston Dressler: There was little fanfare in 2008, when the 5-foot-7 slotback joined the Roughriders. He went on to become the league's rookie of the year, and a six-time 1,000-yard receiver in the CFL.

Richie Hall: The 5-foot-6 defensive back/punt returner was an established CFLer by the time he arrived in Saskatchewan in 1988, via a trade with the Calgary Stampeders, but how many players of that dimension are able to enjoy long and productive careers? Hall is the only person to have been part of three Roughriders championship teams as a player or coach. He played for the 1989 champions and earned Grey Cup rings as the defensive coordinator in 2007 and 2013.

Ron Lancaster: A 5-foot-9¾ quarterback? That's an underdog!

Jeff Treftlin: Exhibiting shades of Danny Banda, this 5-foot-8, 170-pound defensive back and punt returner played for Saskatchewan from 1988 to 1991 Treftlin moonlighted at linebacker early in the 1989 season after the Roughriders were decimated by injuries at that position.

The 2009 Roughriders advanced to the Grey Cup, only to lose a 28–27 heartbreaker to the Montreal Alouettes. On the Roughriders' final offensive play, Bagg suffered a broken collarbone.

He was enjoying another strong season in 2010 before suffering a torn anterior cruciate ligament in his left knee. As the 2011 season loomed, he reinjured the knee and was again on the shelf. He returned to the lineup in 2012, only to tear his right ACL three games into the season.

Again undaunted, he refused to listen to the doomsayers and instead immersed himself in rehabilitation.

Bagg's perseverance was rewarded in 2013, when he helped the Roughriders post the first home-field Grey Cup victory in franchise history. By 2017, he was the only Roughrider who had been associated with the team for the entirety of a prosperous decade.

"I'm not sure I would be who I am without all of the doubters along the way," Bagg said. "Even coming out of college and not getting drafted changed my mentality drastically. And then getting that injury in 2010, the first thing that came to mind after having the operation—and perhaps this is unusual or odd, but it makes me who I am—was hearing people say 'that's it' and 'that's over' and 'time to move on and find something else.' That was all I needed to hear to want to get back out there and prove them wrong.

"Certainly, there were moments when I wasn't sure if I'd be able to do it. Tearing it the second time was almost worse because you know how much work went into repairing the other side and getting back to where you wanted to be. It's kind of overwhelming to look at the long road ahead, but I just had great people around me who helped me break it down into steps and weekly goals.

"I can't imagine how I would feel today had I given up on my dream and listened to all the people who suggested I should [retire] back then."

The dream was made possible when Roughriders GM Eric Tillman placed Bagg on the negotiation list shortly after the 2007 draft. In some circles, Bagg was dismissed as a training-camp body, but he wouldn't hear any of that.

Tillman and head coach Kent Austin were so impressed with Bagg that there was never any serious consideration of releasing him.

There was only one snag: he was going back to school.

"I remember knowing that it was cutdown day, obviously," Bagg recalled. "We were still in the Luther College dorms. Joe

Womack was The Reaper, or the guy who was coming around and grabbing guys and asking for their playbook.

"I remember him walking by my room. I had my door open and I kept saying, 'Mr. Womack, I really do need to talk to you guys.' Joe said, 'Everything's all good, Robbie. We'll talk to you. I've just got to get a couple of guys first.'

"I just remember that the day felt like a very long one. He never came to my door, and eventually the guys said there was a meeting in the auditorium. I went to the auditorium, sat beside [linebacker] Mike McCullough, and told him what I was planning on doing. He said, 'Don't do it. You need to talk to someone.'

"By that night, I was packing my bags and headed home. It certainly wasn't a decision that came easily, and I certainly thought that perhaps I could have made the wrong one on that long flight home, but I guess it was meant to be, in a sense.

"I did go back to school and I felt that I proved that I should have been drafted the year past by having a pretty solid fifth-year campaign."

The final season at Queen's was highlighted by a nine-catch, 341-yard, three-touchdown explosion against the University of Toronto Varsity Blues on October 20, 2007.

"It just felt that when I didn't get drafted I needed to show everyone that I should have been, and that was the manner in which I felt like I needed to do that," Bagg said. "One thing led to the next and fortunately I got another opportunity with the Riders the following year."

And for many great years thereafter.

69 Jack, Bill, and Ill Will

Jack Gotta and Bill Quinter formed a mutual abhorration society.

They coolly co-existed for two years at the helm of the Roughriders' football-operations department until, late in 1986, the situation was deemed to be unsustainable. So, it was time for the team to start over…again.

Gotta and Quinter were at the forefront of a rebuilding initiative late in 1984, after head coach Reuben Berry and general manager John Herrera were fired. Gotta was hired to succeed Berry, after which Quinter was appointed GM.

Instant problem. An irresolvable one at that.

Ordinarily, a team hires a general manager, who then selects the coach. But everything was out of order, in more ways than one, when Gotta and Quinter were installed.

The Roughriders' management committee had made overtures to Gotta, a three-time CFL coach of the year, during the week of the 1984 Grey Cup.

"They thought Jack would be a good hire because he had some success in Calgary. He had been [in Saskatchewan] on Eagle Keys' staff when they won the Grey Cup [in 1966]," Quinter recalled.

All the right things were said at the outset of the Gotta-Quinter regime, but the atmosphere soon soured. It didn't help matters that Saskatchewan lost eight of its final nine games (including six in a row) after winning four of its first seven in 1985.

Friction was evident well before the season concluded. With five games remaining, Gotta appeared on CKCK Television's *Sports Journal* and was asked by Dale Isaac whether he thought the calibre of recruiting had hurt the team in 1985. "You hit the nail on the head," Gotta responded, in effect criticizing Quinter.

How toxic was it?

"It was bad," said Alan Ford, who was an administrative assistant at the time. "It would be a chill, or no information travelling between them. Jocko gets ahold of an agent and says, 'We want to bring this guy in. Quinter doesn't know about it.' Who was actually running the football side? Who was running the business? Who had the overall control? Why is Bill Quinter standing out there at practice with his hands on his knees in his coaching shorts with a whistle?

"It was dysfunctional."

Gotta sounded an ominous tone after the 1985 season, telling reporters that the team would "only need one bullet" if the Roughriders' woes persisted…which they did.

The team improved marginally in 1986, responding to a five-win season by registering six victories and a tie. The three-point hike led to fireworks, but not in a positive manner, as sparks continued to fly in a fractured front office.

After the 1986 campaign, with both men having one season remaining on their contracts, there was a division of opinion. Gotta believed he would remain, with Quinter being ousted. Quinter viewed the inverse scenario as being the most likely, especially after he outlined a blueprint for 1987 that, of course, excluded Gotta.

"The areas where we broke down most were leadership and head coach," Quinter told the *Leader-Post* in a post-mortem of 1986. "I don't think he had a strong coaching staff, in terms of teaching."

The committee took Quinter's advice and sacked Gotta—but cashiered the GM at the same time. So ended the two-year tenure of Gotta-Quinter.

"It never worked," Bob Hughes wrote in the *Leader-Post*, "because it never had a chance."

70 The First Cup Was the Sweetest

Brendan Taman waited a long time to celebrate an elusive second championship.

Taman first won a title in Grade 11, as the manager of the city-champion Aden Bowman Bears senior boys basketball team in his hometown of Saskatoon. Another 30 years elapsed before he once again savoured that winning feeling—as general manager of the 2013 Roughriders.

"One was career-defining. One was a nice moment," Taman reflected. "Bowman was career-defining."

That statement was made, in jest, in Taman's typically deadpan fashion. In reality, he cherished the opportunity to be part of a championship team in the CFL, having worked his way up from the bottom rung to the pinnacle of success, Canadian football style.

His introduction to the Roughriders, albeit as the smallest cog in the wheel, took place in 1982 when the team moved its training camp to Saskatoon.

Taman was conscripted as a "gofer," performing sundry odd jobs during seemingly interminable days, one of the more glamorous responsibilities being to pick up a then-anonymous kicker named Dave Ridgway—a future Hall of Famer—at the Saskatoon airport.

Gradually and diligently, Taman worked his way up the chain, to the point where he was named a player personnel assistant in 1987 (at age 20).

He joined the Ottawa Rough Riders in 1989 (the year Saskatchewan won its second Grey Cup) and was their manager of football operations for four years. Then it was back to Saskatchewan in 1993 to begin a four-year stint as the assistant director of player personnel.

Taman moved to Vancouver in 1997—naturally, the Roughriders reached the Grey Cup that year—and was the B.C. Lions' director of player personnel until being named the Winnipeg Blue Bombers' assistant GM in 1999. (The Lions won the Grey Cup in 2000. Notice a pattern here?)

He was promoted to general manager by the Blue Bombers in 2004 and held that position until 2008. The highlight (sort of) for Taman in that span was a trip to the 2007 Grey Cup game, won 23–19 by (you guessed it) Saskatchewan.

The home province beckoned again in 2009, when Taman spent his first of two seasons as the Roughriders' director of football administration. Early in 2010, he succeeded Eric Tillman as the team's GM. (The Taman curse continued, as the Roughriders lost to the Montreal Alouettes in the 2009 and 2010 Grey Cup games.)

The fortunes quickly cratered in 2011, as the Roughriders won only five games. Part of the problem was an unwieldy front-office arrangement that called for Taman, the putative GM, to answer to vice-president of football operations Ken Miller.

Noting the flaws of the format, president-CEO Jim Hopson gave Taman a vote of confidence and, crucially, autonomy. His first major move was to hire Corey Chamblin as the head coach—the very same Corey Chamblin whom Taman had recommended a year earlier, when Miller had instead opted for Greg Marshall (only to make a coaching change and return to the sideline after the Roughriders' 1-7 start).

Taman and director of player personnel Craig Smith proceeded to remake the Roughriders, adding key players such as guard Brendon LaBatte, centre Dominic Picard, wide receiver Taj Smith, and tailback Kory Sheets in 2012.

An "all-in" mindset prevailed in 2013, with the Grey Cup to be held in Regina. Taman signed free agents such as defensive ends John Chick and Ricky Foley, middle linebacker Rey Williams, and defensive back Dwight Anderson, in addition to trading for future Hall of Fame receiver Geroy Simon.

A talented, veteran-laden roster proved to be championship material. Although the Roughriders finished 11–7 and second in the West, they upset the 14–4 Calgary Stampeders in the division final before downing the Hamilton Tiger-Cats in the championship game.

Appropriately, a Saskatchewan-born GM had assembled the first Roughriders team to win a Grey Cup on home soil.

"His contributions were key," former Roughriders president-CEO Jim Hopson said of Taman, who was fired (along with Chamblin) after Saskatchewan lost its first nine games in 2015.

"Brendan left, unfortunately, under less-than-great terms, but the Grey Cup is truly a high point. You won't meet a more decent, honest man than Brendan. He has one passion in life and that's the CFL—and, within the CFL, the Riders. Understated. No big ego. He absolutely loved this job and loved the team.

"Over the years, he had been kicked around a little bit, so I was so happy for him. He really was the architect of that championship team."

71 A Sack-cessful Career

Roughriders great Bobby Jurasin left his mark in the CFL while sporting a trademark bandana.

The future Hall of Fame pass rusher adopted the look in 1984, as a junior with the Northern Michigan University Wildcats.

"My mother-in-law picked up this rising-sun bandana because she thought it symbolized what I was about—being a kamikaze," Jurasin said. "After I started wearing it, I had good luck."

Even so, he proceeded with some caution upon being introduced to the pro ranks.

"When I went to rookie camp, I didn't wear the bandana," Jurasin said. "I was there to win a job. I wanted to attract the attention of the coaches, but I didn't want to attract the attention of the veterans.

"It wasn't until the middle of my rookie year that I started wearing the bandana, and even then it wasn't the bandana. It was just a rising-sun headband."

Jurasin was a rising star by 1987, when he registered 22 sacks to set a Roughriders single-season record. Eleven years later, having played his final CFL game, he was third on the league's all-time sacks list (142) and a lock to be enshrined in the Canadian Football Hall of Fame (which came calling in 2006).

Jurasin also found his calling in Saskatchewan, embracing the team and the province—to the extent that he was adopted by the community as much as any Canadian player.

"I'm from upper Michigan," he noted. "We're basically Canadians as it is, anyway. We're a stone's throw across [the lake].

"I don't know if it was the Saskatchewan mentality of the hard work and the farmers or whatever, but that's all I knew how to do, and that's all they knew how to do, and they appreciated it. There was nothing fake about it. I had to work my nuts off to succeed, period.

"Making it is one thing. Staying is the other."

Staying on the field was a key for Jurasin. Beginning in 1987, he missed only nine of a possible 198 regular season games over 11 years. He seemed impervious to pain, especially while helping Saskatchewan win the 1989 Grey Cup.

"If you watch the game closely, you'll see that I had a little hitch in my giddy-up," said Jurasin, who had 16 sacks in 1989 despite seriously injuring a knee in Week 3. "Just with the sheer excitement of the Grey Cup, I made 'er through. Then, two days

Bobby Jurasin and his famous bandana in 1990. (Don Healy, *Regina Leader-Post*)

later, I was in the hospital getting reconstruction. I was just getting over the hangover, and into the hospital you go. You do what you've got to do to play."

At times, he played on artificial turf that would not have been suitable for someone's deck. He shrugged off pain, critics, and the elements while revelling in every minute he spent with the Roughriders.

"A lot of people ask me for the best memory of the CFL," he said. "I say, 'Taylor Field.' I walked on Taylor Field and there was the turf, and our locker room was old, and I said, 'This is the best place I've ever been.' I fell in love with that place from the first day I set foot on that field.

"Saskatchewan just fit great for me. I had my chances and this and that to go to other places and make more money, but it wasn't about making more money. It was about being happy where you're at.

"You can't be greedy. I got paid well in Saskatchewan. It didn't matter what a guy would have made in Edmonton. It didn't matter what he would have made in different markets. Saskatchewan fit me. I liked it. Regina wasn't a huge city, but it was big enough. It was perfect for me."

72 Just for Old Times' Sake

It can be challenging to document the feats of players who toiled for the Regina Rugby Club and Regina Roughriders.

Statistics from that era, if they even exist, are often incomplete. Video footage is virtually non-existent. Eyewitness accounts are scarce.

But the players who blazed the trail for the Saskatchewan Roughriders should not be forgotten—especially when the objective is to write a book of considerable breadth.

Accordingly, here is a list of some gridiron greats who played for the Regina Rugby Club (RRC), or the Roughriders, before the "Saskatchewan" label was attached in 1948.

Steve Adkins: Caught 11 passes for 231 yards in a 1934 game; that club single-game receiving-yardage record stood until 1983, when Chris DeFrance exploded for 260.

Gordon Barber: A fine lineman who played in four consecutive Grey Cups, beginning in 1929; Plaza of Honour member (POH).

Fred Brown: Outside wing with the Riders, 1928 to 1930; scored the first interception-return touchdown in Canadian football history, 1929; first Western player to score a touchdown in a Grey Cup, 1930.

Jack "Jersey" Campbell: A Roughrider from 1929 to 1935; in 1929, he threw the first forward pass in Grey Cup history.

Howard Cleveland: Nicknamed "Highpockets," this explosive halfback was the Western Interprovincial Football Union's most valuable player in 1939.

Jerry Crapper: His 99-yard touchdown jaunt was the Roughriders' longest fumble return until 1984, when the record (since eclipsed) was tied by Steve Johnson.

Rollo "Swede" Edberg: One of the Riders' first star receivers; West All-Star, 1939.

Eddie James: Nicknamed "Dynamite," he spent three seasons (1928, 1929, 1931) with the Roughriders; he also starred for Winnipeg before eventually entering the Canadian Football Hall of Fame.

Johnny Garuik: Debuted on the line with the Roughriders in 1930 and played his last game with the team in 1943; POH.

Greg Grassick: Talented Roughriders halfback from 1927 to 1932; played in five Grey Cups; Riders' player-coach in 1929; also coached the Riders in 1934; later served as the club's travel and accommodations manager and on the executive; POH; Saskatchewan Sports Hall of Fame inductee, 1982.

Dean Griffing: Beginning in 1936, the Kansas-born Griffing spent seven seasons on the Riders' line and was also the head coach; later managed the Roughriders in the 1950s; Canadian Football Hall of Fame inductee; POH.

Paul Kirk: Starred at halfback from 1934 to 1937; scored 20 points to lead the West in scoring, 1937; the year before, he returned an interception 105 yards for a TD.

Howie Milne: Debuted for the RRC in 1921; part of the transition to the Roughriders, for whom he played until 1929; known for his tackling prowess; coached the Riders, 1926 to 1928; POH.

Angie Mitchell: An effective quarterback despite weighing only 130 pounds, he also caught the first home-field touchdown pass in club history (thrown by Fred Goodman, 1931); a Rider from 1928 to 1932.

Ralph Pierce: Game-breaking halfback with the Riders, 1934 to 1937.

Howard "Tare" Rennebohm: His nine seasons with the team, which he joined in 1916, were only the beginning; later managed the Riders and served as equipment manager, spending nearly 40 years with the organization; POH.

Fred Ritter: Quarterbacked and coached the RRC to its first three provincial titles (1911 to 1913) and two Western Canada crowns (1911, 1912); also served on Regina city council.

Fritz Sandstrom: Versatile star with the RRC and Roughriders for most of 1920s, and in the early 1930s.

Curt Schave: Early 1930s Roughrider, from North Dakota; one of the team's first game-breakers and import players; in 1931, he rushed for 225 yards—a team single-game record that endured until George Reed's 268-yarder in 1965.

Jack Thompson: Nicknamed "Tiny," he was a key member of the Roughriders' offence for most of the 1930s.

Brian Timmis: Starred in the offensive backfield and on the defensive line for the RRC, 1920 to 1922, before completing his playing career in the east and ending up in the Hall of Fame.

Al Urness: The father of Hall of Fame centre Ted Urness, Al played on the Riders' line from 1926 to 1931, and again in 1937; POH.

Al Urquhart: An original member of RRU in 1910, he played his final game in 1922.

Bob Walker: A dominating lineman from 1934 to 1939, and again in 1941; two-time West All-Star; POH.

Maurice Williams: This two-time West All-Star spent five seasons with the Riders over a period spanning 1939 to 1948; under-sized, yet effective, two-way lineman; POH.

Fred Wilson: One of the RRC's first stars, the diminutive ball-carrier—also an excellent kicker—joined the team in 1911 and didn't wrap up his playing career until 1930; POH.

73 Fabulous '50s Footballers

The Roughriders of the 1950s touched both extremes—reaching the Grey Cup with a charismatic quarterback and enduring a one-win season to round out the decade.

A common thread was the presence of stars who are fondly remembered. For example:

Ron Atchison: Began his 17-year tenure as a Riders defensive tackle in 1952; Canadian Football Hall of Famer (CFHOF); Plaza of Honour (POH) inductee.

Mel Becket: Named the West's All-Star centre in 1956, shortly before being killed in a plane crash.

Johnny Bell: This talented pass-catcher completed his seventh and final season with the Riders in 1952; POH.

Alex Bravo: Took off on a team-record 98-yard run, 1956.

Ferd Burket: Scored a team-record five touchdowns in one game, 1959.

Mike Cassidy: Two-way star lineman from 1948 to 1955; POH.

Ken Carpenter: Scored 18 TDs, a Riders single-season record, in 1955; West's leading scorer and MVP, 1955; POH.

Ken Charlton: An eight-year Rider whose final season was 1954; dangerous runner and receiver who could also unleash soaring punts; POH; CFHOF.

Bill Clarke: A 14-year Riders lineman, beginning in 1951; two-time All-Star; POH; CFHOF.

Mario DeMarco: An All-Star guard in 1953, he was killed in the 1956 plane crash after his fourth season with the Roughriders.

Glenn Dobbs: The popular passer/punter/personality captivated the province in 1951, when he was named the West's most valuable player; POH.

Red Ettinger: Ex–New York Giant was the West's All-Star centre, 1951.

Cookie Gilchrist: Rushed for 1,254 yards in 1958, which was his only season with the Riders.

Sully Glasser: The versatile veteran played halfback and chipped in elsewhere over 12 seasons; POH.

Neil Habig: An outstanding centre and linebacker for seven years, beginning in 1958; POH.

Mike Hagler: The diminutive all-purpose back had two punt-return TDs, 1958.

Jack Hill: Caught 60 passes for 1,091 yards and 14 TDs, 1958; also had league-high 145 points; POH.

Larry Isbell: First-round draft pick of Washington Redskins, 1952; he was a skilled receiver, defensive back, and punter over five seasons with the Roughriders, beginning in 1954; POH.

Herb Johnson: Returned a punt 109 yards for a TD, 1953.

Harry Lunn: Played for the Riders from 1955 to 1958; West's outstanding rookie, 1955; returned two punts for a touchdown, 1958.

Bobby Marlow: A Giants first-rounder, 1953; this eight-year Rider, who debuted with the team in 1953, was impactful as ball-carrier, linebacker, or defensive back; POH.

Pete Martin: An excellent guard for Riders, 1946 to 1951; POH.

Jack Nix: Caught seven TD passes in the 1951 regular season and added one more score in the Grey Cup game.

Bob Pelling: A reliable receiver from 1947 to 1953; averaged 21.5 yards per catch and scored three TDs, 1951.

Martin Ruby: Formidable two-way lineman, 1951 to 1957; named a West All-Star offensive *and* defensive tackle, 1954 and 1956; POH; CFHOF.

Jack Russell: Posted a team-high nine touchdown receptions with the first-place Riders, 1951.

Mac Speedie: Starred for the Cleveland Browns before leading the 1953 Riders in catches (57), receiving yards (817), and TD grabs (seven).

Harry Smith: Nicknamed Blackjack; reached the 1951 Grey Cup in his only season as Riders' head coach.

Clarence "Toar" Springstein: Two-time All-Star tackle for Riders, with whom he played from 1939 to 1941, and 1946 to 1952; talented kicker; POH.

Gord Sturtridge: A two-time All-Star defensive end, and the West's rookie of the year in 1953, he was killed in the 1956 plane crash.

Ray Syrnyk: Played guard for the Riders, 1954 to 1956; killed in the 1956 plane crash.

Frank Tripucka: The second great Roughriders passer, following Dobbs; POH.

Del Wardien: A two-time All-Star halfback during seven seasons with the Riders; a skilled defender, he was credited with 27 tackles during a game in Winnipeg in 1948 (long before tackles were an official stat); POH.

Reg Whitehouse: A 15-year Riders offensive lineman, beginning in 1952; POH.

Stan Williams: Excelled as a receiver and defensive back, 1953 to 1957; POH.

John Wozniak: An All-Star guard in three of his four seasons with the Riders; POH.

74 Quarterback Quandaries

Nothing can turn a green coach red faster than the mere mention of a quarterback controversy.

That was evident in November of 1989, during the week leading up to the Grey Cup game.

There was some debate at the time about whether Kent Austin or Tom Burgess should start behind centre for the Roughriders against the Hamilton Tiger-Cats.

In fact, a local TV station conducted a poll in which viewers were asked to choose between Austin and Burgess. The latter pivot received the approval of 54 per cent of the respondents. The poll itself, however, did not receive the endorsement of the head coach.

"Can you believe it?" an incredulous John Gregory told reporters three days before the big game. "They phoned me at the hotel last night and told me they were doing this really neat thing. Neat? That isn't neat. It can divide a team. Why do it now?"

Gregory, who had the only vote that counted, opted for Austin early in the week—a decision that was validated during the Roughriders' 43–40 victory. Austin threw for 474 yards and three touchdowns en route to receiving Grey Cup offensive MVP honours.

In the West Division final, though, Austin had injured a knee in the second quarter. Burgess, whose 22 touchdown passes led the team during the regular season, threw for two more scores in the second half to help Saskatchewan upset the Edmonton Eskimos 32–21.

Burgess and Austin shared the quarterbacking in 1988 and 1989, a period in which their comparative merits were consistently debated. A similar situation existed in 1994 and 1995, when Burgess and Warren Jones took turns at quarterback.

One flammable quarterback controversy erupted near mid-season in 1997. With starting quarterback Reggie Slack faltering, there was a vocal and vigorous lobby in favour of Kevin Mason.

For most of the week leading up to a Labour Day weekend matchup with the Winnipeg Blue Bombers, head coach Jim Daley held off on naming a starter. Slack eventually got the nod and continued to struggle, whereupon Mason entered the game to con-siderable applause—and fared even worse.

There was one positive to extract from the 43–12 home-field loss, as humbling as it was.

The quarterback controversy was over, at least for the time being, as Slack took over and enjoyed an excellent playoff run. But fans can be fickle.

During Darian Durant's career, for example, there were often calls for his understudy to receive more playing time—the backup quarterback often being the most popular person in town.

Durant's detractors were strangely silent, though, during a November to remember which was capped by his three-touchdown-pass performance in the Roughriders' 2013 Grey Cup victory.

75 Green Screen

For some ex-Roughriders, film work wasn't restricted to the meeting room.

Bobby Hosea, for example, played the lead role in *The O.J. Simpson Story*, which was broadcast on FOX in 1995—14 years after Hosea's second and final season as a defensive back for Saskatchewan.

"After his vivid portrayal of Simpson, Hosea's acting career stalled, he thinks because his portrayal of Simpson was just too real," read a portion of a 2016 story that appeared on *Inside Edition*'s website.

The story also noted that Hosea and Simpson worked together in an HBO situation comedy, *1st and 10*. That was before Simpson was accused of brutally murdering his ex-wife, Nicole Brown Simpson, and her friend Ronald Goldman in 1994.

"I said, 'Hey, Juice, I'm working with you today,'" Hosea told *Inside Edition*. "He looks me up and down and he never says another word to me."

Like Simpson, a former USC Trojans star, Hosea played college football in southern California at UCLA. As a Roughrider, he intercepted two passes in 1980 and four the following year. He was released by Saskatchewan before the 1982 season.

Hosea, incidentally, isn't the only tie between Simpson and Saskatchewan. O.J.'s close friend, Al Cowlings, played on the defensive line for four games with Montreal. One of those contests was the Alouettes' 35–35 tie at Taylor Field on October 8, 1978. During that abbreviated CFL stint, Cowlings scored one touchdown, on a 22-yard fumble return.

The Hollywood influence was more visible at Taylor Field on August 9, 1991, when actor/comedian John Candy—then a part-owner of the Toronto Argonauts, along with Wayne Gretzky and Bruce McNall—accompanied the team on a road trip to Regina (travelling by plane and automobile, but not by train).

Candy stood on the sideline during the game and happily accommodated fans who wanted an autograph, a picture, or a brush with greatness.

"He was legitimately interested in the CFL," former Roughriders president John Lipp said. "He attended some board of governors' meetings and was very interested and involved. He didn't goof around. He was serious."

Tommy Reamon was a serious game-breaker for a portion of the Roughriders' 1977 season. The World Football League's leading rusher in 1974—whatever happened to the Florida Blazers? —Reamon had a short CFL stint three years later. Post-football, he appeared in the original version of the movie *North Dallas Forty* and in several episodes of *Charlie's Angels* (TV version).

TV viewers were also treated to an episode of *The Simpsons*, in which Homer opted against attending a barbecue hosted by Ned Flanders, choosing instead to watch the 1991 CFL draft on TV. The Roughriders were one of the CFL teams mentioned in a Season 3 episode, "When Flanders Failed."

The following year, "A Bird in the Hand…"—an episode of *Columbo*, a detective show—included footage from an early-1990s game between the Roughriders (quarterbacked by Kent Austin) and Edmonton Eskimos.

To quote that noted authority on all things Hollywood and Canadiana, Wikipedia: "As the footage showed Kent Austin playing and wearing the No. 5 jersey, the actor playing the quarter-back wore a jersey bearing that number throughout the television episode. When a scene required seeing the quarterback in play, they used footage of Kent Austin."

Hanks for the Memories

With all due respect to everyone who played or coached in the 2013 Grey Cup game, the star of the day was a 57-year-old American who had only a fleeting familiarity with the three-down game.

Welcome to Regina, Tom Hanks.

A few hours before the hometown Roughriders faced the Hamilton Tiger-Cats for CFL supremacy, Hanks boarded a private jet and flew to Regina with his son (Colin), actor Martin Short (a huge Tiger-Cats fan), and Short's son (Oliver).

After landing at Regina International Airport, the group was hustled over to Mosaic Stadium for a pregame show appearance with TSN's Brian Williams. Hanks then greeted fans and posed for selfies before cheerfully consenting to a brief interview with this author. The first question pertained to his thoughts on being in Regina for the Grey Cup.

"It's exciting," Hanks responded. "I came along with my good Canadian friends and here we are, in order to take in everything—the people, the game, the cold, the temperature, the Rider Nation, the 'Oskee Wee Wee,' the whole bit. It's a dream come true."

Hanks added, "I never thought I'd see a Grey Cup in my lifetime. I'm a lucky man."

Appropriate words from someone who earlier that year had played the lead role in *Lucky Guy* on Broadway.

The interview having concluded, Hanks and friends headed over to Mosaic Stadium's east side.

At one point, the cameras zoomed in on Hanks—business as usual—as he donned a Tiger-Cats toque. The image was shown in the stadium, whereupon Roughriders fans joined in the fun by booing. He quickly saved the day by removing the Hamilton headgear and replacing it with green garb.

And there were more cheers for screen icon Tom Hanks.

Another former Roughriders quarterback, Henry Burris, played a minor role in Oliver Stone's football flick, *Any Given Sunday*. Smilin' Hank was among the players who participated in sessions that were turned into game footage.

"You won't see me in the movie," Burris lamented. "I was only able to throw passes. All you would see is Jamie Foxx throwing the pass. Once the pass is gone, that is actually somebody else throwing the ball. All you would see of me is the ball I throw. It's like, 'Hey, that's my spiral!'"

And the review?

"Out of five stars, I'll give it four," Burris said with a laugh. "It doesn't get five stars because I'm not in it."

76 Caught Rhett-handed

Rhett Dawson made the most important catch Ron Lancaster never saw.

The iconic Roughriders quarterback was knocked to the turf a millisecond after he intuitively threw a pass in the direction of Dawson, with a game against the host Calgary Stampeders—and first place in the Western Conference—on the line.

Dawson made the grab for a three-yard major as time expired on both teams' regular seasons.

"I just remember squeezing that ball as tightly as I could," Dawson recalled of a 33–31 victory Saskatchewan posted on November 7, 1976. "What a great moment."

And what a great example of the telepathic relationship Lancaster and Dawson enjoyed in the mid-1970s.

In an interview with Tony Proudfoot for his fine book, *First and Goal: The CFL and the Pursuit of Excellence*, Lancaster described the play in exacting detail.

"I called for Rhett Dawson…to run a deep seam route between the safeties," said Lancaster, who spearheaded the Roughriders' rallies from deficits of 24–0 and 27–8. "When the ball was snapped,

Too Close to Tragedy

One of Rhett Dawson's special guests for his 2006 Plaza of Honour induction was his brother, Red, who was present only because of a quirk of fate.

William "Red" Dawson was an assistant coach with the 1970 University of Marshall Thundering Herd football team, which was decimated by a plane crash.

However, Dawson was spared because, along with graduate assistant Gale Parker, he drove home from a game against East Carolina in a car he was using on a recruiting trip.

On the car radio, Dawson and Parker learned that the Herd's chartered DC 9 had crashed in foggy conditions just short of the runway in Huntington, West Virginia. All 75 people on board were killed.

Under ordinary circumstances, Dawson would have been travelling with the team. With that in mind, he spent considerable time thanking his lucky stars.

But he doesn't always feel that way. "There have also been times when I wasn't so sure that I wouldn't have been better off being one of them," he said in a 2006 interview. "I had feelings of guilt. I've had feelings of shame that I should have been with the players. It doesn't make sense, but that doesn't keep you from being real."

The Thundering Herd was honoured in the movie *We Are Marshall*, which was released two-and-a-half months after the Plaza of Honour induction. The role of Dawson was played by someone he befriended during the production of the Warner Brothers motion picture, Matthew Fox.

For the longest time, Dawson would not discuss the crash and its aftermath. The topic became somewhat easier to tackle over time.

"If I sat down and wrote a book about it, nobody would believe what some of us went through after that," said Dawson, who eventually did write a book, in 2015. "It was unbelievable. I was 27 years old and I'd never been to a funeral. I'd never seen a dead person. And yet, before it was over, I was out at the National Guard armoury trying to help with identifications.

"You'd be walking around campus in those days and you'd pass people who were openly crying. Hell, I remember that a bunch of times I was one of them. It was hard times. We got through it.

"For 30-some years, I didn't want to talk about it. There's no way in the world I could have talked to you about this a year and a half ago," he said. "It has been kind of healing for me, no question."

the defensive rush was in my face sooner than I had expected, and I was forced to throw the ball sooner than I wanted to.

"I knew I was not going to be able to execute the deep seam pass I had called in the huddle, and I threw the ball deep to the sideline—not to the area where the receiver was supposed to be. I had a sense that Rhett recognized the predicament I was in by the defensive alignment, and he modified his route, knowing I wouldn't be able to throw a long pass down the middle of the field.

"As I unleashed the ball, I was flattened, and it wasn't until I heard the crowd roar that I knew it was a long completion. Rhett and I smiled about that play for years to come."

The mere mention of Dawson also produced a smile.

"I loved playing with him," Lancaster said in 2006, when Dawson entered the Roughriders' Plaza of Honour. "He was an outstanding receiver. He was a great guy to work with and even more of a fun person."

Lancaster added that Dawson came "probably about as close as anybody could" to emulating another ace Roughriders receiver, Hugh Campbell.

In their first game together—on September 29, 1974—the Lancaster-Dawson combo collaborated for two aerial touchdowns in a 34–10 home-field victory over Calgary. The Roughriders' new No. 25 had arrived in Regina only four days earlier.

"It was as if Ronnie and I already knew each other and had known each other for a long, long, long time," reflected Dawson, a former Florida State Seminoles star who spent time in the NFL with the Houston Oilers and Minnesota Vikings.

"I could go on and on about Ronnie. Ronnie was a player-coach. I would wander over to the coffee shop down below the coaches' office, which was on the second floor [of the Hill Avenue Shopping Centre], about the time I knew the coaches' meeting was ending. Ronnie would come downstairs and we'd sit down and drink coffee before we went over to practice and draw pass patterns on paper napkins."

All that extra work paid dividends, and in historic fashion, one chilly afternoon in Calgary.

The result was Dawson's last of 23 regular season touchdowns as a Roughrider. Before the 1977 season, while at a stalemate with team management over a contract, a newly married Dawson decided to remain in the United States to concentrate on his family and an off-field vocation.

At 28, he was suddenly a retired football player.

"To walk away from it was one of the hardest things I ever did," Dawson reflected. "It's an unresolved matter in my head. There's a giant part of me that wishes I would have come back and played five or 10 more years, because it was my true love. I cherish my days in Regina."

77 Sask-ATCH-Ewan

Ron Atchison hailed from a hamlet and, dramatically at times, made a lot of plays for the Roughriders.

"Atch," born in the tiny Saskatchewan community of Mullingar, played 17 seasons of professional football with the home-province team—experiencing assorted highs and lows during a career that was honoured by the Canadian Football Hall of Fame.

He endured the loss of four teammates in a 1956 airplane crash, along with subsequent seasons of one and two victories, before finally experiencing what he called the "beautiful satisfaction" of helping Saskatchewan win the 1966 Grey Cup game.

By then a stalwart on the Roughriders' defensive line, he did not play in a championship game until his 15th season, at age 36.

But, really, what was the likelihood that he would end up playing for the Roughriders, let alone be a part of the landmark conquest?

Atchison, a graduate of the junior Saskatoon Hilltops, attended the Green and White's training camp in 1952.

Cliff McClocklin, who had watched Atchison with the Hilltops, kept telling the strapping youngster that he should try out for the Roughriders. Finally, he took the advice and journeyed to Regina.

"I came down and just walked into camp and told them that I was a Hilltopper and wanted to try out," Atchison recalled in 2006. "They accepted me and I played for the next 17 years…I was just a walk-on. You never know who's going to walk on, right?"

A Hush Comes Over the Stadium

Ron Atchison wasn't nervous during a 1967 playoff game against the Calgary Stampeders, but he still had cold feet.

So did everyone who played on Taylor Field in the Roughriders' 11–9 victory, which evened the best-of-three Western Conference final at 1–1.

Along with the adverse weather conditions, there was the matter of footing, or lack thereof. Atchison's cleats were not providing anything close to satisfactory traction.

"After the rainstorm, it froze, so the field was just a piece of ice," he said. "They sanded down the middle of it. I went to our waterboy and asked him to help me out. He had to go back to the exhibition grounds—and that wasn't just going next door—and get my Hush Puppies. When I had put my Hush Puppies on and they had sanded the middle of the field because it was ice, I had very good traction. I was looking pretty damn good and I made plays that I could never have made with cleats."

Atchison was so pleased with the unconventional football footwear, in fact, that he wore the Hush Puppies home after the game.

The non-invitee to training camp ended up earning West All-Star honours on six occasions, chewing up rival offensive linemen with his ferocious, uncompromising style of play.

"He was two different people," Roughriders great George Reed said. "Away from the field, he was a very mild-mannered guy. He had time for everyone and did what he could in the community. On the football field, he was quite a different guy."

Ultimately, the Roughriders virtually had to pull Atchison off the field. He attended training camp in 1969 and was prepared for an 18th season, but head coach Eagle Keys had other ideas.

"I never quit until they fired me," Atchison said with a laugh. "I wanted to play some more. After spring training, I thought I was slowing down, and I was a little concerned. After the training camp, Eagle Keys said, 'Atch, I'd like to see you in my office.' Well, I felt about the same way when my mom died. I just thought, 'Well, this is it, Atch. He's calling me in to tell me,' because they don't call you in if you've made it.

"I remember how badly I felt. Eagle softened the blow as much as anybody could. He said, 'Atch, you're at an age where you should retire. I don't want to cut you.' So he let me announce that I'd retired. If I didn't announce my own retirement, he'd have had to cut me.

"I was devastated. I told Eagle, 'I was hoping to get a couple of more years in.' He said, 'Atch, you've worked hard.' He gave me the old story, but he said, 'We've got a little something for you.' I said, 'Yeah, I can imagine. *Very* little.'

"I got the whole year's salary and they lined me up a job with Saskatchewan Government Insurance, doing promotion and advertising. I was a goodwill ambassador for the insurance company."

Atchison's career was honoured by the team during halftime of a game in September of 1969. The *Leader-Post* marked "Ron Atchison Day" by publishing a full-page tribute that featured the headline SaskATCHewan.

A dinner was held to recognize Atchison, who was showered with gifts in addition to one special form of recognition. The provincial government announced that a lake near Meadow Lake had been named after Atchison. That was quite the distinction for someone who, as an unheralded 22-year-old, had tested the waters with the Roughriders in 1952.

Atchison received more laurels in 1978, when he was enshrined in the Canadian Football Hall of Fame. He died in 2010 at age 80.

78 Visit the Rider Store

Once upon a time, Jim Hopson couldn't have imagined what was in store for the Roughriders.

A cramped retail outlet was an appendage to the team's offices at Taylor Field, and, for quite some time, it was only open on game days.

"I don't think any of us saw the potential that it had," said Hopson, who in 2005 began an immensely successful 10-year run as the team's first president-CEO. "We were doing okay, but we weren't doing great. We weren't winning any championships."

Nonetheless, there was an appetite for team merchandise, to the extent that a second Rider Store opened in 2003 at Regina's Northgate Mall. That gave the team more retail space, although steps were still taken to expand even further.

"We took my office and made it part of the store," Hopson said with a chuckle. "People used to say, 'Don't leave your desk, because Hopson will take your office and turn it into something else.'"

The operation became something else, all right. A transformational 2007 season, which culminated in a Grey Cup championship, resulted in a mushrooming of interest in and revenue for the Roughriders. In 2013, when Saskatchewan won a Grey Cup on home turf, there was also a voracious appetite for Roughriders-related items of virtually any description.

"During those two Grey Cup years, we sold a lot of stuff and did very well, but it really exploded in 2007," Hopson noted. "People didn't just want the 'trash and trinkets,' as we used to jokingly call it. They wanted nice golf shirts and things like that, and it really started to take off.

"I'd be lying if I said I thought we'd end up selling millions of dollars of merchandise a year, but that's what it turned into. The province was booming, the team was winning, and there was an insatiable desire for all things Riders."

The demand is reflected by the fact that the Rider Store, in addition to having an online component (theriderstore.ca), now has five locations—three in Regina (Mosaic Stadium, Northgate Mall, Grasslands) and two in Saskatoon (The Centre, Lawson Heights).

79 Rider Pride Day

Rider Pride was on the home team's side on October 28, 1979.

The Roughriders set a franchise single-game attendance record (since surpassed) when 28,012 spectators—406 more than the seating capacity of a newly expanded Taylor Field—watched their team's second and final victory of a generally gruesome season.

That edition of the Green and White customarily played before several thousand empty seats, exacerbating the woes that were evident on the field. In Year 1 of a massive rebuilding initiative, undertaken by rookie head coach Ron Lancaster, the Roughriders did not record a victory until Game 13.

The long-awaited win was a shocking 26–25 conquest of the visiting Edmonton Eskimos, who would soon win their second of an unprecedented five consecutive Grey Cup championships. The Roughriders' ice-breaking victory did fuel some excitement for their next home game, to be held two weeks later.

To spur interest and provide an infusion of cash to a team that was destined to incur heavy financial losses, "Rider Pride Day" was launched.

The objective was to pack Taylor Field for an October 28 game against the B.C. Lions. Initially, it seemed like an unattainable goal, because the attendances rarely crept much over 20,000.

Not one for pessimism, Winnipeg-based sports writer/broadcaster John Robertson—formerly of the *Leader-Post*—went above and beyond in his attempts to heighten enthusiasm for the pack-the-park promotion.

Robertson made five trips to Regina in the 10 days leading up to the game, absorbing all travel and accommodations expenses. He also declined a $500 speaker's fee for the Roughriders' $200-a-plate dinner.

"There is a magnet here," he told the dinner patrons. "It's like an old lover I keep coming back to."

He also returned to an old love, the *Leader-Post*, and wrote a column that appeared as part of a full-page advertisement for "Rider Pride Day."

"I know that many thousands of you have grown to love the Roughriders over the years, as if they were your own sons," Robertson wrote. "And I know that you don't quit being proud of your sons just because they lose a few football games. But if you're like me, sometimes you're so busy telling them what they are doing wrong, you forget to tell them that you still love them as much as ever.

"Sometimes you forget to tell them how proud you are of them, even when they make mistakes—and recent Rider teams and their executives have made more than their share of mistakes. Sometimes you let them grow away from you—perhaps because they stopped reminding you how much they needed your support—until one day when you decided to put on your coat and go and see them, you discovered to your horror that they were gone...forever."

The horror show was put on hold when the Roughriders downed the Lions 26–12.

"When I got to the park and was exposed to that nationally covered standing ovation just prior to the game, I can tell you I was emotionally moved," said Gordon Staseson, the Roughriders' president from 1979 to 1981.

"I stood under the stands and watched our team being introduced and it was even greater than being at the Grey Cup in those great days when we were in the playoffs. I was overcome,

Fans Go Wild(er)

Willie Wilder played in only eight games for one of the worst Roughriders teams ever. Yet, 40 years after his final game, his name is fondly remembered. Ditto for his nickname.

Willie "Touchdown" Wilder.

The 1979 Roughriders were winless when they faced the Calgary Stampeders on September 16 at Taylor Field. It had been more than a month since Saskatchewan had scored a touchdown.

But then it happened, on an innocent-looking play. Craig Juntunen, one of five quarterbacks to start for the Roughriders that season, threw a short pass to Wilder, who caught the ball near the left sideline. The speedy University of Florida Gators alumnus, a running back turned receiver, caught the pass, slipped a tackle, and raced down the sidelines, with nary a soul nearby.

The result was a 96-yard score that snapped the touchdown drought at 266 minutes, 48 seconds.

But the Roughriders' offence didn't get any wilder after that. Saskatchewan lost 52–10.

particularly so later in the afternoon when we played so well and won the game.

"The slogan, Rider Pride, hit it right on the head. We have a wave of fans out there and it was almost like a religion. The fans showed up that day and let the players know they were there to help pay the bills."

The overflow crowd provided an $80,000 boost to the Roughriders, who nonetheless lost more than $400,000 on their 1979 operations. As a counterbalance, the team gained a slogan.

"That was the beginning of Rider Pride," Lancaster said in 2008. "That slogan caught on and it has been around forever."

80 "Don Swann" Makes It Big

Don Narcisse was able to catch long before he caught on with an organized football team.

"I was always able to focus on the ball and catch it," recalled Narcisse, whose 13 standout seasons with the Roughriders were a ticket to the Canadian Football Hall of Fame. "I could catch with one hand. I just could catch the football. I probably couldn't run from here to there, but if you threw the ball to me, I was going to catch it.

"Everybody around the house knew that 'Donald could catch the football.' I always thought I was Lynn Swann or Drew Pearson. They used to call me Don Swann around the house. That's all I did—catch the football. I didn't worry about anything but catching the ball. We would play in the streets all day long."

Dorothy Narcisse had her reservations.

"My momma didn't want me to play any sports—none at all," a proud son said. "I had a heart murmur and I had asthma.

"She wanted me to be in a band, like my brothers. I played the trumpet in the fifth and sixth grades. I just couldn't do it. I still remember that the keys to my trumpet used to stick. I put the trumpet in the bathtub to wash it out, and the trumpet just came apart. I said, 'Shoot, I guess I don't have to play the trumpet no more,' but they went and rented one for me. I was like, 'Man…!'"

Narcisse's pass-catching talents were not widely trumpeted until his 12th grade year at Lincoln High School in Port Arthur, Texas. A standout senior season landed Narcisse a scholarship at Texas Southern University in Houston.

"That was my first time leaving home," Narcisse said. "It was time for my momma to go to work and she said goodbye. When she did, I started crying so hard. She walked out the door and came back and gave me a hug again. I didn't want to go."

But he eventually hit the road and, despite standing only 5-foot-9, ultimately put up some big numbers. As a senior at Texas Southern, he caught 88 passes for 1,074 yards and 15 touchdowns, leading the NCAA Division 1-AA in receiving and earning first-team All-American honours.

Despite receiving those laurels, he was not chosen in the 1987 NFL draft. The St. Louis Cardinals took notice, though, and signed him as an undrafted player—with a $5,800 bonus. The alternative was to join the Roughriders, whom he had impressed at a free-agent camp in Shreveport, Louisiana.

While with the Cardinals, he was introduced to quarterback Kent Austin, who would also join the Roughriders in the fall of 1987 after being cut by St. Louis.

Narcisse made his CFL debut on September 19, 1987, catching a touchdown pass from Jeff Bentrim in a 34–13 loss to the Edmonton Eskimos. So began Narcisse's league-record streak of 216 consecutive games with at least one reception.

He remained a Roughrider through the 1999 season, retiring with a since-eclipsed league record of 919 receptions. Just as impressively, he must have set a standard for most fans' birthday parties attended by a CFL player.

While excelling on the field, Narcisse was equally valued in the community, helping to launch "Catch for KidSport"—a fundraiser that enabled children from low-income families to take part in sports programs.

At every stop, Narcisse would sign autographs, perform his rubber-legged touchdown dance, and chat amicably with everyone. Appropriately, the fans turned out en masse in August 2010, when he was inducted into the Canadian Football Hall of Fame. August 12 was designated "Don Narcisse Day" by the provincial government.

He was to give a speech outside Regina city hall, but the elements intervened. The wind blew away his prepared address, leaving him no choice but to speak extemporaneously.

"I never visualized this day," he told the crowd. "My dream was to be a Heisman Trophy winner, but this is far beyond that."

81 Hooray for Ray

A remarkable combination of brains and brawn made Ray Elgaard a one-of-a-kind player.

The 6-foot-3, 225-pound slotback was equally capable of running over or past would-be defenders, which he did to the tune of 830 catches and 13,198 yards over 14 seasons with the Roughriders—a career that was honoured in 2002 with enshrinement in the Canadian Football Hall of Fame.

"I think I was more of a slotback type in a tight end shape," Elgaard reflected. "After all the years of playing rugby, I wasn't a lineman. I was a runner. I was a guy who carried the ball all the time and knew how to shake and shimmy and all that stuff, and I was hard to tackle."

That was obvious in 1983, when Elgaard—a second-round draft pick (12th overall) out of the University of Utah Utes—attended his first CFL training camp.

"By the time I got to Saskatchewan, I was in a tight-end-sized body," he continued. "There were probably three or four things that I thought were helpful for me, and the first one was brains. I'm not much for, 'Look how smart I am,' because I'm stupid with a lot of things, but I got it. I understood it.

"I knew how to get open. I understood routes and angles and directions and change of pace and using your skills against somebody who had some other skills and paying attention to what they're being taught and how they're being coached to cover you and using all that information to your advantage. That was, in my mind, issue No. 1."

And one reason why he was No. 1 on the CFL's all-time list in catches and receiving yards when he retired in 1996.

"There are tons of guys who are super-fast or super-strong or whatever but, for whatever reason, they could never get open," said Elgaard, a four-time CFL All-Star who was named the league's outstanding Canadian in 1988, 1990, and 1992.

"You can have all the skills, but if you don't really get it as a receiver, you won't make it. Everybody who has made it has gotten it. I think I got it more than a lot of other people."

Elgaard enhanced his command of the game by paying attention to what the quarterbacks and defensive backs were being taught. By understanding positions that also had a bearing on how a receiver performed, he had a complete command of all elements when the time arrived to make it happen on the field.

Welcome to the CFL...and Good-Bye

Dan Farthing still laughs at the story, one that he always enjoys telling—one that defines Ray Elgaard.

"A defensive back who ended up going against him in training camp was not familiar with Ray at all," Farthing, a fellow Plaza of Honour slotback, said while recalling the early 1990s. "He wasn't familiar with Ray's history, his style of play, or his attitude on the football field, which is fairly intense.

"Ray was running a route on a freshly watered field in and around [Saskatoon's] Griffiths Stadium and ended up slipping in his route and going down on the turf. The ball got thrown pretty much to air and it was an easy interception.

"This young defensive back caught the ball, to his credit. To his discredit, though, he spun the ball in Ray Elgaard's face after he picked it off. Ray took exception to that.

"The one-on-one period continued for a good 30 minutes and, in that 30 minutes, every time it was Ray's turn to go, he would work out the route with the quarterback and then he would look back in the defensive-back lineup and call out that guy to come and face him—time after time after time. He went from smashing this guy and running right over the top of his chest plate, to a finesse swim move that left the guy grasping air, to a juke that also left him turning the wrong way.

"They ran the route tree, from zero to nine. They took this guy to town and beat him up on every single play. To this day, I still don't know whether this gentleman was cut or whether he quit, because it was pretty humiliating to have happen to you.

"It was quite a display and quite a spectacle. It's who Ray Elgaard is. He's definitely old-school in some of his approaches. He spiked the ball hard when he got a touchdown but, in terms of all the other pomp and circumstance that surrounds football, that's not part of who Ray Elgaard was. And every time he spiked the ball, you thought it would pop.

"He definitely taught a lesson, number by number."

Elgaard also had the number of B.C. Lions defensive back Anthony Drawhorn.

"Ray decided he wasn't going to run a route," quarterback Kent Austin recalled. "He got up to Drawhorn, grabbed him, bowled him over, head-butted him, and pancaked him. Ray wasn't one to talk on the field but, that time, he came back to the huddle and said, 'Anything you want the rest of the night.' I'll never forget that. He ended up catching passes for umpteen zillion yards."

"If you want the ball, the best thing to do is be where the guy who's throwing it wants you to go," Elgaard explained. "That's one of the things I figured out pretty early. I could be 10 yards in the clear, but if I'm not where the quarterback thinks I'm going to be, it doesn't matter, because he doesn't have all day to find me and figure it out.

"I think the combination of those two things—understanding routes and angles, and then understanding what the quarterbacks wanted from you—was issue No. 1. That would all fall under the category of brains or knowledge or whatever. But that isn't enough. You can't just be smart. You've got to have more.

"Issue No. 2? I was always a b---h. People always said, 'He's not that fast. He's not this or that.' B------t. I was plenty fast. I knew what I was doing, and I wasn't going to let anybody stop me from doing it. That was the second thing.

"I had a focus about it. I cared about it. I thought it was important. I felt responsible to get it done, and I got it done."

In the open field, there was never anyone quite like the Roughriders' No. 81, who used size and strength to flatten rival defenders.

"It was a gas," he said. "You get tackled. You're not superhuman. Guys figure out how to get you on to the ground. If you really work to make them take you down, you will break some tackles and you will get away sometimes, but it wasn't like you're playing with kids or anything.

"It's part of your job. It's what you're supposed to do. When you do it and do it well and you leave a trail of bodies behind you now and then, you feel damned good about yourself."

82 Keeping Up with the Jones

One week, give or take a day or two, made such a difference on both ends of Chris Jones' tenure with the Roughriders.

He was named the team's head coach, defensive co-ordinator, general manager, and vice president of football operations on December 7, 2015—only nine days after coaching the Edmonton Eskimos to a Grey Cup championship.

Following three seasons in Saskatchewan, Jones signed a contract extension that carried through 2020, only to tender his resignation one week later to join the Cleveland Browns' coaching staff.

"That's pro football," Roughriders president-CEO Craig Reynolds said. "Nothing surprises you.

"Obviously, when you hire somebody in that role, and you hire a very senior person to run your football organization, you hope they're here for a long time, and Chris was here for three years. We were certainly hoping that he would be here longer, but I also understand the reality of the situation. When you have an opportunity like he had with the Cleveland Browns, I understand how that's very appealing from his perspective."

Reynolds' original signing of Jones was the opposite of what used to occur.

Back in the days when the Roughriders were a virtual charity, rival teams with considerably greater resources routinely helped themselves to the better coaches.

Unmatchable contract offers led to the departures of Roughriders head coaches Bob Shaw (to the Toronto Argonauts), Eagle Keys (to the B.C. Lions), and Don Matthews (to Baltimore's short-lived

CFL franchise). The tables turned after the Roughriders became a financial powerhouse, a surge of success that began in 2007.

In a period spanning 2007 to 2013, the Roughriders made four Grey Cup appearances and won two titles. By 2015, though, the team had become a doormat—albeit an affluent one—and a monumental rebuilding project was imperative.

Hence the wooing of Jones, who had gone 12–6 and 14–4 in his two seasons in Edmonton.

Reynolds sought and received permission to approach Jones, who was then offered a lucrative contract.

Never before had the Roughriders contemplated, let alone executed, such a power play.

"When I grew up, it was unimaginable," said Reynolds, who is from Foam Lake, Saskatchewan. "I think it spoke to where we're at as a franchise. We had, and have, become a place where people want to be. In fact, it is, in many cases, the place where people want to be, and I think we saw that with Chris and the interest he had in that job. People wanted to be here.

"I think they want to be here because they know the fan support is here and players feed off of that and it allows you an opportunity to be successful. They know we have resources which allow us to make sure that we're doing things right.

"At the time, the new stadium was certainly on the horizon and people were seeing what an amazing facility this was, and that was different."

When Jones arrived, the Roughriders were in a sad state even though they were preparing to move into new Mosaic Stadium in 2017.

"We were a team that was in rough shape coming out of a 3–15 season, much like some seasons in the '90s, but it was just different in that people saw an opportunity to be successful here," Reynolds said, "whereas I think in the '90s it was such a challenge to get

The Defence Never Rests

The 2018 Roughriders were so explosive that, the odd time, they even got a big play from their offence.

Defensively, they were unlike any other edition of the Green and White, registering 11 touchdowns when the opposition had the football.

In the process, they tied the 1987 B.C. Lions' league records for defensive touchdowns (11) and return touchdowns (15) in a season.

Saskatchewan's defence was so potent that the team posted two of its 12 regular season victories without even scoring an offensive touchdown. Willie Jefferson, a 6-foot–7 defensive end, had an interception return for a touchdown in both of those victories.

Jefferson was named the Roughriders' most outstanding player for 2018, thanks primarily to his game-changing capabilities. He took over three key West Division games that helped Saskatchewan nail down its first home playoff game since 2013:

September 8: With Saskatchewan trailing 10–0 in Winnipeg, Jefferson intercepted the Blue Bombers' Matt Nichols and took off on a 97-yard touchdown return. Later, Jefferson disrupted Nichols' timing on a pass that was intercepted by Samuel Eguavoen and returned 103 yards for another major. The only two Roughriders touchdowns were scored by their defence in a 32–27 victory.

October 8: The Edmonton Eskimos were leading 12–9 late in the fourth quarter when Jefferson intercepted Mike Reilly and motored 49 yards for what turned out to be the game-winning touchdown. Roughriders 19, Eskimos 12.

October 27: Jefferson made two massive plays in a 35–16 victory over B.C.—a result that clinched the aforementioned home playoff game. He tipped a pass to cause an interception (by Tobi Antigha) and strip-sacked Travis Lulay (leading to a Zack Evans fumble recovery for a touchdown).

"What made this defence so good is the mindset we had from Week 1, knowing that we were going to be the most physical, most athletic team out there," Jefferson told reporters in advance of a 23–18 loss to Winnipeg in the West Division semifinal. "Once the season started, it seemed like we just got rolling."

Jefferson is the only defensive lineman in franchise history with two interception-return touchdowns in one season. He shares the

Roughriders' single-season record for pick-sixes with Glen Suitor (1987), Bryce Bevill (1996), LaDouphyous McCalla (2000), Jackie Mitchell (2003), Chris McKenzie (2011), and Nick Marshall (2018).

Marshall and Jefferson combined for half of Saskatchewan's eight pick-sixes—another team record—in 2018. The Roughriders eclipsed the previous team standard of six, set in 1976.

The 2018 Roughriders' non-offensive touchdowns break down as follows:

Eight interception returns: Jefferson (2), Marshall (2), Antigha, Eguavoen, Ed Gainey, and Duron Carter

Three fumble returns: Eguavoen, Evans, and Charleston Hughes (Eguavoen blocked a punt and returned it for a touchdown—a special-teams situation, it would seem—but the league categorized the return as a defensive major.)

Three punt returns: Kyran Moore (2) and Christion Jones

One kickoff return: Marcus Thigpen

One close call: On September 2, Matt Elam intercepted Nichols and returned the ball 53 yards to Winnipeg's 1-yard line. Saskatchewan later scored on a quarterback sneak.

As it was, 37.5 per cent of the Roughriders' touchdowns (or 15-of-40) were not scored by the offence.

The team's puny total of touchdown passes (11) matched that of 1959 and 1996. Only the Roughriders of 1961 (eight) and 1979 (nine) connected for fewer passing touchdowns.

One notable difference: the 1959, 1961, 1979, and 1996 Roughriders had a combined winning percentage of 20.5. Those four teams collectively posted 13 victories, only one more than the 2018 edition.

people to come here because they didn't necessarily have the same belief that you could be successful here, for a variety of reasons.

"But we've proven over the last decade that you have a great opportunity to be successful here and, with things like the stadium coming on, you can be successful for a long time if you do the right things."

The results were not immediately apparent, despite Jones' pedigree of success in the CFL as an assistant and head coach. The

Roughriders won but one of his first 11 games as the team's head coach, finishing the 2016 season at 5–13.

The 2017 edition was 0–2, 1–3, and 2–4 before reversing its fortunes and finishing 10–8. In the playoffs, Saskatchewan was one defensive stop away from defeating Toronto and advancing to the Grey Cup. However, the Argonauts converted a third-and-five play late in the game and went on to win 25–21.

Saskatchewan continued to progress in Year 3 under Jones, finishing 12–6—second-best in the West—and clinching its first home playoff game since 2013. Although the Roughriders were eliminated in the first round of the playoffs, Jones was named the CFL's coach of the year.

At the time, Jones had one season remaining on his contract. The deal was lengthened by one year shortly before the Browns, who hired Freddie Kitchens as the head coach on January 12, 2019, approached the Roughriders and asked for permission to talk to Jones. The deal was quickly sealed.

Kitchens was a quarterback at the University of Alabama in 1997 when Jones was a graduate assistant with the Crimson Tide. Kitchens and Jones also lived in the same apartment complex.

"I love Saskatchewan," Jones told the *Leader-Post*'s Murray McCormick one day after joining the Browns as their senior defensive assistant. "It has been a great ride and it was exactly what I thought was true.

"The people get up in the morning and the first thing they do is think about Roughriders football. There is no place better for that in the league. It's a testament to how much football means to people in Saskatchewan, and it was fun to be involved with."

83 "A Special Place"

While employed exclusively as the Roughriders' special-teams co-ordinator, Craig Dickenson knew he was part of a special team.

Those sentiments were underlined on January 25, 2019, when Dickenson was named the 47th head coach in franchise history.

"This is a special place," Dickenson said at his introductory media conference. "Football means something out here. It means something more here than it does in other places.

"The support here is unbelievable. I don't think you could ask for a better organization from the top down. They give you what you need to be successful.

"People are interested and passionate about the game. You're going to take some lumps sometimes, but there's never a question about whether people care out here. You want to go where football is important and where you have the support that gives you a chance. This place has that and more."

That includes more pressure than a head coach would customarily face in other CFL centres.

"But I think that's good, because people care out here," Dickenson noted. "People are going to scrutinize what you do, both good and bad, and they're going to have an opinion. We respect that and we acknowledge that. That sort of scrutiny, that sort of expectation level, is what makes this the best job in the CFL as well."

Dickenson has won two Grey Cups—with the 2008 Calgary Stampeders and 2015 Edmonton Eskimos—as a CFL assistant coach.

Of his first 17 seasons in the league, 14 were spent as a special-teams co-ordinator. He was also an assistant special-teams

A New Day Under O'Day

Jeremy O'Day was born near Buffalo but, ultimately, Saskatchewan fit the bill.

He became a fixture with the Roughriders, and in Regina, during a 14-year playing career that concluded in 2010.

After retiring from the gridiron, he spent another eight years with the organization in an administrative capacity before becoming the vice-president of football operations and general manager on January 18, 2019.

"When you get named a general manager in a place that you've been for a long period of time, you know the people in the province," O'Day said. "You know the fans. You know what makes up the culture of the province. For me, it means something.

"If Saskatchewan people's beliefs and toughness would filter into our locker room, I've always thought that we'd be in great shape. It's something I believe in.

"This is home to me. All my kids were born here. My wife was born and raised here. I've made it home. I take a lot of pride in being from here and being with this organization for a long time.

"It means a lot to me to be the general manager, but I want it to be more than that. I don't want to be hired because I've been here for a long time. I don't want to be hired because I was a good football player. I want to be hired because I was the right candidate."

After attending Edinboro University in Pennsylvania, O'Day spent two seasons with the Toronto Argonauts before signing with Saskatchewan as a free agent in 1999.

He soon became entrenched on the Roughriders' offensive line, being named a West Division All-Star centre in six of his 12 seasons with Saskatchewan.

In fact, O'Day decided to retire as a player after the 2010 season, despite once again having been an All-Star.

"I was asked in that [retirement] press conference what my aspirations and goals were," O'Day recalled. "The answer for me was a simple one: I wanted to become a general manager."

He was the Roughriders' assistant GM for four-and-a-half seasons before being named interim GM midway through the 2015 season, following the firing of Brendan Taman.

After the 2015 campaign, O'Day applied for the GM's job, which president-CEO Craig Reynolds eventually handed to head coach Chris Jones when he took over the Roughriders' football operations.

O'Day remained in the front office and spent three seasons as the assistant vice-president of football operations and administration.

"I'd be lying if I said I didn't think I was ready to become a general manager [in 2015], but I do believe in being patient," O'Day said. "I believe that you can learn from everyone. Anytime you really want something really badly and you don't get it, you'll have some disappointment with that, but I actually give Craig a lot of credit.

"We had a good conversation when he had to actually break the news to me in '15 that I wasn't the candidate. He said, 'This is going to be a good situation for you. You're going to be able to learn from another general manager. You'll have an added role, with Chris coming in in a dual role.'

"There was an opportunity for me to learn the rest of the stuff that I needed to learn to become a general manager. Craig was right with what he said to me that day. Anytime you gain more experience, you're going to gain more readiness."

As it turned out, O'Day was ready, willing, and able to assume the general manager reins after Jones resigned in mid-January of 2019.

"The best candidate for the job was already working for us," Reynolds said, "and I knew that."

coordinator in the NFL with the San Diego Chargers (2000 and 2001) and Oakland Raiders (2010).

Dickenson was the Roughriders' special-teams co-ordinator during two stints (2011 and 2012; 2016 to 2018) before being promoted following the surprising departure of head coach Chris Jones, who joined the Cleveland Browns' staff.

"I love the game and I love coaching," said Dickenson, who maintained his special-teams role in addition to assuming the head-coaching reins.

"This job, in a lot of ways, found me, but I chose to be a member of the Saskatchewan Roughriders. The stars seemed to align on this one. Being a head coach wasn't a career goal of mine.

Being a good coach, working with good people, and doing a good job to the best of my ability always was the goal. Ultimately, I hoped to get an opportunity, and I'm grateful that it's here."

That opportunity, as Dickenson put it, was "the perfect job with the perfect people at the perfect time."

Dickenson took the job with the encouragement of his younger brother, Dave, who is Calgary's head coach.

"We've competed our whole lives," Craig Dickenson said. "I'm thrilled to be able to coach in the same league as my brother.

"He said, 'Go for it! It's a good job. Everybody in the league knows that.' It's a really good job."

Upon first taking a job with the Roughriders, back in 2011, Dickenson began immersing himself in his new surroundings. He pored over history books about the team, with the objective of fully understanding the football culture in Saskatchewan.

"This is a storied franchise and it's got great tradition, great history," he said. "You hear stories about people donating trucks of grain to try to raise money, doing what they needed to do to try to support the team. So I will always respect and really admire the folks who pay good money to come out and watch us.

"I appreciate that and we're going to do our best to make sure that the people who pay good money to watch us play have a quality product to watch.

"It's an honour to be a part of this organization."

84 Buy a Riders Share

The Green Bay Packers were delighted to share information about shares—which helped the Roughriders emulate the NFL's only community-owned team.

Early in 2004, the Roughriders announced their first share offering, with each Class A version being available for $250. The program was designed as another fundraiser for a CFL team that had just declared itself debt-free for the first time in nearly 20 years.

Tom Robinson, who was then completing his term as the Roughriders' president, described the share campaign as a "springboard to the future," the objective being to use the revenues to help the team recruit and retain players in addition to improving the game-day experience at Taylor Field.

The issuing of shares also allowed "owners" to vote on certain issues at the annual general meeting, such as the election of the board of directors.

A restriction of 20 shares per buyer was applied to the number of Class A (voting) shares to ensure that a company or a bloc of voters could not seize control of the football team. An unlimited number of Class B (non-voting) shares was also made available.

Series I shares included images of Ron Lancaster, George Reed, and Roger Aldag. Series II shares, released in 2010, commemorated the club's 100th anniversary. Series III shares, featuring the images of Kent Austin, Bobby Jurasin, and Don Narcisse, were released in 2011 to honour the 1989 Grey Cup champions. Series IV (2017) celebrated the inaugural season at new Mosaic Stadium, along with Taylor Field and the team's history.

Shares are still available for the original cost—visit riderville.com for more information—with one of the longtime perks being a 15 per cent discount at the Rider Store. Additionally, a shareholder who also owns a season ticket receives preferred seat-exchange priority.

85 Join the Pep Band

Rhonda Kerr-White has played for the Roughriders since 1993.

She is an original member of the Rider Pep Band.

"It really has evolved over the years," said Kerr-White, who is the band's organizer in addition to playing the trumpet. "Now we've got such a youth component in the band that we'll play some of the songs that you hear on the radio."

The ensemble usually has 40-plus members, ranging in age from 19 to 70. With a repertoire of 75 songs, the group plays at Roughriders home games, every Grey Cup and, well, virtually anywhere to which it is invited.

"It's all about performing," Kerr-White said. "We love playing music for diehard Rider fans. There's something special about being associated with Rider fans across the country and across the world, and it's something that people can relate to."

One does not require a doctorate in music to audition for, let alone play in, the band. However, a modicum of musicianship—and a passion for football—are prerequisites.

So, to a large extent, is the willingness to fundraise for the group's annual trip to the Grey Cup. The Pep Band has appeared at every national football festival since the orchestra was founded by Bob Mossing.

Kerr-White and Russ Lowey, who plays the baritone sax, are the two remaining original members of the band. Kerr-White is the only one who has made every Grey Cup trip.

"It's all about having fun," she said. "We see people every year that we only see at the Grey Cup. People say, 'Hey, the Grey Cup can begin! The Pep Band's here!' We might as well toot our own horns, so to speak."

The band is also proud of one rather unique feat—being penalized on September 9, 2000, when the Roughriders played the B.C. Lions. Visiting quarterback Damon Allen, a future Hall of Famer, complained to referee Ken Lazaruk that the band's musical interludes were preventing the Lions' offensive players from hearing the signals. The Roughriders were promptly assessed a 10-yard delay-of-game penalty.

"We were playing when the Lions were out of the huddle," Kerr-White recalled. "They thought we were being directed by the Riders' bench, but we were fans in the stands, and we had instruments instead of voices."

The Pep Band played an instrumental role in celebrations of the team's Grey Cup victories of 2007 (in Toronto) and 2013 (Regina).

"After we won in 2007, we sauntered back to the hotel, playing our songs," Kerr-White said. "When we looked back, there were three blocks of people behind us."

The musicians' dedication is truly a "cymbal" of the degree to which Rider Pride is infectious and joyous.

New members are always welcomed. There is a minimum age of 19—because the band sometimes plays in licensed establishments—and musicians cannot be beginners.

Any interested party who meets those requirements, in addition to having a passion for the Roughriders, can email riderpepband@ accesscomm.ca or visit the group's Facebook page.

86 Path to a Prolific Passer

The Roughriders' courtship of a legendary quarterback triggered a chain of events that ultimately put the team in position to acquire someone who also became an iconic passer.

If not for the Roughriders' unsuccessful pursuit of former NFL star quarterback/punter Sammy Baugh, who was offered the head-coaching position in 1958, Ron Lancaster may not have ended up in the CFL and, ultimately, with Saskatchewan.

The Roughriders' brass, led by president Sam Taylor, wooed Slingin' Sammy after terminating head coach Frank Filchock. Baugh, who was the head football coach at Hardin-Simmons University in Abilene, Texas, told the *Abilene Reporter News* that Saskatchewan had wooed him with a three-year contract "for the most money I'll ever be offered in coaching."

Although Baugh had two years left on his deal at Hardin-Simmons, he had been granted permission to leave if he was suitably enticed by the Roughriders' offer. Baugh was tempted, but he decided to stay put when Hardin-Simmons administrators and school alumni came through with a five-year contract extension.

"Baugh is as fine a person as I've ever met," Taylor told the *Leader-Post*. "He would have been a natural with the Riders, but they like him so well in West Texas that they simply wouldn't let him go."

The Roughriders promptly hired George Terlep as head coach. He lasted until September 30, 1959, at which time the 0–9 team had been outscored 334–93.

Terlep quickly resurfaced as the Ottawa Rough Riders' backfield coach and, in 1960, was promoted to general manager.

Not long after assuming that position, Terlep was contacted by Bill Edwards, the head football coach at Wittenberg College.

Previously, Edwards had been the head coach at Vanderbilt University, where his staff had included Terlep.

Edwards called his one-time colleague to tout the abilities of Lancaster, who had been Wittenberg's starting quarterback and was looking to play professional football.

The 5-foot-9¾ Lancaster ended up journeying northward and making Ottawa's roster, which also included a promising pivot named Russ Jackson. Lancaster and Jackson were teammates for three full seasons before Ottawa resolved its quarterbacking dilemma.

Ottawa head coach Frank Clair decided to make Jackson the uncontested starter, so Lancaster was dealt to Saskatchewan for $500, along with the provision that Ottawa would have the first right of refusal if the Roughriders tried to trade him back to the Eastern Conference.

Terlep was no longer Ottawa's GM by the time Lancaster was traded, having resigned after the 1962 season, but you are free to wonder how the Little General's career would have unfolded if not for a chain of events that began when the Roughriders' overtures toward Baugh were unsuccessful.

87 Berry Interesting

Former Roughriders head coach Reuben Berry has to be the franchise's all-time leader in sayings.

Although the Green and White had a 10–15–1 record under Berry, the man who brought us "Saskatchewan Tough"—and so much more—left a lasting imprint with his unique turn of phrase while coaching the team for part of the 1983 season and all of 1984.

Reuben Berry in 1984. (Roy Antal, *Regina Leader-Post*)

So how else to begin a chapter on memorable quotations in Roughriders history except to lead off with the best of Berry?

- "There are two seasons in Saskatchewan—football and winter—and you have to be tough to survive them both."
- "I want players who can stand bare-chested facing into the north wind in the winter and not let it bother them."
- "I want to be on the bridge of the Titanic. I want challenges."
- "We were chopping, chopping, but no chips were flying."
- "When you're green, you're growing, and when you're ripe, you're rotten."
- "I coach from the eyebrows up."
- "We want to be like high water rolling over low ground."
- "I want old heads on young shoulders."
- "I want guys who will go into the trenches with you—guys who will be in the foxholes with you."
- "Losing is worse than dying because you've got to live with losing."

We now turn the floor over to other Roughriders luminaries:

- "You can only go to The Gold so often."—Defensive lineman Gary Dulin, 1985, lamenting the perceived lack of nightlife in Regina.
- "One damn play, and it ruins the whole damn season."—Safety Ted Provost following a last-minute loss to the Ottawa Rough Riders in the 1976 Grey Cup game.
- "Inhumane!"—Montreal Alouettes president Ted Workman, following a 44–0 loss in Regina in 1966.
- "It was three or four o'clock in the morning and I didn't want to go to sleep, because as soon as you wake up, it's the next day and you're not a champion that day."—Offensive lineman Vic Stevenson, recalling the aftermath of the 1989 Grey Cup victory.

- "Austin is now a god. He's maybe the all-time MVP of this franchise."—Offensive lineman Gene Makowsky to Steve Simmons of the *Toronto Sun* after Kent Austin coached Saskatchewan to the 2007 Grey Cup title, having quarterbacked the Riders to a championship 18 years earlier.

- "They said there were all these seasons in Saskatchewan—the wind blew in the winter, the spring, and the summer, and Lancaster would blow playoff games in the fall."—Ron Lancaster, 2006.

- "That wasn't a pass. It was a catch."—Lancaster, on a 25-yard, one-handed touchdown catch by tight end Bob Richardson in the 1976 Western Conference final against the Edmonton Eskimos.

- "If they dropped a bomb on Regina, there would only be 67 cents damage."—Disgruntled receiver Sammy Greene after being cut by the Roughriders in 1984.

- "Get the monkey off my back, please. Please!"—Darian Durant after quarterbacking Saskatchewan to a Grey Cup victory in 2013.

- "I guarantee it. We will win on July 12."—Head coach Jim Eddy before a season-opening 33–11 loss in Winnipeg on July 12, 1977.

- "We've made history today."—Regina mayor Henry Baker to CBC on November 26, 1966, following the first Grey Cup victory in the Roughriders' 56-year history.

- "Don't feel too badly if you had a little trouble with Ottawa. I've had some trouble with Ottawa myself."—Saskatchewan premier Tommy Douglas, addressing the Roughriders after their 21–14 loss to the eastern Riders in the 1951 Grey Cup.

- "They're tired, they're fat, they're wobbly. They're fat and sassy pigs."—Defensive tackle Scott Schultz describing the B.C. Lions' offensive linemen, 2003.

- "You've got to pit the teams up against each other, head-to-head. It comes down to, does Henry want to play for Danny Barrett and the Saskatchewan Roughriders or does he want to play for Tom Higgins and the Calgary Stampeders? That's how I look at it."—Head coach Danny Barrett in mid-February 2005, shortly before quarterback Henry Burris signed as a free agent with the Tom Higgins–coached Stampeders.

- "It's like playing in the Prison League."—Defensive tackle Colin Scrivener in 2002, about playing at Hamilton's Ivor Wynne Stadium.

- "It's like dog years and it felt like a month and a half." —Quarterback Kevin Glenn, jokingly, in 2015 after being asked what it was like to be out of the lineup for six weeks.

- "Maybe I should have listened to my old man when he suggested I take up accordion playing."—Head coach George Terlep during training camp in 1959, which turned out to be the worst season in franchise history (1–15).

- "You can have your fancy drills—your split-T formation, your reserves, your option plays. It doesn't mean a thing if you can't get down there on the dirt and beat the gizzard out of the guy across from you."—Head coach Steve Owen, 1962.

- "We've still got a lot of unfinished business."—Chris Jones on January 8, 2019, one week before resigning as the Roughriders' head coach, general manager, and vice-president of football operations to join the Cleveland Browns' coaching staff.

- "What do Riders do? Ride!"—Ken Miller, Roughriders head coach, 2008 to 2011.

88 The (S)elect Few

Oft-used sports cliché: "(Athlete X) is so popular that he could run for mayor."

Some Roughriders alumni have done just that.

At least three former Saskatchewan players—Corey Holmes, Eddie Lowe, and Galen Wahlmeier—have held the highest-ranking position in civic government.

Holmes was the mayor of Metcalfe, Mississippi, from 2009 to 2017. A two-time CFL special-teams player of the year, he was elected two years after helping Saskatchewan win a Grey Cup.

Lowe, a linebacker with the Roughriders from 1983 to 1991, won the mayoralty race in Phenix City, Alabama, in 2012 and was elected to a second term in 2016.

Wahlmeier, a centre/linebacker who made his CFL debut in 1959 and signed off with the Roughriders in 1967, stayed in Saskatchewan after his playing career and was a two-term mayor of Estevan (1976 to 1982). He also served on city council.

Similarly, fullback Chris Szarka was a Regina city councillor from 2009 to 2012. The Canuck Truck played for the Roughriders from 1997 to 2010.

Szarka's former teammate, offensive lineman Gene Makowsky, was elected to the Saskatchewan Legislative Assembly in 2011, shortly after the last of his 17 seasons with the Roughriders. Based in Regina, Makowsky was re-elected in 2016—one year after being inducted into the Canadian Football Hall of Fame.

"[Politics] has been very interesting," said Makowsky, who was appointed a cabinet minister by the governing Saskatchewan Party. "Just like any job, any profession, there's ups and downs and disappointments and things that are great.

"It's a unique type of job. I think football might help a little bit in that. There's a lot of leaders on a football team and that's what political parties look for—community leaders and people who care about their community and want to give back. A lot of guys on a team are given that opportunity, and that continues to this day.

"There's also some aspect of dealing with the media. You get to do that sometimes in the football world. You learn to have thick skin at times and I think that has also served me well. You're in the public eye when you play with the Roughriders, certainly in Saskatchewan. Those are some of the things that might prepare you or might help."

As a player, Makowsky had a connection to two people who had some association with American politics.

Ken Miller, a member of the Roughriders' coaching staff from 2007 to 2011, was 18 and in college when he campaigned for John F. Kennedy in 1960.

"I did some lightweight campaigning, trying to influence people," recalled Miller, who grew up near Dufur, Oregon. "JFK was charismatic. He just attracted people. I thought that he had a tremendous vision. There was the idea of serving—that government serves and you should serve your country. It's not what our country can do for us, but what we can do for our country."

There was also a Republican influence of note in the Roughriders' dressing room at one time. Quarterback Jimmy Kemp spent 10 games with the Roughriders in 1996, the same year in which his father (Jack Kemp) was the vice-presidential candidate on the GOP ticket, alongside Bob Dole.

Coincidentally, the Roughriders of 1996 employed a Kemp (Jimmy) and a Dole (offensive line coach Bill Dole).

Kemp-Dole was not a success on either side of the border in 1996. Clinton-Gore won the electoral college, 379 votes to 159, and the Roughriders went 5–13.

89 "Hennnn-ry!"

Henry Burris was revered and reviled by Roughriders fans for the better part of a generation.

The ebullient Burris was immensely popular during two stints as Saskatchewan's quarterback, but was otherwise the target of a derisive "Hennnn-ry!" chant every time he visited Regina.

The serenade was born in 2005, after Burris left the Roughriders to sign as a free agent with the Calgary Stampeders. Many Roughriders loyalists felt jilted and, as a result, voiced their frustrations—usually in unison—when he was in town.

Even so, part of his heart will always remain in Saskatchewan.

"I'm always truly proud to say that I'll always bleed green," Burris said after wrapping up a sure-fire Hall of Fame career by guiding the Ottawa Redblacks to the 2016 Grey Cup title.

Burris first donned green in 2000, signing with Saskatchewan as a free agent after spending his first three CFL seasons in Calgary.

He was an immediate sensation, throwing for 4,647 yards and 30 touchdowns in 16 starts for the 2000 Roughriders. Off the field, he signed every autograph, posed for every picture, and lived up to the moniker of Smilin' Hank.

Burris parlayed a standout season into an NFL look-see. He was with the Green Bay Packers (in 2001) and Chicago Bears (2002) before returning to the CFL, and Saskatchewan, in 2003.

He assumed the starter's role early in the 2004 season—after Nealon Greene suffered a broken leg—and guided the team to a berth in the West Division final.

Burris' third touchdown pass of the game gave the Roughriders a 24–21 lead late in the fourth quarter, but the B.C. Lions forced overtime with a last-second field goal and ultimately won 27–25.

Little did anyone suspect at the time that Burris had played his final game as a Roughrider. He did not conceal his desire to re-sign with the team as a free agent, but then-general manager Roy Shivers was more guarded.

"We have a No. 1 quarterback already [in Greene]," Shivers told the *Calgary Herald* shortly after the 2004 season. "Henry's a bonus for us."

The Stampeders wooed Burris with more intensity, and more money, and he was soon donning a cowboy hat at a press conference in Calgary.

"When there's a GM that you didn't want to play for at the time, for various reasons, it was time to move on," Burris said. "Calgary was a place where I began my career, and if I had a chance to get back there, I wasn't going to say no."

Roughriders fans had other things to say in 2005 when Burris returned to Regina, this time as a member of the Stampeders. The furore was such that a T-shirt, bearing a message that was unflattering to Burris, was manufactured and sold.

One of the purchasers was Burris, who donned the T-shirt and made a surprise visit to a fans' luncheon in Regina as the game loomed. He was, of course, grinning ear-to-ear as he welcomed attendees to the function.

Fan fervour reached a crescendo on November 24, 2013, when the Roughriders played a home-field Grey Cup game for the first time. Fittingly, the visiting quarterback was Burris.

"When I came back there as a Hamilton Tiger-Cat to play in the 2013 Grey Cup, we knew we were walking right into a trap," Burris said. "We had guys catching frostbite with their fingers and such during the week of practice."

The Roughriders built a 31–6 halftime lead and went on to win 45–23.

Although Burris was 38 at the time, he would play in two more Grey Cup games—both with Ottawa.

Henry Burris with the Roughriders in 2004. (Roy Antal, *Regina Leader-Post*)

In 2015, the Edmonton Eskimos defeated Ottawa 26–20. Despite the outcome, the Redblacks could derive considerable satisfaction from having reached the championship game in only their second year of existence. Burris led the way, amassing a league-high 5,693 passing yards en route to winning CFL most-outstanding-player honours at age 40.

That was a prelude to a storybook signoff for Burris, who in 2016 piloted Ottawa to a 39–33 overtime victory over Calgary in the 104th Grey Cup game. At 41, he completed 35-of-46 passes for 461 yards and three touchdowns (including the 18-yard game winner to Ernest Jackson in OT) in what turned out to be the personable passer's final game.

Not long after announcing his retirement on January 24, 2017, he made several public appearances in Saskatchewan, at sports banquets and the like.

"I always look forward to coming back and helping out," he said, "and giving back to one of the greatest places in the world."

90 Jon Ryan Comes Home

Until 2019, Jon Ryan had only dressed up as a Saskatchewan Roughrider for events such as Halloween.

Then, at age 37, he made his long-awaited debut with his hometown CFL team.

The Regina-born Ryan grew up watching, and even worshipping, the Roughriders. At the same time, he was developing into someone who would excel at football in high school (with the Sheldon-Williams Spartans) and with the University of Regina Rams.

The Winnipeg Blue Bombers took notice, selecting Ryan—a star receiver and punter in college—in the third round of the 2004 CFL draft.

He made history as a second-year pro, averaging 50.6 yards per punt—a league single-season record—for Winnipeg.

That success was parlayed into an NFL contract with the Green Bay Packers, with whom he spent two seasons before enjoying 10 years with the Seattle Seahawks. He helped Seattle win a Super Bowl in 2014 while becoming one of the most popular players on the team.

Despite all those accomplishments, he had not yet played for the one team that helped to ignite his passion for football.

Ryan turned eight on November 26, 1989, when there was a province-wide celebration. That was the date on which the Roughriders defeated the Hamilton Tiger-Cats 43–40 to win the Grey Cup.

"I was more nervous for that game than I was for most of the games I have ever played," Ryan recalled.

Ryan was only four years old when he attended his first CFL game in 1985. He was a Roughriders season-ticket holder from 1990 to 2004.

"I remember that season tickets were $110 and I had to raise $55 in the winter, shovelling walks and whatnot, and I had to save my allowance to pay for my half of the season ticket," he said. "I think green and white will always be in my blood."

With that in mind, it made eminent good sense for Ryan to sign with Saskatchewan on May 14, 2019. He had worked out for the team at a free-agent camp six weeks earlier in Vero Beach, Florida.

"Looking back on my career, I've been so happy and so fortunate, right from playing touch football in Regina and coming up through the system there," he reflected. "With all the opportunities that I've been given, this is kind of a cherry on top of a dream."

91 Record Collection

The Roughriders established two longstanding team records—only one of them is a highlight—in the same season.

In 1991, Saskatchewan scored the most points in franchise history (606) but didn't come close to making the playoffs.

The problem was that the Roughriders allowed 710 points, setting team and league records in that category, while posting a 6–12 record and missing the playoffs.

The average score: Opponent 39, Roughriders 34.

The plight of the 1991 Roughriders was such that they lost games despite scoring 47, 41, 36, 35, and 35 points.

The victorious opposition, at various times, lacerated the alleged Saskatchewan defence for point totals of 62, 54, 50, 49, 49, and 48.

As a small measure of solace, at least the team was entertaining, regardless of the outcome.

Despite missing five full games due to injury, Kent Austin threw for 4,137 yards and 32 touchdowns.

Six of those scoring tosses, another team record, were registered on September 21, 1991, in a 49–47 victory over the host B.C. Lions.

In that game, Jeff Fairholm caught two touchdown passes. On the season, he led the Roughriders in receiving yards (1,239) and touchdowns (13). One of his majors was a 99-yarder.

"I do remember a couple of times sitting on the bench when our defence would give up a touchdown and we'd be like, 'Oh, okay. Gotta go score again,'" Fairholm recalled. "We had that attitude.

"We were so proficient at scoring and running our offence. Hey, defence gives up points. That's what they do. You can't be perfect, and the other team is paid to play, too. But there were times when it was, 'Okay, let's go. Let's go score again.' Sometimes it almost felt easy, which is fun, too."

92 Good Times, Bad Times

The Roughriders have figured in some noteworthy blowouts, experiencing life as both the router and routee.

Here is a flashback to some long days for the Roughriders or their opposition:

Most Points Scored by the Roughriders
Saskatchewan 58, Ottawa 22 (August 7, 1989)
Playing against his former team, the Roughriders' Tom Burgess threw four touchdown passes—two to Jeff Fairholm—at Taylor Field before being replaced by Kent Austin early in the third quarter, by which point the game was out of hand. Tim McCray rushed for 107 yards and another two touchdowns.

Saskatchewan 56, Winnipeg 4 (September 3, 1995)
Ray Elgaard caught two touchdown passes and Darren Joseph, who rushed for 100 yards, added two scores on the ground. Oddly enough, the Blue Bombers defeated the visiting Roughriders 25–24 one week later, meaning that the teams split a home-and-home set even though Winnipeg was outscored 80–29.

Saskatchewan 56, Edmonton 8 (August 28, 1964)
Ed Buchanan lit up the Eskimos' defence for 301 yards from scrimmage at Clarke Stadium. He rushed 19 times for 199 yards (including a 73-yard touchdown) and caught three passes for 102

yards. Hugh Campbell had 10 receptions for 146 yards while catching three of Ron Lancaster's four touchdown passes.

Saskatchewan 56, Winnipeg 23 (September 1, 1991)
Austin threw for 461 yards and four touchdowns and ran for another major.

Saskatchewan 55, Winnipeg 10 (September 13, 2009)
The Roughriders turned eight Blue Bombers turnovers into 31 points in Winnipeg. Wes Cates ran for two touchdowns and scored on a reception. "I almost want to walk out of here with a bag on my head," Bombers defensive end Gavin Walls told Kirk Penton of the *Winnipeg Sun*.

Most Points Allowed by the Roughriders
Hamilton 67, Saskatchewan 21 (October 15, 1962)
Joe Zuger, making his first start as a pro quarterback, threw eight touchdown passes—a CFL single-game record. Frank Cosentino added two more scoring tosses for the Tiger-Cats. After the game, a reporter pointed out to Roughriders head coach Steve Owen that he was reputedly a defensive genius. "If I hadn't been a f----- genius, it would have been 100–0!" replied Owen, the CFL's coach of the year in 1962.

Hamilton 63, Saskatchewan 17 (August 5, 1999)
The Tiger-Cats converted six Saskatchewan turnovers (including five interceptions) into 38 points. Hamilton led 39-14 at halftime. The tone was set the day before, when Roughriders quarterback Reggie Slack missed the team's flight. Steve Sarkisian and John Rayborn handled the quarterbacking for Saskatchewan. A few days later, Slack announced at a media conference that he had a "medical addiction."

Montreal 62, Saskatchewan 7 (August 3, 2000)

The host Alouettes led 41–7 at halftime, whereupon the fans were treated to the closest matchup of the day—a pro wrestling tussle between Jacques Rougeau and King Kong Bundy. Rougeau won by pinfall, to the delight of a partisan crowd at Montreal's Percival Molson Stadium.

Toronto 62, Saskatchewan 10 (August 15, 1991)

Michael "Pinball" Clemons scored three touchdowns and Raghib "Rocket" Ismail added his first two CFL majors as the Argos ran wild at home.

Winnipeg 61, Saskatchewan 8 (August 29, 1959)

A *Leader-Post* headline summed it up: RIDERS HUMILIATED. Jim Van Pelt threw seven touchdown passes (then a league record) and Ernie Pitts had five scoring grabs (also a record) for a Winnipeg team that piled up 34 second-quarter points against Saskatchewan, which had lost 55–0 to Edmonton five days earlier. Blue Bombers head coach Bud Grant mercifully kept Van Pelt on the bench for most of the second half at a silent Taylor Field. One coincidence: Saskatchewan's lone touchdown was on an eight-yard pass from Don Allard to lineman Jim Marshall, who scored on a tackle-eligible play. Marshall later starred on the defensive line with the Grant-coached Minnesota Vikings.

93 States of Confusion

The CFL's fortunes were going south, so the United States was a logical—and last-ditch—destination.

Expansion revenues were a lifeblood for the established franchises in the mid-1990s, including the Roughriders.

"If we didn't have the expansion, we never would have survived," said Alan Ford, Saskatchewan's general manager from 1989 to 1999.

"We had a feeling that it probably wasn't the best move to make as quickly as we did, and it just never caught on. We had lousy [American] owners. We had people who just wanted to jump in and say, 'I own a team.'"

Others, such as Jim Speros (Baltimore Stallions) and Fred Anderson (Sacramento Gold Miners, San Antonio Texans), were credible, committed owners. But, for the most part, the league threw around expansion franchises like confetti, hoping that the infusion of desperately needed cash would keep the ship afloat.

Hence the arrivals of the Las Vegas Posse, Shreveport Pirates, Memphis Mad Dogs, and Birmingham Barracudas.

From a Saskatchewan perspective, two home games against American teams stand out.

The first visit by a U.S.-based franchise—Sacramento—drew 33,032 spectators, then a Roughriders record crowd—on August 27, 1993. Saskatchewan won 26–23 on a late field goal by Dave Ridgway.

The final game played by an American team—Baltimore—was the 1995 Grey Cup, held at Taylor Field. The Stallions defeated the Calgary Stampeders 37–20, after which the CFL's three-year American experiment ended.

Although U.S. expansion often turned the league into a punch line, Jeff Fairholm enjoyed the change of pace.

"It was great," the former Roughriders slotback recalled. "Just visiting different places and playing in different stadiums was fun. In the CFL, if you have any kind of career, it does get a little old. You're playing Edmonton four times a year, for example. There's a comfort level where almost every stadium becomes a home game, because you're used to the locker room and you know what you're doing and you know what hotel you're staying in. It's almost a grind.

"It's somewhat rejuvenating when you get to go to these different places. As goofy as the stadium was in Memphis, you're still going to Memphis. You still get to check out the city. It was fun—different weather, different teams, different cities. It just added some flair to a season."

Not always in a good way. In 1993, for example, the Roughriders played in Edmonton on a Wednesday (July 21) before travelling to Sacramento for a Saturday scorcher.

"It was 100 degrees in Sacramento," Fairholm said. "I was so exhausted. I actually dropped two passes in that game. I'll never forget it. I tell my kids I never dropped anything, but I did."

"I still had open wounds from the Edmonton game when we played in Sacramento," fellow Riders slotback Dan Farthing added. "I remember Willie Pless tackled me in Edmonton and got his face mask into my back a little bit. It was still an open wound when I was playing on Saturday. It took us a full quarter and a half to actually warm up, because we just were bumped and bruised. You can't play a football tournament, and that's basically what that was."

The conditions were also stifling on July 16, 1994, when the Roughriders played in Las Vegas—winning 32–22 in overtime.

"It was a very tough game, because it was 116 during the day," said Farthing, still wincing at the thought. "I remember the sun still being up when we were doing warmups and even partway through the first quarter. There was a bit of a breeze, and it was exactly the opposite of what a minus-15 wind chill day would do to you. It was that hot. Your sweat couldn't stay on your skin long enough to actually cool you down. It would just evaporate, and your eyeballs would dry out—I'm not joking—if you didn't blink frequently. It was that hot.

"I remember going through about six pairs of glass-cutter gloves because you could literally just wring them out. I remember guys being on IVs after the game because they'd lost so much fluid. I remember guys jumping into the big tin tub that soft drinks were in after the game. One guy jumped right in because he thought he was going to die. He was fully submerged below his nose.

"It was an interesting time, for sure."

94 Lightning Hits the Outhouse

CHAOS BY THE CREEK—A placeline conventionally kicks off a newspaper article, not a book chapter, but what better way could there be to initiate a reminiscence about the Roughriders' Reign of Error?

That term was coined by peerless *Leader-Post* columnist Bob Hughes in the 1980s, while the Roughriders were mired in an unmatched CFL playoff drought that eventually swelled to 11 seasons.

Hughes also began many columns with the aforementioned placeline, while often referring to the team's front-office and/ or player-personnel moves as "shuffling the deck chairs on the Titanic."

Each non-playoff season had its own name—Revival IV, Revival V, Revival VI, etc.—as the miseries persisted. At times, one could only laugh, with Jack Gotta providing many of the punch lines during his two seasons (1985 and 1986) as the Roughriders' head coach.

After one especially gruesome loss, Gotta noted, "When lightning hits the outhouse, the whole joint stinks."

Gotta also commented on the team's lack of enthusiasm for tackling by quipping, "They weren't exactly like a bunch of hungry dogs chasing after a meatball, were they?"

Gotta's predecessor, Reuben Berry, articulated his desire to have the team adopt what was termed a "Saskatchewan Tough" mentality after assuming the head-coaching reins in August of 1983. However, the tough losses continued.

Saskatchewan's protracted dry spell began with a heartbreaking 23–20 loss to the Ottawa Rough Riders in the 1976 Grey Cup. The Roughriders did not appear in another playoff game until 1988.

During the 11-year drought, there was only one winning season (the 9–7 mirage of 1981) and one .500 campaign (8–8, in 1977). The low points included a pair of 2–14 ordeals (1979 and 1980).

"As a 15-year-old in 1979, I saw a game at McMahon Stadium between the Bombers and the Stamps," longtime Roughriders fan Ron Podbielski recalled. "I ducked under the stands at halftime to see if I could buy any Rider memorabilia. In those days, it was pins, ribbons, and the odd cap.

"I found a table vendor carrying some stuff from every team in the CFL—except the Riders. A nervous kid, I asked the vendor, 'Where is the Rider stuff?' He answered, to my sadness and chagrin, 'There is nothing. We don't carry anything from those losers.' It was a sad and sobering moment that stayed burning within me until 10 years later, when the Riders won the Grey Cup. I wish I could have found that vendor and told him to stuff it."

A Grey Cup title seemed inconceivable during the Reign of Error—as was the case in 1984, when the Roughriders had just a win and a tie after eight games.

Some dissatisfied customers wore bags over their heads. Defensive lineman Rick Mohr was so fed up that, at one point, he gave the fans the finger. (Or, perhaps, he was updating the fans on the team's victory total to that point.)

Hughes weighed in, classically, noting that quarterback Joe Paopao "is close to considering having his sweater number unlisted."

Paopao, always a class act, tried to make the best of the situation.

"You can't take it personally, except for one time when they were throwing batteries—those little AAA things—at our bench," he said. "I remember Rick Mohr was so mad that he got up and charged up into the stands. That was a wild moment.

"Someone turned to me and said, 'What do you think, Pao?' I said, 'If those batteries work, let's keep them. We'll get something out of this thing.'"

Hughes, for his part, emerged with some priceless columns, although he was amenable to pursuing a different angle had the circumstances warranted.

"I'd go to games and think they were starting to turn it around," Hughes recalled in 2009, four years before his death. "Out they'd come and, after the first series, they'd be behind already. I always thought, 'I'll start a column with 'VICTORY BY THE CREEK,' but, by the end of the second quarter, it was always 'CHAOS BY THE CREEK' again."

95 Taylor Field Mile-Stones

In early October of 2006, the "S" on the Roughriders' logo could have stood for "Satisfaction."

Mick Jagger and the Rolling Stones played two wildly successful concerts at Taylor Field, events with which the Roughriders were heavily involved.

"The key was that, other than the handful of city workers who were there, we were the only ones who knew how to operate the stadium, the ticket office, the concessions, and everything else," said Jim Hopson, who was then in his second season as the Roughriders' president-CEO. "After they announced the concert, they realized, 'We'd better have the Riders onside with this, because how are we going to make this work?'

"Of course, we said yes. We were wanting to be great partners with the city. We also saw a revenue opportunity, because they gave us a split of the merchandise."

But not before some Roughriders staffers endured some splitting headaches as a result of extra toil that could be exasperating and exhausting.

"Those were some of the most tiring, frustrating days of my career, with us being a big part of that, but it was really cool," Hopson said. "Who would have thought that we would host the Rolling Stones?"

City of Regina-owned Ipsco Place (now Evraz Place), which has traditionally brought shows to the exhibition grounds, took the lead in arranging the Stones' visit. One concert was initially scheduled, but the voracious appetite for tickets created demand for a second show. The concerts, held October 6 and October 8, each drew 40,000-plus people.

"It's one thing to think about doing a stadium concert, but to do the biggest in the world for your first ever was a little bit mind-blowing," recalled Neil Donnelly, who was integrally involved in the Stones' concerts during his tenure as Ipsco Place's vice-president of marketing and sales.

"There just isn't anything bigger or higher-pressure than dealing with the Rolling Stones. They have legal teams and press teams and just every single person you want to deal with at the biggest level in the business. For me, it was six months of no sleep and serious stress, because everything was the biggest and the best in the world, but they were the toughest people to deal with, the toughest negotiators.

"That one, for sure, stands out the most because it paved the way for all the other ones."

Taylor Field also played host to AC/DC (in 2009), Bon Jovi (2010), and Paul McCartney (2013).

96 Visit Riderville

The Roughriders always have a big presence at the Grey Cup, regardless of whether the team is actually playing in the game.

Riderville has become a phenomenally popular venue at the annual national football fest, having evolved from a small-scale site into a gathering point for football fans (and socializers in general) from across Canada and beyond.

"In 2004, just after I was appointed [Roughriders president-CEO], I went to Ottawa for the Grey Cup," Jim Hopson said. "We had Riderville, but it was in an old bar and it was run by volunteers, who would set it up. It was always well-attended and well-liked, but it wasn't anything like it is now."

The catalyst for Riderville's explosion was the 2007 Grey Cup festival in Toronto. Saskatchewan ended up advancing to, and winning, the championship game.

"It was then that we realized that we needed to take it over," Hopson recalled. "We still wanted to have the volunteers support us but book the venue ourselves and so on. The Grey Cup of '07 just blew the doors right off it. Riderville was in the Metro Toronto Convention Centre and the lineup was still around the block."

When Saskatchewan next won the Grey Cup, in 2013, Riderville was at the epicentre of everything. The festival, after all, was held in Regina.

The main, albeit unexpected, attraction the night before the game was Roughriders quarterback Darian Durant, who appeared on stage to greet and thank the fans. The next day, he threw three touchdown passes to pilot Saskatchewan to a 45–23 victory over the Hamilton Tiger-Cats, helping to engineer a Riderville party like none other.

"It has become such a big event for not only Roughriders fans, but football fans," Hopson noted. "If you go to the Grey Cup, you go to Riderville."

97

Goofy Gridiron Gems

There have been a few quirky contests in Roughriders history.

November 6, 1943: The All-Service Roughriders, a wartime team, lost 1–0 to the host Winnipeg Royal Canadian Air Force in the opener of a two-game, total-points Western semifinal. Winnipeg completed only one pass—the offence didn't exactly live up to the "air force" label—but that connection set up the decisive rouge. "We licked them out there and they know it," one Roughrider said within earshot of the *Leader-Post*'s Dave Dryburgh. "That one point doesn't mean a thing." Ironically, the player was correct. Winnipeg won 11–0 in Regina five days later to secure the West crown.

November 6, 1948: A 4–4 tie with the visiting Calgary Stampeders was noteworthy for two reasons: First, a playoff game ended in a draw, of all things; and second, it was the only blemish on the record of the 1948 Stampeders, who were ahead after 60 minutes in each of their other 14 games (including the Grey Cup). Nevertheless, the Roughriders and Stampeders were even at four after the opener of a two-game, total-points West final. Calgary prevailed 17–6 five days later and soon completed an undefeated season—the only one in Canadian professional football history.

November 11, 1949: The Roughriders came tantalizingly close to defeating Calgary in a two-game, total-points West final (won 22–21 by the Stampeders) and advancing to the Grey Cup. Saskatchewan missed two attempts at a series-clinching field goal late in the game. The first miss, by Buck Rogers, was washed away by an offside penalty against Calgary player-coach Les Lear. Instead of calling upon Rogers to attempt the second kick, from five yards closer, head coach Fred Grant asked Del Wardien to handle the placement. Wardien, too, was unsuccessful, settling for a meaningless rouge. "I feel sure that I would have been successful the second time," a disconsolate Rogers said after the game. Saskatchewan won the series finale 9–4, but an 18–12 loss in the opener barely provided Calgary with the sufficient cushion. In Game 1 at Taylor Field, the Roughriders had been stopped on Calgary's 1-yard line on the final play.

October 25, 1954: The Roughriders played 54 in '54. The regular season finale, against the B.C. Lions, was called by Western Interprovincial Football Union commissioner Sydney Halter when, as The Canadian Press put it, "The soupy British Columbia fog made play impossible." Back then, the league would ordinarily order a replay of the game under such circumstances, but the proximity to the playoffs was taken into consideration. "As it was the final game of the season, and as the standing of the league cannot be altered or affected, I see no purpose of the game being replayed either wholly or partially," Halter said. "Accordingly, I'm going to rule that the game stand as a completed game." Saskatchewan won the 54-minute contest 15–9. That was the only weather-shortened game in Canadian professional football history until August 9, 2019, when the Roughriders were credited with a 17–10 victory over the host Montreal Alouettes. That game was called with 2:41 remaining in the third quarter, following a one-hour delay that was caused by thunder and lightning.

September 18, 1970: Saskatchewan won 23–22—but, more accurately, B.C. lost the game. Leading 22–20 with just 44 seconds left, the Lions had the football on their 9-yard line. Three turnover-free plays would have exhausted the clock and ensured a B.C. victory. The problem: on second down, Lions quarterback Paul Brothers did not call for the snap before 20 seconds had elapsed. As a consequence, the Lions were penalized for a time-count violation and the clock stopped with 11 seconds remaining, necessitating a

Lions punt. Jim Walter fielded the punt on B.C.'s 50-yard line. His 11-yard return gave Saskatchewan possession in field-goal range with three seconds remaining. Jack Abendschan then made the kick from 47 yards to give the Roughriders a miraculous win.

October 3, 1982: The Roughriders received unaccustomed, North America–wide exposure when an NBC crew trekked northward to televise a Sunday afternoon game against the visiting Stampeders. The NFL was on strike at the time and, with NBC looking to fill the football void, the CFL was the best option. One problem: a 53–8 Roughriders victory, while a rare source of satisfaction to the home fans during a 6–9–1 season, was unlikely to hold the audience.

98 One Game, Enduring Fame

The Calgary Stampeders' Doug "Tank" Landry was Robbed—by Rob Bresciani.

Landry was seemingly poised to intercept the Roughriders' Kent Austin during an October 8, 1989, game at McMahon Stadium. But then Bresciani intervened, stealing the football from the Calgary linebacker for a first-down reception.

That was part of Bresciani's game of a lifetime, a dominating effort that helped the injury-plagued Roughriders win 39–26.

The Regina-born receiver caught six passes for 194 yards on a day when Saskatchewan was without star slotbacks Jeff Fairholm (who was hurt on the opening play) and Ray Elgaard (knee injury).

During the third quarter, Bresciani scored his only CFL touchdown—a 59-yarder—in accidental, yet scintillating, fashion after Austin threw over the middle to Tim McCray. The all-purpose

One-Year Wonders

Holland Aplin: Also known as Holly, he was the Roughriders' most productive receiver in 1952, with 41 catches for 801 yards and six touchdowns.

Rick Eber: The former NFL player was a favourite target of Ron Lancaster in 1973, catching 46 passes for 730 yards and seven touchdowns. At the University of Tulsa, Eber had played under head coach Glenn Dobbs—an ex-Roughriders quarterback and field boss. (In one 1967 game at Tulsa, Eber caught 20 passes for 322 yards and two touchdowns.)

Don "Red" Ettinger: Credited by some as the inventor of the blitz, Ettinger was an All-Star with a 1951 Roughriders team that reached the Grey Cup.

Cookie Gilchrist: One of football's all-time characters, Gilchrist was a Saskatchewan sensation in 1958, rushing for 1,258 yards. He also had stints with the Hamilton Tiger-Cats and Toronto Argonauts before starring in the American Football League.

Bobby Johnson: What might have been? Johnson was a sensation with the 1986 Roughriders, rushing for 869 yards in 13 games en route to earning CFL All-Star honours. However, he suffered a career-ending neck injury in Week 14.

Curtis Marsh: Unlike everyone else on this list, Marsh played more than one year with the Roughriders—spending all of the 2000 season and part of 2001 in green and white. But his one monster year merits mention. As a first-year CFLer, he had league-high totals of 102 catches and 1,560 receiving yards, despite missing one regular-season game. He also enjoyed a strong start in 2001 before suffering a knee injury and fading out of the picture.

Jack Nix: The talented pass-catcher spent one season with the San Francisco 49ers before joining the Roughriders in 1951, when he caught 46 passes for 599 yards and seven touchdowns on the way to earning All-Star honours. In his final CFL game, a 21–14 Grey Cup loss to the Ottawa Rough Riders, he caught a touchdown pass from Dobbs.

Ray Purdin: A la Marsh, we are making an exception by listing a player who was with Saskatchewan for more than one season. Purdin, a Roughrider from 1961 to 1963, peaked in the middle season when he scored 14 touchdowns. In 1962, he rushed for 809 yards (averaging 6.1 yards per carry) and added 34 receptions for 771 yards (22.6 yards per reception). He scored on a 93-yard run and a 104-yard reception.

Neal Smith: After being named the Roughriders' rookie of the year and a West All-Star in 1999, when he led the team in sacks (nine), he retired from pro football.

Barry Wilburn: A shutdown cornerback who had two interceptions for the Washington Redskins in their 1988 Super Bowl victory, he was an All-Canadian with Saskatchewan in 1993.

tailback was juggling the ball as Bresciani passed by, plucked the pigskin from McCray's fingertips, and took off toward the end zone.

"It was just one of those days," said Bresciani, who also made a spectacular, one-handed catch along the sideline. "I should have bought a lottery ticket."

Bresciani played 38 career regular season games, catching 15 passes for 320 yards while playing for Saskatchewan, Calgary, and the Ottawa Rough Riders. In the aforementioned 1989 game, he registered 60.6 per cent of his career receiving yards while making a timely, memorable contribution to a team that ultimately won the Grey Cup.

Some other one-game wonders in Roughriders history:

Ferd Burket: In 1959, Burket scored five touchdowns—all in one day—to set a franchise single-game record that, as of this writing, had yet to be broken. The five scores represent 36 per cent of his career total (14 majors). He spent four of his five CFL seasons with Saskatchewan.

Rocky Butler: A surprise starter at quarterback in the 2002 Labour Day Classic against the Winnipeg Blue Bombers, Butler—who was Saskatchewan's fourth-string quarterback at one point in the season—rushed for three touchdowns in a 33–19 win.

Stu Foord: The Regina-born running back had a dream that he would score the first time he touched the ball in a CFL game—and he did. On September 20, 2008, Foord produced an 18-yard major on his introductory CFL carry. Later in the game, he scored on a 55-yard reception in a 27–21 home-field loss to the B.C. Lions. Over a six-year pro football career, spent with Saskatchewan and B.C., he played in 99 games and scored four touchdowns.

Mark Guy: An often-forgotten member of the Roughriders' receiving corps in 1989, he registered back-to-back gains of 18 and 10 yards to set up Dave Ridgway's game-winning field goal in the 1989 Grey Cup. That was part of Guy's four-catch, 100-yard performance. He had 10 receptions for 114 yards during the regular season.

Willie Jones: Once a pass-rushing threat with the Oakland Raiders, Jones played in only one game with the Roughriders—registering 1.5 quarterback sacks (along with six defensive tackles) in a 46–24 road victory over Ottawa on July 29, 1984. Injuries prevented him from ever returning to the lineup.

Tim Kearse: Mere days after catching a game-winning, 19-yard touchdown pass with 1:02 left in the fourth quarter against Calgary on August 20, 1988, Kearse was released. He had set up the decisive touchdown by making a 13-yard reception on third-and-six.

Pete Van Valkenburg: The Flying Dutchman, once a backup to O.J. Simpson with the Buffalo Bills, scored all three of his CFL touchdowns on August 20, 1976. He caught two touchdown passes and rushed for a 90-yard major during a 38–13 victory in Calgary. However, he struggled in the weeks following and was released before season's end.

Brian Walling: Seldom used during his brief time with the Roughriders, Walling nonetheless scored one of the most important touchdowns in Roughriders history. With 1:38 remaining in the fourth quarter of the 1989 West semifinal, he scored on a

50-yard run after the Roughriders called a draw play on second-and-10. The touchdown put Saskatchewan ahead to stay as it won 33–26 in Calgary. The Roughriders won the Grey Cup two weeks later.

99 Did Sullivan Stick Around? Neigh!

Six years after winning a Heisman, Pat Sullivan met the horsemen.

Sullivan, who in 1971 received the Heisman Trophy as the outstanding player in U.S. college football, landed in Saskatchewan in September of 1977 after exhausting his NFL options.

Just like that, the University of Auburn Tigers legend was practising with the Roughriders in the infield at Regina Exhibition Track.

A *Leader-Post* photo showed Sullivan walking to the practice field alongside fellow quarterback Ron Lancaster, the accompanying caption reading, "The first thing you need to learn, Pat, is check for horses before you cross the track."

That being done, Sullivan became the first Heisman winner to practise with the Green and White. That was on September 21, 1977, just five days before he returned home to Birmingham, Alabama.

"Pat kind of got mixed up on the five-day trial thing," Roughriders head coach Jim Eddy explained. "He thought it was five straight days and didn't realize it lasted until later this week. And he wanted a decision…he wanted to know if he would be added to the roster. I told him it didn't look like it for this game (a September 25 contest in Calgary)…that I couldn't guarantee him that."

The initial hope was that Sullivan would be the heir apparent to Lancaster, who was in his penultimate season as the Roughriders' No. 1 quarterback. Sullivan briefly joined a quarterbacking equation that, along with Lancaster, included Mike Nott and Eric Guthrie.

Sullivan and assorted other Heisman candidates have spent some time, however minimal, with the Roughriders. The biggest names, Sullivan excepted, are Vince Young and Trent Richardson—both of whom had stints with Saskatchewan in 2017.

Young, a University of Texas Longhorns great who was second to the USC Trojans' Reggie Bush in 2005 Heisman voting, attempted to make a comeback in the CFL at age 33. That experiment ended when he injured a hamstring during a training-camp scrimmage. He wasn't the Young of old—simply an old Young.

Richardson, the third-place finisher in 2011 as a member of the University of Alabama Crimson Tide, was reasonably successful in four games with the Roughriders. He rushed for 259 yards, averaging 5.4 yards per carry, and scored two touchdowns. However, he opted against returning to the CFL in 2018.

The Green and White has also welcomed these Heisman candidates:

Sherman Lewis: A star running back with the Michigan State Spartans, Lewis was third in 1963 Heisman voting. He played in one game with the 1965 Roughriders, gaining 14 yards on a run and two yards on a reception.

Major Harris: After quarterbacking the University of West Virginia Mountaineers, the third-place finisher in the 1989 Heisman race had CFL stints with B.C. and Saskatchewan. While with the Roughriders in 1991, he was actually included in a locally distributed player-card set but never took a snap for the team during an abbreviated stay.

Michael Bishop: In 1998, Bishop—a dynamic quarterback with the Kansas State Wildcats—was the runner-up to Heisman winner Ricky Williams (Texas). A decade later, Bishop became part of a chaotic quarterbacking situation in Saskatchewan. In 10 regular season games with the 2008 Roughriders, Bishop threw for 2,226 yards, with seven touchdown passes and 12 interceptions. He was released after a disastrous showing in a 2008 playoff loss to B.C.

Colt Brennan: Someone named Colt would have been a perfect fit for a team that practised in the middle of a horse-racing track. Alas, he did not arrive until 2012, with a resume that included two strong Heisman bids (sixth in 2006; third in 2007) as a member of the University of Hawaii Warriors. Brennan, who threw 53 touchdown passes for the Warriors in 2006, struggled in training camp with Saskatchewan and was released.

100 Numbers

For Chapter 100, it is only appropriate that we provide an admittedly subjective list that denotes the best Roughriders player to wear each of the 100 numbers. Ready, set...

0, Tobi Antigha: A rare defensive end who can also line up at safety, he made several eye-popping plays in 2018.

1, Kory Sheets: 2013 Grey Cup MVP after rushing for 197 yards.

2, Ralph Pierce: Outstanding two-way player in the 1930s.

3, Omarr Morgan: Three-time CFL All-Star cornerback.

4, Darian Durant: Quarterbacked the Riders to three Grey Cup games, including 2013 win.

5, Kent Austin: Prolific passer; 1989 Grey Cup offensive MVP.

6, Rob Bagg: A highly respected Riders receiver for a decade.

7, Weston Dressler: Five-time 1,000-yard receiver with the Riders.

8, Darren Davis: 1,000-yard rusher in both of his seasons with Saskatchewan.

9, Reggie Hunt: Four-time West All-Star had a 16-tackle game, 2006.

10, Dan Farthing: Reliable receiver was a popular Rider from 1991 to 2001.

11, Ed Gainey: Led CFL with 10 interceptions in 2017; two-time All-Star.

12, Dale West: 10 interceptions in 1963, when three of his five receptions went for a TD.

13, Bob Walker: West All-Star lineman, 1938 and 1939.

14, Tim McCray: Most outstanding player on Cup-winning 1989 team.

15, Lance Frazier: West All-Star defensive back, 2009.

16, Tom Burgess: Led Roughriders in TD passes, 1988 and 1989.

17, Joey Walters: 1,715 receiving yards in 1981 is a longtime club record; amassed 1,692 yards the following year.

18, Jeff Fairholm: Game-breaking slotback from 1988 to 1993.

19, Corey Holmes: Two-time CFL special-teams player of the year.

20, Ken McEachern: Two-time CFL All-Star; 10 interceptions in 1980.

21, Alan Ford: Mr. Versatility helped the Riders in many ways from 1965 to 1976.

22, Bill Clarke: Hall of Fame defensive lineman also wore 42, 60, and 67.

23 (retired), Ron Lancaster: The Little General was twice the CFL's most outstanding player.

24, Bob Kosid: Spent nine years in the Riders' secondary en route to Plaza of Honour.

25, Rhett Dawson: 10 TD catches for the Riders, 1975 and 1976.

26, Dean Griffing: Three-time All-Star centre over eight seasons.

27, Glen Suitor: Riders' all-time-leading interceptor (51).

28, Toar Springstein: All-Star tackle in 1940 and 1949; spent 10 seasons with Riders.

29, Eddie Davis: Hall of Fame defensive back spent nine seasons in Saskatchewan.

30, Bruce Bennett: Six-time West All-Star safety.

31, Hugh Campbell: A remarkable technician who had 60 TD catches in six seasons.

32, Mike Saunders: All-purpose running back scored 15 TDs in 1994.

33, Chris Szarka: The Canuck Truck was money in short-yardage situations.

34 (retired), George Reed: Iconic fullback rushed for 16,116 yards.

35, Johnny Bell: Star end, 1946 to 1952.

36 (retired), Dave Ridgway: Hall of Fame placekicker.

37, Roger Goree: CFL All-Star linebacker with the 1976 Riders.

38, George White: Tackling machine in 2000 and 2001.

39, David Albright: 118 defensive tackles in 1987.

40 (retired), Mel Becket: All-Star centre in 1956, his fourth season with Saskatchewan; killed in 1956 plane crash.

41, Tyron Brackenridge: CFL All-Star safety, 2013 and 2014.

42, Eddie Lowe: One of the finest linebackers in Riders history; crunching hit changed 1989 West final in Edmonton.

43, Ted Urness: Hall of Fame centre and six-time CFL All-Star.

44 (retired), **Roger Aldag:** Hall of Fame offensive lineman; CFL lineman of the year, 1986 and 1988.

45, **Glenn Dobbs:** Iconic quarterback had magical 1951 season.

46, **Jorgen Hus:** Ultra-reliable long snapper.

47, **Maurice Lloyd:** CFL All-Star linebacker, 2008.

48, **Rey Williams:** Linebacker with 2007 and 2013 Grey Cup champions.

49, **Jeff Knox Jr.:** 112 tackles for 2015 Roughriders.

50, **Wayne Shaw:** Six-time All-Star linebacker.

51, **John Terry:** Three-time All-Star offensive tackle.

52, **Jim Hopson:** Four-year Riders offensive lineman was team's first president-CEO.

53, **Jack Abendschan:** Hall of Fame guard and a fine place-kicker in his day.

54, **Jeremy O'Day:** Four-time CFL All-Star centre.

55 (retired), **Mario DeMarco:** West All-Star guard, 1954; killed in 1956 plane crash after fourth year with Riders.

56 (retired), **Ray Syrnyk:** Killed in 1956 plane crash after his third season with Riders; played guard and linebacker; captained Saskatoon Hilltops to 1953 Canadian junior championship.

57, **Brendon LaBatte:** CFL's most outstanding offensive lineman, 2013; six-time All-Star with Riders.

58, **Ken Reed:** Fine defensive end and linebacker is in Plaza of Honour.

59, **Ralph Galloway:** Five-time All-Star offensive lineman.

60, **Gene Makowsky:** Hall of Fame offensive lineman; CFL's lineman of the year, 2004 and 2005; runner-up in 2008.

61, **Ed McQuarters:** Hall of Fame defensive lineman; CFL's top lineman in 1967.

62, **Reg Whitehouse:** Venerable offensive lineman signed off as a member of the 1966 Grey Cup champions.

63, **Martin Ruby:** Hall of Famer was a dominant two-way lineman (also wore 36).

64, Ron Atchison: Hall of Fame defensive lineman was a 17-year Rider (also wore Nos. 14, 16, 41, and 54).

65, Bill Baker: Hall of Fame defensive lineman (also wore 76).

66, Al Benecick: Hall of Fame offensive lineman.

67, Clyde Brock: Four-time CFL All-Star offensive tackle.

68, Andrew Greene: CFL's top offensive lineman, 2003.

69, George Wells: All-Star defensive end, 1975 and 1976; five sacks in 1975 West semifinal.

70, Steve Mazurak: Reliable receiver, 1974 to 1980, and a favourite target in the clutch.

71, Bobby Jurasin: Hall of Fame pass rusher.

72, Jim Worden: CFL All-Star tight end, 1966.

73 (retired), Gord Sturtridge: West All-Star defensive end, 1955 and 1956; killed in 1956 plane crash.

74, Dan Rashovich: 13-year Rider was fearless at linebacker and on special teams.

75, Garner Ekstran: CFL All-Star defensive end (1962, 1963) and linebacker (1967).

76, Doug Killoh: Riders defensive lineman, 1953 to 1960; Plaza of Honour inductee.

77, Wally Dempsey: Seven-year Riders linebacker is in the Plaza of Honour.

78, Vince Goldsmith: CFL rookie of the year, 1981; 20 sacks in 1983.

79, Gary Lewis: Two-time All-Star defensive tackle.

80, Don Narcisse: Hall of Famer has a club-record 919 catches.

81, Ray Elgaard: Hall of Fame slotback amassed 13,198 receiving yards.

82, Frank Tripucka: Star quarterback in 1950s.

83, Andy Fantuz: CFL's top Canadian, 2010, after 87-catch, 1,380-yard year.

84, Jordan Williams-Lambert: West Division's rookie of the year, 2018.

85, Mike Hagler: Dynamic receiver, runner, and returner in 1958.

86, Bob Pelling: Riders receiver from 1947 to 1953; averaged 19.9 yards per catch.

87, Sully Glasser: Riders halfback from 1946 to 1957 (also wore Nos. 1, 9, 16, and 47).

88, Ken Charlton: Hall of Fame halfback.

89, Chris Getzlaf: Two-time 1,000-yard receiver; 2013 Grey Cup's top Canadian; led 2013 champions in receiving yards.

90, Jack Hill: 14 TD catches, 1958.

91, Cookie Gilchrist: Rushed for 1,254 yards, 1958.

92, Bobby Marlow: Two-way star in 1950s.

93, Brian Timmis: Punishing runner with Regina Rugby Club, 1920 to 1922.

94, Larry Isbell: All-around star was a three-time All-Star defensive back; known for towering punts.

95, Ricky Foley: Standout defensive end for 2013 Cup winners; 12 sacks in 2014.

96, Scott Schultz: Plaza of Honour defensive tackle.

97, John Chick: CFL's top defensive player, 2009; starred in 2007 and 2013 Grey Cup wins.

98, Jearld Baylis: CFL's outstanding defensive player, 1993.

99, Ken Carpenter: Roughriders record 18 TDs, 1955.

Bibliography

Books

Calder, Bob, and Garry Andrews. *Rider Pride: The Story of Canada's Best-Loved Football Team.* Saskatoon: Western Producer Prairie Books, 1984.

Calder, Robert, Darrell Davis, Julie Folk, Bob Hughes, Dan Marce, Gordon Staseson, and Rob Vanstone. *Saskatchewan Roughriders: First 100 Years.* Regina: The Leader-Post Carrier Foundation Inc./Centax Books, 2009.

Chaput, John. *Saskatchewan Sports Legends: One Hundred Years of Athletic Distinction.* Calgary: Johnson Gorman Publishers, 2005.

Chaput, John. *Saskatchewan Tough: The Lives and Stories of Homegrown Saskatchewan Roughriders.* Regina: Centax Books, 2013.

Gifford, Frank. *The Glory Game: How the 1958 NFL Championship Changed Football Forever.* New York: Harper Perennial, 2009.

Hopson, Jim, with Darrell Davis. *Running the Riders: My Decade as CEO of Canada's Team.* Regina: DriverWorks Ink, 2015.

Kelly, Graham. *Green Grit: The Story of the Saskatchewan Roughriders.* Toronto: HarperCollins, 2001.

Phillips, Curt. *Saskatchewan Roughriders Player Reference, 1960-1996.* Self-published, 1997.

Proudfoot, Tony. *First and Goal: The CFL and the Pursuit of Excellence.* Bolton: Fenn Publishing Company Ltd., 2006.

Reed, George, with John Chaput. *George Reed: His Life and Times.* Regina: Centax Books, 2011.

Vanstone, Rob. *The Greatest Grey Cup Ever.* Regina: The Leader-Post Carrier Foundation Inc./Centax Books, 2010.

Vanstone, Rob. *West Riders Best*. Regina: The Leader-Post Carrier Foundation Inc./Centax Books, 2009.

Yuen, Edward. *92 Years of Roughrider Football*. Self-published, 2002.

Interviewed for This Book

Rob Bagg

Bob Calder

Duron Carter

Lori Dattilo

Darian Durant

Weston Dressler

Dylan Earis

Jeff Fairholm

Dan Farthing

Norm Fong

Alan Ford

Trent Fraser

Ivan Gutfriend

Jim Hopson

Lorne Kazmir

Sheila Kelly

Rhonda Kerr-White

Phil Kershaw

Brendon LaBatte

John Lipp

John Lynch

Gene Makowsky

Paul McCallum

Ken Miller

Maureen Miller

Judith Milliken

Darren Mitchell

Rod Pedersen

Ron Podbielski

Dan Rambo

George Reed

Craig Reynolds

Dave Ridgway

Don Rice

Tom Shepherd

Brendan Taman

Eric Tillman

Interviewed for Author's Previous Books/Articles

Roger Aldag

Sandy Archer

Kent Austin

Don Bahnuik

Bill Baker

Joe Barnes*

Al Benecick

Gord Brown

Rob Bresciani

Tom Burgess

Hugh Campbell

Wes Cates

Geoff Currier

Rhett Dawson

William "Red" Dawson

Blake Dermott*

Glenn Dobbs

Neil Donnelly

Larry Dumelie

Ray Elgaard

Dave Elston

Greg Fieger*

Sharla Folk

Tony Gabriel

Richie Hall

Bob Hughes

Kerry Joseph

Bobby Jurasin

Mike Kerrigan

Eagle Keys

Chris Knox

Ron Knox

Mark Kosmos

Ron Lancaster

Ed McQuarters

Don Narcisse

Joe Paopao

Ken Ploen

Bob Poley

Ray Purdin

Bill Quinter

Ken Reed

Jon Ryan

Larry Robinson

Bob Shaw

Wayne Shaw

Kory Sheets

Geroy Simon

Harry Skipper*

Gordon Staseson

Glen Suitor

Mark Urness

Ted Urness

Joey Walters

Brad Watson

Dale West

Reg Whitehouse

Gene Wlasiuk

Lyall Woznesensky*

*interviewed by researcher Mitchell Blair